WALT WHITMAN: THE CRITICAL HERITAGE

THE CRITICAL HERITAGE SERIES

GENERAL EDITOR: B. C. SOUTHAM, M.A., B.LITT. (OXON.)
Formerly Department of English, Westfield College, University of London

---

For list of books in the series see back end paper

WALT WHITMAN

THE CRITICAL HERITAGE

Edited by
MILTON HINDUS
Professor of English, Brandeis University

BARNES & NOBLE, Inc.
NEW YORK
PUBLISHERS & BOOKSELLERS SINCE 1873

First Published
in Great Britain 1971

Published in the United States of America 1971
by Barnes & Noble Inc, New York, N.Y.

ISBN 0 389 04208 0

Printed in Great Britain

General Editor's Preface

The reception given to a writer by his contemporaries and near-contemporaries is evidence of considerable value to the student of literature. On one side, we learn a great deal about the state of criticism at large and in particular about the development of critical attitudes towards a single writer; at the same time, through private comments in letters, journals or marginalia, we gain an insight upon the tastes and literary thought of individual readers of the period. Evidence of this kind helps us to understand the writer's historical situation, the nature of his immediate reading-public, and his response to these pressures.

The separate volumes in *The Critical Heritage Series* present a record of this early criticism. Clearly, for many of the highly-productive and lengthily-reviewed nineteenth- and twentieth-century writers, there exists an enormous body of material; and in these cases the volume editors have made a selection of the most important views, significant for their intrinsic critical worth or for their representative quality.

For writers of the eighteenth century and earlier, the materials are much scarcer and the historical period has been extended, sometimes far beyond the writer's lifetime, in order to show the inception and growth of critical views which were initially slow to appear.

In each volume the documents are headed by an Introduction, discussing the material assembled and relating the early stages of the author's reception to what we have come to identify as the critical tradition. The volumes will make available much material which would otherwise be difficult of access and it is hoped that the modern reader will be thereby helped towards an informed understanding of the ways in which literature has been read and judged.

B.C.S.

Contents

1865–92

1893–1914

CONTENTS

A Note on Sources

In assembling materials for this volume, I have drawn in part upon four earlier gatherings of writings about Whitman. These four works, which are now virtually unobtainable, are referred to in the headnotes by short titles, as follows:

Bucke Richard Maurice Bucke, *Walt Whitman* (Glasgow, 1884).

Dowden Edward Dowden, ed., 'English Critics on Walt Whitman', printed as Appendix to Bucke (above).

Imprints *Leaves of Grass Imprints. American and European Criticisms on 'Leaves of Grass'* (Boston, 1860). A 65-page volume published anonymously by Whitman and distributed to the public free of charge as advertising for the third edition.

In Re *In Re Walt Whitman*, edited by his literary executors, Horace L. Traubel, Richard Maurice Bucke and Thomas B. Harned (1893).

I should like to thank Professor Gay Wilson Allen for his kind permission to include Evie Allison Allen's translation of Knut Hamsun's criticism of Whitman, originally published in Professor Allen's volume *Walt Whitman Abroad* (Syracuse, 1955).

I wish to acknowledge some useful bibliographical material placed at my disposal by Professor William White of Wayne State University, editor of the *Walt Whitman Review*, who is now compiling the bibliography of the new collected edition of Whitman's writings which is in process of publication by the New York University Press.

Introduction

THE BATTLE FOR RECOGNITION: 1855–60

Libraries of criticism have grown up around those literary works which humanity has found most challenging, but it seems safe to say that there has never been a book more intimately bound up with the history of its reception than *Leaves of Grass*. From the moment it made its appearance in the world early in July 1855, it was the destiny of this singular imaginative production which, the author later implied, was to be taken less as a work of art than as a piece out of a man's life, to be 'enveloped in the dust of controversy'.

In tracing the development of the conflict of opinion, there is a certain logic in grouping the responses around the dates of the nine successive American editions which appeared during Whitman's lifetime (1855, 1856, 1860, 1867, 1871, 1876, 1881, 1888 and 1892). The decisive years were those in which the first three editions appeared. In later years, as Whitman's fame grew without ever quite overcoming his notoriety, grave men of letters felt almost compelled to take sides either for or against his work, and they brought subtlety and erudition to the task. Yet the early reviews, though not as refined and analytical as some later criticism, retain a surprising amount of freshness and interest, if only because, as Anatole France suggests in *La Vie littéraire* with regard to the classics, the early readers of a work alone are free and spontaneous in their responses to it. Later readers are to some degree constrained by the consensus that time has brought about, even when they are moved to rebel against it.

The first sign that the new book, as unconventional in its appearance as it was in content, would not fail to find its mark was given by Ralph Waldo Emerson in his famous letter to Whitman (No. 1) written from his home in Concord, Massachusetts, on 21 July 1855, about seventeen days, according to the most reliable calculations, after its publication by the author in Brooklyn, New York. The last paragraph of the letter indicates that for a time at least Emerson suspected that the book might be a hoax of some kind. There was no name of an author on the title-page, only a picture of the supposed author in most informal attire and pose (open collar, no tie, hand nonchalantly placed on hip, workingman's shirt and trousers, tilted hat) facing it. The name Walter Whitman was printed in tiny letters on the following page in the copyright notice, and the name Walt Whitman appeared unobtrusively in one of the odd verses of the book, like the careless signature of a painter stuck away in the corner of his canvas and barely noticeable at first glance.

Cicero observed caustically that even the most pessimistic philosophers took pains to identify the personal authorship of their dispiriting treatises, and Emerson's interest may have been aroused by the contrast between the near anonymity of this volume and the 'omnivorous' egotism which seemed to inform it. His letter, after more than a century, still preserves the sense of excitement with which he made his discovery. It may be comparable in a way to the experience recorded by Keats in his sonnet on Homer, and it was historically more important, not because Whitman is comparable to Homer but because Homer should have existed on the map of the world's literature whether or not Keats found him there in translation, while Emerson's recognition and encouragement were of incalculable importance in placing Whitman there. It is certainly fatuous to assert, as the Norwegian novelist Knut Hamsun once did in a lecture on Whitman at the Copenhagen Student Union in 1889 (No. 46), that 'if he had not received that letter from Emerson his book would have failed, as it deserved to fail', yet the letter no doubt served as a catalyst to hasten a process that might otherwise have been slower.

The earliest printed notice of the book, written by Charles A. Dana and published in *New York Daily Tribune* on Monday, 23 July 1855 (No. 2) appeared before Emerson's letter could have reached Whitman, and its tone, while far from being as hostile and mocking as some later reactions were to be, was less encouraging and more equivocal than a sanguine author hopes for. The paper gave its notice of the new publication a leading place that day and it was both liberal in space and tasteful in its choice of excerpts from Whitman's Preface and his poems, but its very opening sentence expressed an attitude of critical scepticism concerning the worth of the author and, after saying some better things later about his work, it concluded on a rather pinched and grudging note.

The mixed feelings of Dana presaged, more accurately than the enthusiasm of Emerson, the conflict which for so long has swirled about the book. The ambivalence of Dana is echoed in a review by the New Englander Charles Eliot Norton, which appeared in *Putnam's*

Monthly, published towards the end of the summer in which the book appeared, September 1855 (No. 3). We could hardly guess, judging from Norton's flippant tone, that, behind the visible scene of public print, he was, very soon thereafter, participating in another drama with regard to Whitman's book. On 23 September 1855, in a letter to his good friend James Russell Lowell (No. 5a), Norton called *Leaves of Grass* to his attention confidently with the assurance that the book must have something good in it to have recently 'excited Emerson's enthusiasm. He has written a letter to this "one of the roughs" which I have seen, expressing the warmest admiration and encouragement.' The time was only a few weeks before Whitman permitted Dana to publish Emerson's letter to him in the *New York Tribune* of 10 October (which Emerson complained to Samuel Longfellow was 'a strange rude thing' to do) and long before he caused a striking sentence from it ('I greet you at the beginning of a great career') to be embossed in gold on the spine of the second edition of the book in 1856. But if Norton had hoped to interest Lowell sufficiently to tempt him to undertake a review of the book, his hopes were dashed by the reply from Lowell (No. 5b) on 12 October: 'No, no, this kind of thing you describe won't do. When a man aims at originality he acknowledges himself consciously unoriginal, a want of self-respect which does not often go along with the capacity for great things.'

Another New Englander, however, was less reserved. Edward Everett Hale undertook to review the book in the *North American Review* for January 1856 (No. 8). Apart from Emerson's letter, this was the most understanding appraisal that the book had received, and Whitman himself was so well pleased with it that he gave it the leading place in a pamphlet of advertisements for himself entitled *Leaves of Grass Imprints*, which was distributed with the third (Boston) edition of the book in 1860. But it is significant that, even then, the reviewer's tone, while admiring, is also defensive and somewhat apologetic. He concludes with the observation that 'there is not a word in it meant to attract readers by its grossness, as there is in half the literature of the last century, which holds its place unchallenged on the tables in our drawing-rooms'.

The polemical note sounds like an answer to the bombardment of abuse against the book's indecency which must have begun in conversation before it reached the stage of print. Since many Americans at that time, though independent enough politically, were still colonial in their cultural attitudes, the effect of the negative verdicts pronounced in the London periodicals is not difficult to imagine. The *Saturday Review* of 15 March, 1856 had concluded: 'If the *Leaves of Grass* should come into anybody's possession, our advice is to throw them instantly behind the fire.' More vehement and uncompromising still were the pronouncements of the (London) *Critic* (No. 10) of 1 April 1856:

Walt Whitman is as unacquainted with art, as a hog is with mathematics . . . Walt Whitman libels the highest type of humanity, and calls his free speech the true utterance of *a man*; we, who may have been misdirected by civilisation, call it the expression of a beast . . . If this work is really a work of genius—if the principles of those poems, their free language, their amazing and audacious egotism, their animal vigour, be real poetry and the divinest evidence of the true poet—then our studies have been in vain, and vainer still the homage which we have paid the monarchs of Saxon intellect, Shakspere, and Milton, and Byron . . .

The reviewer concluded with the statement that the most generous assumption he could possibly make was that the writer was mad!

The review in the *Boston Intelligencer* (No. 11) of 3 May 1856, which Whitman thought representative enough to bind into an Appendix entitled 'Opinions' printed in the second edition of the *Leaves* later that year, made a valiant attempt to surpass the billingsgate of these reactions overseas:

We were attracted by the very singular title of this work, to seek the work itself, and what we thought ridiculous in the title is eclipsed in the pages of this heterogeneous mass of bombast, egotism, vulgarity and nonsense. The beastliness of the author is set forth in his own description of himself, and we can conceive no better reward than the lash for such a violation of decency as we have before us. The *Criterion* says: 'It is impossible to imagine how any man's fancy could have conceived it, unless he were possessed of the soul of a sentimental donkey that had died of disappointed love.'

This book should find no place where humanity urges any claim to respect, and the author should be kicked from all decent society as below the level of a brute. There is neither wit nor method in his disjointed babbling, and it seems to us he must be some escaped lunatic, raving in pitiable delirium.

To compensate somewhat for these vilifications, those men who were most directly under the influence of Emerson—Moncure Conway, Thoreau and Bronson Alcott—confirmed the validity of their chief's appraisal of the new American literary phenomenon. As early as 17 September 1855, Moncure Conway, writing to Emerson from

Washington (No. 4) after visiting Whitman in his home, said: 'I came off delighted with him. His eye can kindle strangely; and his words are ruddy with health. He is clearly his Book—and I went off impressed with the sense of a new city on my map, viz., Brooklyn, just as if it had suddenly risen through the boiling sea.' Later, at the end of 1856, in a letter to Harrison Blake, Thoreau (No. 14) characterized *Leaves of Grass* in a sentence that has often been quoted: 'Though rude and sometimes ineffectual, it is a great primitive poem,—an alarum or trumpet-note ringing through the American camp.'

Emerson himself, however, had soon begun to waver, unfortunately. Whether this was due to annoyance at the use to which his private letter had been put for publicity by Whitman himself or to the unrelenting power of the reaction which Whitman had evoked in many reviewers or to genuine doubts as to the accuracy of his own judgment, it is now impossible to say. But as early as 6 May 1856, in a letter to Carlyle, Emerson is clearly beginning to be of two minds about his new protégé:

> One book last summer came out in New York, a nondescript monster which yet had terrible eyes and buffalo strength, and was indisputably American,—which I thought to send you; but the book throve so badly with the few to whom I showed it, and wanted good morals so much that I never did. Yet I believe now again I shall. It is called *Leaves of Grass,*—was written and printed by a journeyman printer in Brooklyn, New York, named Walter Whitman; and after you have looked into it, if you think, as you may, that it is only an auctioneer's inventory of a warehouse, you can light your pipe with it.

What a distance separates these sentiments from the ones with which he had hailed Whitman ten months before ('the most extraordinary piece of wit & Wisdom that America has yet contributed. . . . incomparable things said incomparably well, as they must be. . . . the courage of treatment which so delights us, & which large perception only can inspire. . . . It has the best merits, namely, of fortifying & encouraging. . . .') The truth appears to be that Emerson, like others who have made important discoveries, did not succeed in holding on to his faith in what he had found. Despite all of his vaunted individualism (in theory he was as uncompromising as Ibsen when he said at the end of *Enemy of the People*: 'He is the strongest who stands most alone!'), Emerson was as inclined as other civilized men to yield and conform to social pressures in matters of literary evaluation.

In his later years, Emerson hurt Whitman's feelings by his failure to include a single selection from *Leaves* in his anthology *Parnassus*

(1872). Yet it was Whitman's feeling that, in the deepest sense, Emerson had not changed his mind about his worth since 1855, and in his talks with Horace Traubel in Camden, he added to the written record something that Emerson had said to him as they were conversing on the Boston Common in 1860. Sensing that Whitman, despite his brave demeanour, was feeling somewhat disheartened by all the clamour and controversy which surrounded his book, Emerson said, in an effort to buoy up his spirits: 'You have put the world in your debt, and such obligations are always acknowledged and met.'

After Emerson's death, Whitman's disciples (Traubel, Bucke, Harned, Burroughs, Kennedy, O'Connor) were often critical of Emerson's vacillations. It appeared to them that he had blown hot and cold. Some of his quoted sayings hurt, e.g. that he had expected from Whitman the songs of a nation and had got only its inventories. Yet Whitman himself never questioned Emerson's integrity or the indispensable service his spontaneous letter had performed in getting a sceptical public to grant him a hearing. In later years, he told Traubel mildly that even his own brother George had said to him on one occasion: 'Hasn't the world shown you that it doesn't want your work? Why don't you call the game off?' Walt said he had remained silent in answer to the questions. But, as Felix Adler once said consolingly to Whitman, 'readers must not only be counted; they must be weighed'. An Emerson, though he were alone in his appreciation (which, fortunately, he was far from being), would always carry weight in the world's estimation. And in conversation, Emerson may on occasion have been even more rapturous in his recommendation of Whitman's merits than he was on paper; he is reported, for example, to have said to a friend in the first phase of his enthusiasm over Walt: 'Americans abroad can now come home, for unto us a man is born!' Among the many 'firsts' to be claimed for Emerson in Whitman criticism, the allusion in the concluding part of this sentence is the first known suggestion of a comparison, which appealed to William Douglas O'Connor (No. 30) and many other Whitman enthusiasts in the late nineteenth and early twentieth century between the American poet and Christ.

In retrospect, it appears that the most redoubtable warrior in Whitman's cause at the outset may have been none other than Whitman himself! Though it is doubtful that he ever heard of them, he acted in the spirit of the words attributed to Rabbi Hillel: 'If I am not for myself, who will be for me? But if I am for myself alone, what am I?' He may have hoped, like all authors, for a receptive audience when, in his thirty-seventh year, he finally published a book, but he was mentally prepared for the bitter polemic that ensued. And he was too intelligent not to have realized that, like Molière's character George Dandin, he himself 'had asked for it!' Without being bellicose, he could, when occasion demanded it, be stubborn indeed (as when he rejected Emerson's friendly advice on the Boston Common to meet his respectable enemies half-way by expurgating his own book). There was a marked vein in him of the phlegm and recalcitrance that Motley had noted in the Dutch character. In his seventieth year, he was to use a military image in describing the first publication of his book more than thirty years before. He described it as 'a sortie', the success or failure of which would not be evident for at least a hundred years more. Perhaps the figure that should be employed to describe his action is that of a gambit in chess. Literature was a superior and amusing game which Whitman enjoyed playing seriously against the world, and once his gambit was slashingly accepted and countered by his opponents and a fierce struggle began around his boldly exposed position, he proved willing to defend it as strenuously as was necessary.

Not only was he prepared for the extremely risky and unauthorized use of Emerson's letter (at a time when he could ill afford the loss of his one influential friend or the additional obloquy to which his tactics exposed him) but he went to the length of writing at least three separate reviews of his own book (No. 7) and published them anonymously in different places: the *United States Review*, the *American Phrenological Journal* and the *Brooklyn Daily Times*. Since he made no effort to disguise his characteristic style, the truth was suspected at once and used against him by shrewd contemporary readers (No. 15), and it was officially proclaimed by his literary executors in the volume *In Re Walt Whitman* (1893) after his death. He may have been inspired in this dubious practice, which raises some eyebrows among students still, from having heard of the tradition that the poets Spenser and Leigh Hunt (not to speak of the actor Garrick) had, at various times, all written laudatory accounts of their own performances.

He went still further by adopting (or, it may be, inventing) a technique that has become common in twentieth-century advertising when he made use of the hostile and negative opinions of his book as well as the positive ones (some of them composed by himself) in an effort to intrigue the reader's interest and to compel him to sit in judgment for himself. He was determined, since he evidently would never be an unqualified success, to be at least a controversial one, for he had intuitively grasped the idea, put into words by Oscar Wilde, that the only thing worse than being talked about was not being talked about. In fact, it might have been Whitman whom Irving Babbitt was writing about in *Rousseau and Romanticism*:

As for the lesser figures in the (Romantic) movement their 'genius' is often chiefly displayed in their devices for calling attention to themselves as the latest and most marvellous births of time; it is only one aspect in short of an art in which the past century, whatever its achievement in the other arts, has really surpassed all its predecessors—the art of advertising.

Whitman's penchant for giving prominence to and reprinting almost everything that was ever said about himself and his work, no matter how trivial, obscure or worthless the source, annoyed even some of his greatest admirers and friends. It was John Addington Symonds (No. 48) who observed of Whitman: 'Instead of leaving his fame and influence to the operation of natural laws, he encouraged the *claque* and *réclame* which I have pointed out as prejudicial. . . . Were Buddha, Socrates, Christ, so interested in the dust stirred up around them by second-rate persons, in third-rate cities, and in more than fifth-rate literature?'

The answer may be that it was out of such unpromising materials that Whitman managed in his lifetime to forge a reputation sufficient to attract the attention of Symonds himself though he was separated from him by thousands of miles of ocean and all the tiers of society. But the real justification of Whitman's unorthodox methods should have been, for Symonds, not the simple pragmatic one that they worked but rather the beneficence of the results they accomplished for him and many others. For the healthy spirit and universal sympathies of the American poet moved Symonds, according to his own testimony, more than that of any other book except the Bible. He was one of those readers for whom the *Leaves* seemed nothing less than a religious revelation.

For my own part, [he wrote] I may confess that it shone upon me when my life was broken, when I was weak, sickly, poor, and of no account, and that I have ever lived thenceforward in the light and warmth of it . . . During my darkest hours it comforted me with the conviction that I too played my part in the illimitable symphony of cosmic life.

If, as Whitman suggests in *Democratic Vistas*, the true test of a book is whether or not it is capable of helping a human soul, *Leaves of Grass* had obviously passed the test, and no persiflage or sophistication could erase that simple fact. That is the basic reason why it was able to survive the first five critical years of its existence.

AFTER THE CIVIL WAR: 1865–92

Whitman's record as a volunteer helper in the hospitals in Washington from 1862 on, recorded in part in *Specimen Days*, seemed to many to support the cause of his *Leaves* as well by demonstrating clearly that he was not a writer for whom words are cheap and that the doctrines of sympathy which he expounded so eloquently were of a piece with the conduct of his life. This may not have been a literary argument rigorously logical and pure enough to impress the young Henry James (No. 28) fresh out of Harvard who did not hesitate in dividing the man from the poet and condemning the latter roundly, but it did make Whitman some influential young new friends like William Douglas O'Connor (No. 29) and John Burroughs (No. 53). As a partisan polemicist O'Connor's rhetorical talents were formidable, and in his pamphlet *The Good Gray Poet* (No. 29) he portrayed Whitman as a martyr in the cause of literature because of his discharge from a department of the United States Government on the pretext that he was the author of an indecent book. The portrayal was so persuasive to some contemporaries that Whitman is sometimes described to this day in American newspapers under the sobriquet bestowed upon him by O'Connor.

Whitman was helped, too, by the popular appeal of two of his 'Memories of President Lincoln'. The very unrepresentative, loosely rhymed and metred Song 'O Captain! My Captain!' was soon anthologized and, despite its author's earlier unsavoury reputation, accepted into elementary schoolbooks. 'When Lilacs Last in the Dooryard Bloom'd', on the other hand, impressed the cognoscenti of literature not only in this country but in England. In his study of William Blake, Swinburne magniloquently proclaimed 'his dirge over President Lincoln—the most sweet and sonorous nocturne ever chanted in the church of the world'. It is interesting to trace the stages (No. 32 and 45) by which he passed from this hyperbole to his fulminations in later life against the dangers of 'Whitmania'.

Henry James, however, underwent a change of heart in an opposite direction. From the scathing sentiments of his review in 1865 (No. 28) he proceeded to the relative benignity of his notice of Whitman's letters to Pete Doyle in the volume *Calamus* thirty-three years later (No. 55). There is also the well-known report by Edith Wharton of the positive enthusiasm of James's oral renditions of Whitman's verses in her autobiography, for which she chose a title allusive to one of Whitman's Prefaces, *A Backward Glance*.

Whitman's progress during this period was both a cause and a result of his being 'taken in hand' by reputable publishers and impresarios. In America, Whitman seemed to gain in respectability by being admitted to the list of Osgood (No. 42), though the publisher soon regretted his temerity and drew back before the threat of litigation on grounds of obscenity by the state's attorney. But the greatest 'coup' for Whitman's admission among the poets of the English language was undoubtedly created by the publication of Selections from the *Leaves* edited by William Rossetti in London in 1868 (No. 31). Whitman 'wept and fasted' before consenting to the expurgation that he had obstinately resisted in his own country. But Rossetti, in whom the friend and critic were almost indistinguishable from the impresario, finally prevailed with results so happy that Whitman and his disciples during his last years were inclined to romanticize the experience and to conclude from it that he was but one more illustration of the proposition that prophets are not without honour save in their own country.

The fact is that the most careful student of the growth of his reputation in England, Professor Harold Blodgett, has shown that the barriers to his recognition there were not substantially different from those which confronted him in the United States. But distance lent a certain enchantment on both sides, and the self-confidence of Whitman derived sustenance from the friendship of Rossetti, the politeness of Tennyson, the enthusiasm of Swinburne (before his radical recantation) and Stevenson, the visits and pilgrimages of Anne Gilchrist, Robert Buchanan, Edmund Gosse, Edward Carpenter and others. Signs of affection and esteem from the centre of the English-speaking cultural world certainly produced a stimulating effect upon Whitman's American reputation, just as earlier signs of rejection and distaste there had created a correspondingly depressing effect in the most cultivated circles on this side of the Atlantic.

The final validity of Rossetti's successful enterprise, however, must remain questionable. Of Whitman it may be affirmed by some who are what Scott Fitzgerald called 'quick deciders' that if you've read one of his poems (especially if that one happens to be 'Song of Myself') you have read them all, but it may also be said perhaps with as much truth that unless you have read all of his poems you have not properly read any one of them. No man gains more than he from the mass of his accomplishment rather than by any detail or example of it, however well chosen. All of his words throw light upon the meaning of each, and all of his poems do likewise with regard to each of them separately. No poet, for better or worse, is less *concentrated* in any verse or set of his verses, and if poetry is, as Amy Lowell once said, concentration, then those people are right (including herself) who feel that he may be no poet at all. No poet is less safely, justly or even fairly selected, excerpted or anthologized. And yet this hurrying world requires excerpts, selections and anthologies because it does not have the time or leisure to devote to the elucidation of any writer the attention which he requires to be fully understood. It may have been some such qualms about compromising his integrity that troubled Whitman about Rossetti's proposal of a volume of selections, and, despite the eventual happy outcome of the venture, he may well have been troubled, for, contrary to the dark suspicions and conjecture of Gerard Manley Hopkins (No. 44), Whitman was a man of honour and far from being 'a scoundrel'.

CANONIZATION, KINDNESS AND SOME BRICKBATS: 1892–1914

With Whitman's death in 1892, a predictable process of beatification on the one hand and of demolition on the other began. Some critics, particularly academic ones, attempted to steer a more or less neutral course between these extremes, but this was not easy to do because the passions of the partisans ran even higher at times than when Whitman himself was alive. He remained a source of contention. Hagiography was the first order of the day. Literary remains of the master, tributes, memoirs, a uniform edition of his collected works, including variorum readings—all this was the work of years, of lifetimes actually for his literary executors: Richard Maurice Bucke, Thomas Harned and Horace Traubel. Traubel's voluminous notes alone on the conversations, correspondence and day-to-day life of Whitman's last years have produced five books of over five hundred pages each (the last published in 1964) and the end is apparently not in sight yet almost eighty years after Whitman's death. Symonds' valuable testimony (No. 48) was published the year after Whitman's death (1893) which was also the year of Symonds' own untimely death. The valuable and rare collection of tributes and reminiscences *In Re Walt Whitman* was published by the executors in the same year. Among the more interesting contributions to this volume was one from T. W. Rolleston (No. 49), an Irish admirer and correspondent of Whitman's who was instrumental in helping to translate the *Leaves* into German and thus contributing to the spread of Whitman's European fame.

The year 1896 saw two significant additions to the record by disciples of Whitman, John Burroughs (No. 53) and William Sloane Kennedy (No. 54). The initial posthumous period also saw a large number of cooler though still basically kindly estimates of his significance such as the one by William James (No. 50). Close to this category and yet more neutral in its assessment is that of James's Harvard colleague George Santayana (No. 58), who as early as 1890 when Whitman was still alive had indicated in a philosophical dialogue, which considerations of space forbade us to include here, that he was of two minds about his subject, since he found that Whitman was an author capable of inspiring delight at the very moment he was provoking critical scepticism, not merely in different people at the same time or in the same person at different times but simultaneously within a person. Finally, this period witnessed some ferocious onslaughts against the poet, degenerating at times into *ad hominem* and personal reflections upon him and his work rivalling the worst examples of what had been said about him in the 1850s. These expressions came from those who felt too strongly to heed the ordinary amenities and the cautious Latin admonition to say nothing if not good about the dead. Examples are Max Nordau (No. 51), John Jay Chapman (No. 56) and possibly T. W. Higginson (No. 57).

This period is so rich in examples of all these varying attitudes that we have been compelled, for reasons of space, to omit many items which are intrinsically interesting. We have included nothing, for example, from the disciple Traubel's five volumes of memoirs and reflections. We have likewise sacrificed enthusiastic selections from Edward Carpenter and James Thomson, the author of *The City of Dreadful Night*. Among academic appraisals of various degrees of admiration or hostility, we have not included anything by Bliss Perry, Barrett Wendell, William Peterfield Treat or Paul Elmer More. An *ad hominem* assessment that we regret not having the space for (one of several examples of its kind in different languages) is a 1913 pamphlet by Dr. W. C. Rivers entitled *Walt Whitman's Anomaly*, published in London and, according to its cover, restricted to members of the medical profession. Rivers has little if anything to say about the literary quality of Whitman's work; he treats it solely for the light it is supposed to cast upon its author's putative latent or overt homosexuality. This question (in relation to the *Calamus* section of *Leaves of Grass*) had been raised directly during Whitman's lifetime by Symonds, and Whitman had indignantly denied what he regarded as a shocking imputation. Biographers like Professor Gay Wilson Allen have maintained an agnostic attitude on the point, but Rivers and those critics who have followed him insist on the decisiveness of the internal evidence of the poems themselves to establish the abnormality of Whitman's emotional life. From the point of view of pure literary criticism, of course, this approach, wherever it occurs, represents a bizarre digression. It is a historical curiosity, however, that there have always been those who would reduce Whitman from being primarily a writer to his interest as a 'case'. *Ad hominem* and reductive views of literature (including the Freudian and Marxist varieties) are effectively countered by Marcel Proust in *Contre Sainte-Beuve* with the challenging assertion that 'a book is the product of a different *self* from the self we manifest in our habits, in our social life, in our vices . . .'.

An inference from such a view seems to be that the determination of aesthetic and intellectual worth must finally rest upon some impersonal or objective ground as independent of the judge as it is of the one he judges, and also that it may be asserted with confidence only when arrived at by a broad consensus of readers, as widely separated from each other as possible in space and time. For this reason it has seemed appropriate to conclude this collection with an excerpt from Basil de Selincourt's penetrating study of Whitman (No. 59), first published in 1914. This study has been widely recognized as outstanding, and many of its detailed observations still seem as sensitive, sharp and perceptive as anything written about Whitman before or since. Selincourt's speculative metrical analysis of the opening lines of 'When Lilacs Last in the Dooryard Bloom'd', for example, opened new vistas in the appreciation of Whitman's instinctive technical verbal virtuosity.

It is perhaps as fitting to close this survey of the first sixty years of Whitman criticism with the concrete, practical aesthetic approach of Selincourt as it was to begin it with the broad, sweeping moral generalizations about the effect of the book and its content made by

Emerson. Emerson's letter, Whitman later confided to a friend, presented him with something like 'the chart of an emperor'. How well he utilized the prerogatives granted him by the man whom, in the Preface to the 1856 edition, he saluted as his 'Master', is the subject of Selincourt's critical inquiry.

WHITMAN'S RECEPTION OVERSEAS

Professor Allen for his volume *Walt Whitman Abroad* in 1955 compiled a bibliography of Whitman criticism and translations listing a selection of two hundred and fourteen titles from Germany, France, Denmark, Sweden, Norway, Russia, Bulgaria, Czechoslovakia, Latvia, Poland, the Ukraine, Yugoslavia, Italy, Spain and South America, Israel, Japan and India. Extensive as this listing is, it is hardly exhaustive if only because it leaves out China, about which, especially since the mainland went Communist, information may not have been available to Professor Allen. In the year that his book appeared, however, press dispatches indicated that the centennial of *Leaves of Grass* was marked in China by the appearance of a postage stamp honouring him. One may surmise that Red China's interest in Whitman was of a kind similar to that which explained his vogue in Revolutionary Russia, about which I shall have something to say a little later.

His fortunes in France, which so often sets the style not only in women's dress but in the arts (and which, significantly, has accumulated more Nobel awards for literature than any other country in the twentieth century) are particularly interesting. Some of the most fashionable names in late nineteenth century and early twentieth century France have been among his translators and critics: Jules Laforgue, André Gide and Valéry Larbaud, the translator of James Joyce.

Laforgue's attention to Whitman had been called by one of the French Symbolist poets, Stuart Merrill, who had been born in America. Laforgue published his version in 1886 under the title *Translations of the astonishing American poet, Walt Whitman.* André Gide was impelled to undertake a new translation of Whitman because he was dissatisfied with the idealized versions by Léon Bazalgette, which had become popular in France. Apollinaire wrote a fantastic surrealistic account of Whitman's funeral, supposedly on the authority of someone who had been there. But the turning point came in 1918 when Laforgue's translations were republished together with some by Gide and some by Larbaud who also contributed an important and illuminating essay which fixed Whitman's place firmly on the map of modern avant-garde and experimental literature.

The first seeds of Whitman's German fame were sown in 1868 by Ferdinand Freiligarth, the revolutionary poet who was a friend of Karl Marx and was a political exile residing in London when the volume of Rossetti's *Selections* appeared. Freiligarth reviewed it with boundless enthusiasm for the *Allgemeine Zeitung*. More effective was a monograph in German in 1882 published in New York by a German-American Karl Knortz. Knortz also collaborated with T. W. Rolleston in translating a selection from Whitman's poems, published in Switzerland after the German police had forbidden its publication in Germany.

As had been the case in France, the most sensational advance in the value of Whitman's 'stock' in Germany came with the end of the First World War. Hans Reisiger published a new translation of Whitman in 1919 which, according to one reviewer, succeeded in making the American into a German poet. Thomas Mann described Reisiger's translation as a 'holy gift' to Germany. In the wake of the Second World War, another translation by Georg Goyert, the translator of Joyce, evoked the enthusiasm of critics.

The growth of Whitman's reputation in Russia was given its greatest impetus by the Revolution of 1917, but it had begun a long time before that. Before 1900, Czarist censorship forbade virtually any mention of him or the fame he was achieving in western Europe. Nevertheless, the novelist Turgenev, who was an Anglophile, a traveller, and followed literary developments in the English-speaking literary world with close attention, was impressed enough with Whitman's work to translate some of his poems and offer them to an editor. Turgenev also appears to have spoken to an American writer in 1874 (quite possibly his friend Henry James) and to have told him that while there was undoubtedly a great deal of chaff in Whitman's work there was some good grain there as well. Tolstoy, too, though seemingly even more ambivalent on the subject than Turgenev, suggested the rendition of Whitman into Russian.

Nothing much came of these efforts, however, until 1907 when Kornei Chukovsky took advantage of a relaxation in Czarist censorship after the abortive revolution of 1905 to publish his translations from *Leaves of Grass*, which, by the year 1944, had gone into ten editions. Writing in 1955, Stephen Stepanchev said: 'It would be difficult to overestimate the importance of Walt Whitman in the history of Russian letters of the past fifty years. Whitman's emphasis on pioneering, on building a new, democratic future, on brotherhood and equality elicited a warm response both from youthful Marxists and from partisans of a gentler, more middle-class orientation.' After the Bolshevik Revolution, Whitman's poems appeared with an introduction by the Soviet commissar of culture, Lunacharsky, and his work became the major influence upon the futurist poet Vladimir Mayakovsky. By 1955, according to Stepanchev, 'It is not an exaggeration to say that Whitman is now a Russian as well as an American author.' Whitman's successes in other Slavic countries may perhaps be attributed to Russian influence, but some of them appear to have been achieved independently of it. In Czechoslovakia, for example, Whitman's poems were translated years before Chukovsky's epoch-making version was published in Russia.

Whitman was known early in the Scandinavian countries largely through the efforts of the Danish journalist Rudolf Schmidt. The Norwegian novelist Knut Hamsun, who was very critical of America, reacted against Schmidt's publicity for Whitman by writing one of the most satirical and amusing pieces ever penned against Whitman (No. 46), but another famous Norwegian author, Björnson, was an admirer of his work, and the novelist Johannes Jensen, not only translated Whitman's work into Danish but made the protagonist of his allegorical novel *Hjulet* (*The Wheel*) a character modelled upon Whitman, according to Professor Allen. In 1935, K. A. Svensson brought out a volume of Whitman's poems in Swedish translation.

French critics are credited with first bringing Whitman to the attention of Italian writers. His first influential enthusiast in Italy was Enrico Nencioni, who succeeded in arousing the interest of Carducci and D'Annunzio. Luigi Gambarale published a slim volume of translations from his work in 1887; this was enlarged in 1890 and finally a complete translation appeared in 1907. After the First World War, Giovanni Papini produced an effective proselytizing essay on Whitman's behalf, and after the Second World War the brilliant and ill-fated Cesare Pavese published an essay that is accepted as the most perceptive criticism of Whitman by an Italian. This renewed interest resulted in a complete new translation by Enzo Giachino.

The Cuban journalist José Marti, who had heard Whitman lecture on Lincoln in New York, is credited with introducing him to Latin America in 1887 with an essay that was published in *La Nacíon* in

Argentina and received wide circulation in South America. After the turn of the century, a Whitman cult came into existence in Spain, and a Catalan critic published a study of him and his message in 1913. Miguel de Unamuno published a sensitive and illuminating essay on Whitman entitled '*El canto adánice*' ('Adam's Song'), and the famous Spanish poet Garcia Lorca wrote a poem about him.

Whitman's manifest indebtedness to the Hebrew Bible for both his verse-form and his vision made his appreciation in that language natural. Decades before the establishment of the State of Israel in 1948, the poet Uri Zvi Greenberg was writing about him. In 1950, S. Shalom, a poet and journalist of Tel Aviv, explained why he had undertaken to translate Whitman: 'Whitman's pioneering is very close to us, and so are his Biblical rhythms. To translate him into Hebrew is like translating a writer back into his own language.' The best known and most ambitious translation of Whitman into Hebrew has been made by Simon Halkin, a poet, novelist and critic, who is a retired professor at the Hebrew University in Jerusalem. Professor Sholom J. Kahn of the Hebrew University, an American who has settled in Israel, has written perceptively about Whitman.

Whitman's work has exerted an influence, too, upon Yiddish poetry, and Louis Miller has translated and published selections from *Leaves of Grass* in that language.

Appreciation of Whitman in the Far East may be explained at least in part, as the United States Ambassador to Japan, John M. Allison, once did in opening an exhibit of Whitman materials accumulated by collectors in Tokyo after the Second World War, as a simple human response to the outgoing affection so warmly expressed by the poet who wrote *Salut au monde*:

> Health to you! good will to you all, from me and America sent!
> Each of us inevitable,
> Each of us limitless—each of us with his or her right upon the earth.

In a country like India, however, another factor may enter in that Whitman's mysticism has been thought by some readers to resemble that of the Upanishads, the Bhagavad-Gita and other sacred books. This had already been noticed by a reader like Thoreau who asked Whitman if he had ever read these Indian texts which were just becoming familiar to the West in translation during the nineteenth century. 'No,' Whitman is said to have replied to Thoreau's query, 'Tell me about them.'

CRITICISM AFTER 1914

In an article published in 1928 entitled 'The Critic and American Life', Irving Babbitt recorded his own 'protest against the present preposterous overestimate of Walt Whitman'. In the same year, writing an Introduction to the *Selected Poems of Ezra Pound*, T. S. Eliot assured readers, who may have entertained doubts upon the point, that 'I did not read Whitman until much later in life, and had to conquer an aversion to his form, as well as much of his matter, in order to do so.' He added: 'I am equally certain—indeed it is obvious—that Pound owes nothing to Whitman. This is an elementary observation.' In the light of some scholarly and critical investigations since then, the truth of this observation has turned out to be neither obvious nor elementary. And Eliot himself may have recognized this when he came to write of Pound again in the 1940s. Amy Lowell, too, had felt compelled to deny the influence of Whitman on the Imagist movement in which she was prominent: 'Often and often I read in the daily, weekly and monthly press, that modern *vers libre* writers derive their form from Walt Whitman. As a matter of fact, most of them got it from French Symbolist poets . . .'

The prevailing liberal and literary view of the period, though, increasingly approximated the one which Ludwig Lewisohn formulated with characteristic rhetoric and eloquence in his *Expression in America* (1932) where he had called Whitman 'the most strange and difficult figure in all our letters and perhaps the greatest, certainly the most far-reaching, far-echoing poetic voice'.

In the wake of the Great War (1914–18) many factors had converged to give Whitman pre-eminent stature, at home no less than abroad. The rise of America to world power heightened the interest in the work of a man who had self-consciously proclaimed himself her representative poet and had been accepted at his own estimate by a band of energetic and capable disciples. In the paradoxical post-war world of Prohibition and affluence, those intellectuals leading the struggle for liberation from the repressiveness and inhibitions of Puritan legalism found his frankness and openness, particularly with regard to sexual matters, much to their taste and honoured him as a precursor for the courage and obstinacy of the challenge which he had issued against respectable convention, Victorianism, the genteel tradition and censorship in his time. And many of his fellow-citizens, particularly those of recent immigrant origin, overlooking the nativist and nationalist strains in his work, responded to his internationalism and to his capacious conception of America as 'a nation of nations' (as he had called it in the Preface of 1855) in which none of them need feel alien any more or be compelled to sacrifice any of their distinctive cultural characteristics and background. Amy Lowell made a dour observation that 'it is perhaps sadly significant that the three modern poets who most loudly acknowledge his leadership are all of recent foreign extraction'.

While expatriate Americans (like Eliot and Pound) and some of the 'internal emigrés' in the States who sympathized with them regarded him with distaste and suspicion for those very reasons, other American writers who felt more at home in the melting-pot and were not altogether lacking in talent and prestige continued to testify to the pertinence both of his vision and his style. The most obvious example of Whitman's influence (and it may be one of those whom Amy Lowell had in mind) was no doubt Carl Sandburg, who claimed the whole Whitmanian inheritance—aesthetic, social and political—as his own. This claim can be granted only in part, however, because the extraordinary vivacity of Whitman's imagination and his verbal inventiveness and mimetic precision (e.g. 'The carpenter dresses his plank, the tongue of his foreplane whistles its wild ascending lisp') are never more impressive or clear than when they are contrasted with the laborious effects achieved by even a gifted member of his 'school' such as Sandburg. The sweep of Whitman's majestic vision of America ('The United States themselves are essentially the greatest poem,' he had written in the Preface of 1855) also came into possession of the imagination of a novelist like Thomas Wolfe, as his friend Scott Fitzgerald clearly recognized. Wolfe's dithyrambics to America and the American Dream (when they are separated from their context and grouped together as they are in the volume edited by John Hall Wheelock, *The Face of a Nation*) are quite evidently Whitmanian in quality though they are even wordier than Whitman and though Wolfe's lyricism is more prosaic and drags its plumes along the ground instead of soaring up into the empyrean of song. Yet the reader of Wolfe has the feeling that Whitman himself might have been pleased that his own national ('Unionist') vision had at last found a sympathetic echo in the heart of a Southern writer from the Carolinas.

One of the most impressive of the poetic proselytes that Whitman made in the post First World War period was Hart Crane, who addresses him directly as an inspirer in one of the sections of his epic

The Bridge. Unfortunately, since Crane's ambitious effort was regarded by many academicians at the time as a dismal failure, his intended tribute to Whitman turned into something of a reproach to his master, as is clear from the comment of Yvor Winters in his review in *Poetry* (Chicago) in 1930. According to this reviewer, *The Bridge* merely succeeded in proving 'the impossibility of getting anywhere with the Whitmanian inspiration. No writer of comparable ability has struggled with it before, and with Mr. Crane's wreckage in view it seems highly unlikely that any writer of comparable genius will struggle with it again.'

This forecast did not prove fortunate, and Whitman continued to exercise his fascination upon leading poets of the twentieth century long after 1930, as is evident from a response of William Carlos Williams to this editor's invitation to contribute to a celebration of the centenary of the publication of *Leaves of Grass* in 1955. In the letter accompanying his essay (printed in *Leaves of Grass: One Hundred Years After*), Williams called the *Leaves* 'a book as important as we are likely to see in the next thousand years, especially a book written by an American'.

Succeeding generations of poets and prose writers of varying degrees of talent and prominence from D. H. Lawrence and Henry Miller to Allen Ginsberg, Lawrence Ferlinghetti and David Ignatow have all supplied vivid confirmations of the continuing viability and potency of the Whitmanian muse. The sixties, in America, with their turbulence and social upheaval, have been as hospitable to Whitman, and for many of the same reasons, as the 1930s were. And whatever the future may bring, it seems safe to predict that one facet or another of his many-sided and even contradictory appeal will continue to interest at least some readers and writers. It is not too soon to affirm that the evidence in this book tends to support the conclusion that he belongs not only to history but to living literature as well.

1855–60

1. Emerson's letter to Whitman

1855

Letter from Ralph Waldo Emerson to Whitman, 21 July 1855. Transcribed from facsimile copy in *Walt Whitman: A Selection of the Manuscripts, Books and Association Items*. Gathered by Charles E. Feinberg. Catalogue of an Exhibition Held at The Detroit Public Library, Detroit, Michigan, 1955. The Introduction to this Catalogue by David C. Mearns, Chief of the Manuscripts Division of the Library of Congress, notes that 'This has been called "probably now the most famous letter in American literary history".'

Concord 21 July
Masstts 1855

Dear Sir,

I am not blind to the worth of the wonderful gift of *Leaves of Grass*. I find it the most extraordinary piece of wit & wisdom that America has yet contributed. I am very happy in reading it, as great power makes us happy. It meets the demand I am always making of what seemed the sterile and stingy Nature, as if too much handiwork or too much lymph in the temperament were making our western wits fat & mean. I give you joy of your free & brave thoughts. I have great joy in it. I find incomparable things said incomparably well, as they must be. I find the courage of treatment, which so delights us, & which large perception only can inspire. I greet you at the beginning of a great career, which yet must have had a long foreground somewhere for such a start. I rubbed my eyes a little to see if this sunbeam were no illusion; but the solid sense of the book is a sober certainty. It has the best merits, namely, of fortifying & encouraging.

I did not know until I, last night, saw the book advertised in a newspaper, that I could trust the name as real & available for a post-office. I wish to see my benefactor, & have felt much like striking my tasks, & visiting New York to pay you my respects.

R. W. Emerson.

Mr. Walter Whitman.

2. The first notice

1855

The initial notice of *Leaves of Grass,* so far as is known, appeared in the *New York Daily Tribune* on 23 July 1855. It was written by the editor, Charles A. Dana. Dana (1819–97) served as second assistant-secretary of war under Stanton in 1864–5 and afterwards returned to journalism as editor of the *New York Sun*.

From the unique effigies of the anonymous author of this volume which graces the frontispiece, we may infer that he belongs to the exemplary class of society sometimes irreverently styled 'loafers.' He is therein represented in a garb, half sailor's, half workman's, with no superfluous appendage of coat or waistcoat, a 'wide-awake' perched jauntily on his head, one hand in his pocket and the other on his hip, with a certain air of mild defiance, and an expression of pensive insolence in his face which seems to betoken a consciousness of his mission as the 'coming man.' This view of the author is confirmed in the preface. He vouchsafes, before introducing us to his poetry, to enlighten our benighted minds as to the true function of the American poet. Evidently the original, which is embodied in the most extraordinary prose since the 'Sayings' of the modern Orpheus, was found in the 'interior consciousness' of the writer. Of the materials afforded by this country for the operations of poetic art we have a lucid account:

[here follows a very extensive excerpt from the 1855 Preface beginning with the words 'The Americans of all nations . . .']

Of the nature of poetry the writer discourses in a somewhat too oracular strain, especially as he has been anticipated in his 'utterances' by Emerson and other modern 'prophets of the soul':

[here follows a long passage from Whitman's Introduction beginning with the words: 'The poetic quality . . .']

Such is the poetic theory of our nameless bard. He furnishes a severe standard for the estimate of his own productions. His *Leaves of Grass* are doubtless intended as an illustration of the natural poet. They are certainly original in their external form, have been shaped on no pre-existent model out of the author's own brain. Indeed, his independence often becomes coarse and defiant. His language is too frequently reckless and indecent, though this appears to arise from a naive unconsciousness rather than from an impure mind. His words might have passed between Adam and Eve in Paradise, before the want of fig-leaves brought no shame; but they are quite out of place amid the decorum of modern society, and will justly prevent his volume from free circulation in scrupulous circles. With these glaring faults, the *Leaves of Grass* are not destitute of peculiar poetic merits, which will awaken an interest in the lovers of literary curiosities. They are full of bold, stirring thoughts—with occasional passages of effective description, betraying a genuine intimacy with Nature and a keen appreciation of beauty—often presenting a rare felicity of diction, but so disfigured with eccentric fancies as to prevent a consecutive perusal without offense, though no impartial reader can fail to be impressed with the vigor and quaint beauty of isolated portions. A few specimens will suffice to give an idea of this odd genius.

[here follow extensive excerpts from Whitman's poems beginning with passages now in Section 21 of 'Song of Myself'—as yet untitled in the 1855 edition: 'I am he that walks with the tender and growing night . . .']

The volume contains many more 'Leaves of Grass' of similar quality, as well as others which cannot be especially commended either for fragrance or form. Whatever severity of criticism they may challenge for their rude ingenuousness, and their frequent divergence into the realm of the fantastic, the taste of not overdainty fastidiousness will discern much of the essential spirit of poetry beneath an uncouth and grotesque embodiment.

3. Charles Eliot Norton's review

1855

This review by Charles Eliot Norton (1827–1908) appeared in *Putnam's Monthly* in New York in September 1855. Norton, who was to be the first professor of the history of art at Harvard and the editor, with James Russell Lowell, of the *North American Review*, was impressed enough with Whitman's style to attempt writing some 'free verse' of his own.

Our account of the last month's literature would be incomplete without some notice of a curious and lawless collection of poems, called *Leaves of Grass*, and issued in a thin quarto without the name of publisher or author. The poems, twelve in number, are neither in rhyme nor blank verse, but in a sort of excited prose broken into lines without any attempt at measure or regularity, and, as many readers will perhaps think, without any idea of sense or reason. The writer's scorn for the wonted usages of good writing extends to the vocabulary he adopts; words usually banished from polite society are here employed without reserve and with perfect indifference to their effect on the reader's mind; and not only is the book one not to be read aloud to a mixed audience, but the introduction of terms never before heard or seen, and of slang expressions, often renders an otherwise striking passage altogether laughable. But, as the writer is a new light in poetry, it is only fair to let him state his theory for himself. We extract from the preface:—

The art of art, the glory of expression, is simplicity. Nothing is better than simplicity, and the sunlight of letters is simplicity. Nothing is better than simplicity—nothing can make up for excess, or for the lack of definiteness. . . . To speak in literature, with the perfect rectitude and the insouciance of the movements of animals and the unimpeachableness of the sentiment of trees in the woods, is the flawless triumph of art. . . . The greatest poet has less a marked style, and is more the channel of thought and things, without increase or diminution, and is the free channel of himself. He swears to his art, I will not be meddlesome, I will not have in my writing any elegance, or effect, or originality to hang in the way between me and the rest, like curtains. What I feel, I feel for precisely what it is. Let who may exalt, or startle, or fascinate, or soothe, I will have purposes, as health, or heat, or snow has, and be as regardless of observation. What I experience or portray shall go from my composition without a shred of my composition. You shall stand by my side to look in the mirror with me.

The application of these principles, and of many others equally peculiar, which are expounded in a style equally oracular throughout the long preface,—is made *passim*, and often with comical success, in the poems themselves, which may briefly be described as a compound of the New England transcendentalist and New York rowdy. A fireman or omnibus driver, who had intelligence enough to absorb the speculations of that school of thought which culminated at Boston some fifteen or eighteen years ago, and resources of expression to put them forth again in a form of his own, with sufficient self-conceit and contempt for public taste to affront all usual propriety of diction, might have written this gross yet elevated, this superficial yet profound, this preposterous yet somehow fascinating book. As we say, it is a mixture of Yankee transcendentalism and New York rowdyism, and, what must be surprising to both these elements, they here seem to fuse and combine with the most perfect harmony. The vast and vague conceptions of the one, lose nothing of their quality in passing through the coarse and odd intellectual medium of the other; while there is an original perception of nature, a manly brawn, and an epic directness in our new poet, which belong to no other adept of the transcendental school. But we have no intention of regularly criticising this very irregular production; our aim is rather to cull, from the rough and ragged thicket of its pages, a few passages equally remarkable in point of thought and expression. Of course we do not select those which are the most transcendental or the most bold:—

I play not a march for victors only. . . . I play great marches for conquered and slain persons.
Have you heard that it was good to gain the day?
I also say it is good to fall . . . battles are lost in the same spirit in which they are won.
I sound triumphal drums for the dead . . . I fling through my embouchures the loudest and gayest music to them—
Vivas to those who have failed, and to those whose war-vessels sank in the sea, and to those themselves who sank in the sea.

And to all generals that lost engagements, and to all overcome heroes, and the numberless unknown heroes equal to the greatest heroes known.

I am the mashed fireman, with breast-bone broken . . . tumbling walls buried me in their débris—
Heat and smoke, I respired . . . I heard the yelling shouts of my comrades—
I heard the distant click of their picks and shovels.
They have cleared the beams away . . . they tenderly lift me forth.
I lie in the night air in my red shirt . . . the pervading hush is for my sake.
Painless after all I lie, exhausted, but not so unhappy.
White and beautiful are the faces around me . . . the heads are bared of their fire-caps—
The kneeling crowd fades with the light of the torches.

As to you, life, I reckon you are the leavings of many deaths:
No doubt I have died myself ten thousand times before.
I hear you whispering there, O stars of heaven—
O suns! O grave of graves! O perpetual transfers and promotions, if you do not say anything, how can I say anything.
Of the turbid pool that lies in the autumn forest—
Of the moon that descends the steeps of the soughing twilight?
Toss, sparkles of day and dusk—toss on the black stems that decay in the muck—
Toss to the moaning gibberish of the dry limbs!

Behold a woman!
She looks out from her Quaker cap . . . her face is clearer and more beautiful than the sky,
She sits in an arm-chair, under the shaded porch of the farm house—
The sun just shines on her old white head.
Her ample gown is of cream-hued linen:
Her grandsons raised the flax, and her grand-daughters spun it with the distaff and the wheel.
The melodious character of the earth!
The finish, beyond which philosophy cannot go, and does not wish to go!
The justified mother of men!

Old age superbly rising! Ineffable grace of dying days.

Day, full-blown and splendid . . . day of the immense sun, and action, and ambition, and laughter;
The night follows close, with millions of suns, and sleep, and restoring darkness.

As seems very proper in a book of transcendental poetry, the author withholds his name from the title page, and presents his portrait, neatly engraved on steel, instead. This, no doubt, is upon the principle that the name is merely accidental; while the portrait affords an idea of the essential being from whom these utterances proceed. We must add, however, that this significant reticence does not prevail throughout the volume, for we learn on p. 29, that our poet is 'Walt Whitman, an American, one of the roughs, a kosmos.' That he was an American, we knew before, for, aside from America, there is no quarter of the universe where such a production could have had a genesis. That he was one of the roughs was also tolerably plain; but that he was a kosmos, is a piece of news we were hardly prepared for. Precisely what a kosmos is, we trust Mr. Whitman will take an early occasion to inform the impatient public.

4. Moncure Conway visits Whitman

1855

Letter to Ralph Waldo Emerson, 17 September 1855. Published in *Autobiography, Memories and Experiences of Moncure Daniel Conway* (1904), I, 215–16.

Moncure Daniel Conway (1832–1907) was an American clergyman and author. After studying law for a year he became a Methodist minister in his native state of Virginia. In 1853, Emerson helped him to enter the Harvard Divinity school, from which he was graduated in 1854. His abolitionist views aroused hostility among his neighbours, and he was dismissed from a Unitarian church in Washington, D.C. From 1856 to 1861, he served as minister in the First Congregational Church in Cincinnati, Ohio, and while there edited a liberal periodical named after its eastern predecessor, the *Dial*. During the Civil War, he lectured in England on behalf of the North. For more than twenty years (1863–84), he was minister of the South Place chapel, Finsbury, London. During this time he wrote voluminously for the London Press. In 1884, he returned to his native country to devote himself to literary work. He died in Paris in 1907. Among his works are: *Tracts for To-day* (1858), *Republican Superstitions* (1872), *Idols and Ideals* (1871), *Demonology and Devil-Lore* (1878), *The Wandering Jew* (1881), *The Life of Thomas Paine* (1892) and his *Autobiography* (1904) which is regarded generally as being especially valuable for its sketches of important personages in the nineteenth century who looked upon him as a leader of liberal thought.

My dear Mr. Emerson,—I immediately procured the *Leaves of Grass* after hearing you speak of it. I read it on board the steamer Metropolis on my way to New York the evening after seeing you, and resolved to see its author if I could while I was in the city. As you seemed much interested in him and his work, I have taken the earliest moment which I could command since my return to give you some account of my visit.

I found by the directory that one Walter Whitman lived fearfully far (out of Brooklyn, nearly), on Ryerton Street a short way from Myrtle Avenue. The way to reach the house is to go down to Fulton Street Ferry, after crossing take the Fulton and Myrtle Avenue car, and get out at Ryerton Street. It is one of a row of small wooden houses with porches, which all seem occupied by mechanics. I didn't find him there, however. His mother directed me to Rome's Printing Office (corner Fulton and Cranberry Streets), which is much nearer, and where he often is.

I found him revising some proof. A man you would not have marked in a thousand; blue striped shirt, opening from a red throat; sitting on a chair without a back, which, being the only one, he offered me, and sat down on a round of the printer's desk himself. His manner was blunt enough also, without being disagreeably so.

I told him that I had spent the evening before with you, and that what you had said of him, and the perusal of his book had resulted in my call. He seemed very eager to hear from you and about you, and what you thought of his book. He had once seen you and heard you in the lecture-room, and was anxious to know all he could of your life, yet not with any vulgar curiosity but entire frankness. I told him of the occasions in which Mr. Bartel and others had attempted to read it in company and failed, at which he seemed much amused.

The likeness in the book is fair. His beard and hair are greyer than is usual with a man of thirty-six. His face and eye are interesting, and his head rather narrow behind the eyes; but a thick brow looks as if it might have absorbed much. He walked with me and crossed the Ferry; he seemed 'hail fellow' with every man he met, all apparently in the labouring class. He says he is one of that class by choice; that he is personally dear to some thousands of such in New York, who 'love him but cannot make head or tail of his book.' He rides on the stage with the driver. Stops to talk with the old man or woman selling fruit at the street corner. And his dress, etc., is consistent with that.

I am quite sure after talking with him that there is much in all this of what you might call 'playing Providence a little with the baser sort' (so much to the distress of the Rev. Vaughan's nerves). . . . I could see that he had some books if only a bottle-stick like Alton Locke to read them by; though he told me I thought too much of books. But I came off delighted with him. His eye can kindle strangely; and his words are ruddy with health. He is clearly his Book,—and I went off impressed with the sense of a new city on my map, viz., Brooklyn, just as if it had suddenly risen through the boiling sea.

5. Norton and Lowell disagree

1855

Letters quoted in Kenneth Ballard Murdock's Explanatory Essay in *A Leaf of Grass* (Cambridge, Massachusetts, 1928), a reprint of Norton's review of *Leaves of Grass* in *Putnam's Monthly* (September 1855).

(*a*) Extract from letter from Charles Eliot Norton to James Russell Lowell, 23 September 1855: A new book called *Leaves of Grass* has just come out which is worth knowing about . . . Its author according to his own account is 'Walt Whitman, one of the roughs, a kosmos.' It is a book which has excited Emerson's enthusiasm. He has written a letter to this 'one of the roughs' which I have seen, expressing the warmest admiration and encouragement. It is no wonder that he likes it, for Walt Whitman has read the *Dial* and Nature, and combines the characteristics of a Concord philosopher with those of a New York fireman. There is little original thought but much original expression in it. There are some passages of most vigorous and vivid writing, some superbly graphic descriptions, great stretches of imagination,—and then, passages of intolerable coarseness,—not gross and licentious but simply disgustingly coarse. The book is such indeed that one cannot leave it about for chance readers, and would be sorry to know that any woman had looked into it past the title page. I have got a copy for you, for there are things in it that you will admire.

(*b*) Extract from Lowell's reply to Norton, 12 October 1855: 'I thank you for having thought of me in the copy of Whitman's book . . . I remember him of old—he used to write for the *Democratic Review* . . . No, no, this kind of thing you describe won't do. When a man aims at originality he acknowledges himself consciously unoriginal, a want of self-respect which does not often go along with the capacity for great things. The great fellows have always let the stream of their activity flow quietly—if one splashes in it he may make a sparkle, but he muddies it too, and the good folks down below (I mean posterity) will have none of it.

6. Rufus W. Griswold on Whitman

1855

Unsigned review, *New York Criterion* (10 November 1855). Included in *Imprints*, pp. 55–6.

Rufus W. Griswold was the literary executor of Edgar Allan Poe. He is identified as the author of this review in W. D. O'Connor's copy of *Leaves of Grass*. (See Bliss Perry, *Walt Whitman: His Life and Work*, 2nd ed. rev. (1908), p. 100.)

An unconsidered letter of introduction has oftentimes procured the admittance of a scurvy fellow into good society, and our apology for permitting any allusion to the above volume in our columns is, that it has been unworthily recommended by a gentleman of wide repute, and might, on that account, obtain access to respectable people, unless its real character were exposed.

Mr Ralph Waldo Emerson either recognizes and accepts these 'leaves,' as the gratifying result of his own peculiar doctrines, or else he has hastily indorsed them, after a partial and superficial reading. If it is of any importance he may extricate himself from the dilemma. We, however, believe that this book does express the bolder results of a certain transcendental kind of thinking, which some may have styled philosophy.

As to the volume itself, we have only to remark, that it strongly fortifies the doctrines of the Metempsychosists, for it is impossible to imagine how any man's fancy could have conceived such a mass of stupid filth, unless he were possessed of the soul of a sentimental donkey that had died of disappointed love. This *poet* (?) without wit, but with a certain vagrant wildness, just serves to show the energy which natural imbecility is occasionally capable of under strong excitement.

There are too many persons, who imagine they demonstrate their superiority to their fellows, by disregarding all the politenesses and decencies of life, and, therefore, justify themselves in indulging the vilest imaginings and shamefullest license. But Nature, abhorring the abuse of the capacities she has given to man, retaliates upon him, by rendering extravagant indulgence in any direction followed by an insatiable, ever-consuming, and never to be appeased passion.

Thus, to these pitiful beings, virtue and honor are but names. Bloated with self-conceit, they strut abroad unabashed in the daylight, and expose to the world the festering sores that overlay them, like a garment. Unless we admit this exhibition to be beautiful, we are at once set down for non-progressive conservatives, destitute of the 'inner light,' the far-seeingness which, of course, characterizes those gifted individuals. Now, any one who has noticed the tendency of thought in these later years, must be aware that a quantity of this kind of nonsense is being constantly displayed. The immodesty of presumption exhibited by those *seers;* their arrogant pretentiousness; the complacent smile with which they listen to the echo of their own braying, should be, and we believe is, enough to disgust the great majority of sensible folks; but, unfortunately, there is a class that, mistaking sound for sense, attach some importance to all this rant and cant. These candid, these ingenuous, these honest 'progressionists;' these human diamonds without flaws; these men that have *come*—detest furiously all shams; 'to the pure, all things are pure;' they are pure, and, consequently, must thrust their reeking presence under every man's nose.

They seem to think that man has no instinctive delicacy; is not imbued with a conservative and preservative modesty, that acts as a restraint upon the violence of passions, which for a wise purpose, have been made so strong. No! these fellows have no secrets, no disguises; no, indeed! But they do have, conceal it by whatever language they choose, a degrading, beastly sensuality, that is fast rotting the healthy core of all the social virtues.

There was a time when licentiousness laughed at reproval; now it writes essays and delivers lectures. Once it shunned the light; now it courts attention, writes books showing how grand and pure it is, and prophesies from its lecherous lips its own ultimate triumph.

Shall we argue with such men? Shall we admit them into our houses, that they may leave a foul odor, contaminating the pure, healthful air? Or shall they be placed in the same category with the comparatively innocent slave of poverty, ignorance, and passion that skulks along in the shadows of byways; even in her deep degradation possessing some sparks of the Divine light, the germ of good that reveals itself by a sense of shame?

Thus, then, we leave this gathering of muck to the laws which, certainly, if they fulfil their intent, must have power to suppress such obscenity. As it is entirely destitute of wit, there is no probability that any would, after this exposure, read it in the hope of finding that; and we trust no one will require further evidence—for, indeed, we do not believe there is a newspaper so vile that would print confirmatory extracts.

In our allusion to this book, we have found it impossible to convey any, even the most faint idea of its style and contents, and of our disgust and detestation of them, without employing language that cannot be pleasing to ears polite; but it does seem that some one should, under circumstances like these, undertake a most disagreeable, yet stern duty. The records of crime show that many monsters have gone on in impunity, because the exposure of their vileness was attended with too great indelicacy. *Peccatum illud horribile, inter Christianos non nominandum.*[1]

[1] 'That horrible sin not to be mentioned among Christians.'

7. Whitman's anonymous self-reviews

1855–6

(*a*) Unsigned review, *United States Review* (1855). Included in *Imprints*, pp. 7–13. (See Introduction, p. 14): An American bard at last! One of the roughs, large, proud, affectionate, eating, drinking, and breeding, his costume manly and free, his face sunburnt and bearded, his posture strong and erect, his voice bringing hope and prophecy to the generous races of young and old. We shall cease shamming and be what we really are. We shall start an athletic and defiant literature. We realize now how it is, and what was most lacking. The interior American republic shall also be declared free and independent.

For all our intellectual people, followed by their books, poems, novels, essays, editorials, lectures, tuitions and criticisms, dress by London and Paris modes, receive what is received there, obey the authorities, settle disputes by the old tests, keep out of the rain and sun, retreat to the shelter of houses and schools, trim their hair, shave, touch not the earth barefoot, and enter not the sea except in a complete bathing dress. One sees unmistakably genteel persons, travelled, college-learned, used to be served by servants, conversing without heat or vulgarity, supported on chairs, or walking through handsomely carpeted parlors, or along shelves bearing well-bound volumes, and walls adorned with curtained and collared portraits, and china things, and nick-nacks. But where in American literature is the first show of America? Where are the gristle and beards, and broad breasts, and space, and ruggedness, and nonchalance, that the souls of the people love? Where is the tremendous outdoors of these states? Where is the majesty of the federal mother, seated with more than antique grace, calm, just, indulgent to her brood of children, calling them around her, regarding the little and the large, and the younger and the older, with perfect impartiality? Where is the vehement growth of our cities? Where is the spirit of the strong rich life of the American mechanic, farmer, sailor, hunter, and miner? Where is the huge composite of all other nations, cast in a fresher and brawnier matrix, passing adolescence, and needed this day, live and arrogant, to lead the marches of the world?

Self-reliant, with haughty eyes, assuming to himself all the attributes of his country, steps Walt Whitman into literature, talking like a man unaware that there was ever hitherto such a production as a book, or such a being as a writer. Every move of him has the free play of the muscle of one who never knew what it was to feel that he stood in the presence of a superior. Every word that falls from his mouth shows silent disdain and defiance of the old theories and forms. Every phrase announces new laws; not once do his lips unclose except in conformity with them. With light and rapid touch he first indicates in prose the principles of the foundation of a race of poets so deeply to spring from the American people, and become ingrained through them, that their Presidents shall not be the common referees so much as that great race of poets shall. He proceeds himself to exemplify this new school, and set models for their expression and range of subjects. He makes audacious and native use of his own body and soul. He must recreate poetry with the elements always at hand. He must imbue it with himself as he is, disorderly, fleshy, and sensual, a lover of things, yet a lover of men and women above the whole of the other objects of the universe. His work is to be achieved by unusual methods. Neither classic or romantic is he, nor a materialist any more than a spiritualist. Not a whisper comes out of him of the old stock talk and rhyme of poetry—not the first recognition of gods or goddesses, or Greece or Rome. No breath of Europe, or her monarchies or priestly conventions, or her notions of gentlemen and ladies, founded on the idea of caste, seems ever to have fanned his face or been inhaled into his lungs.

The movement of his verses is the sweeping movement of great currents of living people, with a general government and state and municipal governments, courts, commerce, manufactures, arsenals, steamships, railroads, telegraphs, cities with paved streets, and aqueducts, and police, and gas—myriads of travellers arriving and departing—newspapers, music, elections, and all the features and processes of the nineteenth century, in the wholesomest race and the only stable forms of politics at present upon the earth. Along his words spread the broad impartialities of the United States. No innovations must be permitted on the stern severities of our liberty and equality. Undecked also is this poet with sentimentalism, or jingle, or nice conceits, or flowery similes. He appears in his poems surrounded by women and children, and by young men, and by common objects and qualities. He gives to each just what belongs to it, neither more nor less. That person nearest him, that person he ushers hand in hand with himself. Duly take places in his flowing procession, and step to the sounds of the jubilant music, the essences of American things, and past and present events—the enormous diversity of temperature, and agriculture, and mines—the tribes of red aborigines—the weather-beaten vessels entering new ports, or making landings on rocky coasts—the first settlements north and south—the rapid stature and impatience of outside control—the sturdy defiance of '76, and the war and peace, and the leadership of Washington, and the formation of the constitution—the union always surrounded by blatherers and always calm and impregnable—the perpetual coming of immigrants—the wharf-hemmed cities and superior marine—the unsurveyed interior—the log-houses and clearings, and wild animals and hunters and trappers—the fisheries, and whaling, and gold-digging—the endless gestation of new States—the convening of Congress every December, the members coming up from all climates, and from the uttermost parts—the noble character of the free American workman and workwoman—the fierceness of the people when well roused—the ardor of their friendships—the large amativeness—the equality of the female with the male—the Yankee swap—the New York firemen and the target excursion—the southern plantation life—the character of the northeast and of the northwest and southwest—and the character of America and the American people everywhere. For these the old usages of poets afford Walt Whitman no means sufficiently fit and free, and he rejects the old usages. The style of the bard that is waited for, is to be transcendent and new. It is to be indirect, and not direct or descriptive or epic. Its quality is to go through these to much more. Let the age and wars (he says) of other nations be chanted, and their eras and characters be illustrated, and that finish the verse. Not so (he continues) the great psalm of the republic. Here the theme is creative and has vista. Here comes one among the well-beloved stone cutters, and announces himself, and plans with decision and science, and sees the solid and beautiful forms of the future where there are now no solid forms.

The style of these poems, therefore, is simply their own style, just born and red. Nature may have given the hint to the author of the *Leaves of Grass*, but there exists no book or fragment of a book which can have given the hint to them. All beauty, he says, comes from beautiful blood and a beautiful brain. His rhythm and uniformity he will conceal in the roots of his verses, not to be seen of themselves, but to break forth loosely as lilacs on a bush, and take shapes compact, as the shapes of melons, or chestnuts, or pears.

The poems of the *Leaves of Grass* are twelve in number. Walt Whitman at first proceeds to put his own body and soul into the new versification:

> I celebrate myself,
> For what I assume you shall assume,
> For every atom belonging to me, as good belongs to you.

He leaves houses and their shuttered rooms, for the open air. He drops disguise and ceremony, and walks forth with the confidence and gayety of a child. For the old decorums of writing he substitutes his own decorums. The first glance out of his eyes electrifies him with love and delight. He will have the earth receive and return his affection; he will stay with it as the bridegroom stays with the bride. The cool-breath'd ground, the slumbering and liquid trees, the just-gone sunset, the vitreous pour of the full moon, the tender and growing night, he salutes and touches, and they touch him. The sea supports him, and hurries him off with its powerful and crooked fingers. Dash me with amorous wet! then, he says; I can repay you.

The rules of polite circles are dismissed with scorn. Your stale modesties, he seems to say, are filthy to such a man as I.

> I believe in the flesh and the appetites,
> Seeing, hearing, and feeling, are miracles, and each part and tag of me is a miracle.
> I do not press my finger across my mouth,
> I keep as delicate around the bowels as around the head and heart,
> Copulation is no more rank to me than death is.

No skulker or tea-drinking poet is Walt Whitman. He will bring poems to fill the days and nights—fit for men and women with the attributes of throbbing blood and flesh. The body, he teaches, is beautiful. Sex is also beautiful. Are you to be put down, he seems to ask, to that shallow level of literature and conversation that stops a man's recognizing the delicious pleasure of his sex, or a woman hers? Nature he proclaims inherently clean. Sex will not be put aside; it is a great ordination of the universe. He works the muscle of the male and the teeming fibre of the female throughout his writings, as wholesome realities, impure only by deliberate intention and effort. To men and women he says, You can have healthy and powerful breeds of children on no less terms than these of mine. Follow me, and there shall be taller and richer crops of humanity on the earth.

Especially in the *Leaves of Grass* are the facts of eternity and immortality largely treated. Happiness is no dream, and perfection is no dream. Amelioration is my lesson, he says with calm voice, and progress is my lesson and the lesson of all things. Then his persuasion becomes a taunt, and his love bitter and compulsory. With strong and steady call he addresses men. Come, he seems to say, from the midst of all that you have been your whole life surrounding yourself with. Leave all the preaching and teaching of others, and mind only these words of mine.

Long enough have you dreamed contemptible dreams,
Now I wash the gum from your eyes,
You must habit yourself to the dazzle of the light and of every moment of your life.

Long have you timidly waded, holding a plank by the shore,
Now I will you to be a bold swimmer,
To jump off in the midst of the sea, and rise again and nod to me and shout, and laughingly dash with your hair.

I am the teacher of athletes,
He that by me spreads a wider breast than my own proves the width of my own,
He most honors my style who learns under it to destroy the teacher.

The boy I love, the same becomes a man not through derived power but in his own right,
Wicked, rather than virtuous out of conformity or fear,
Fond of his sweetheart, relishing well his steak,
Unrequited love or a slight cutting him worse than a wound cuts,
First rate to ride, to fight, to hit the bull's eye, to sail a skiff, to sing a song, or play on the banjo,
Preferring scars and faces pitted with small pox over all latherers and those that keep out of the sun.

I teach straying from me, yet who can stray from me?
I follow you whoever you are from the present hour:
My words itch at your ears till you understand them.

I do not say these things for a dollar, or to fill up the time while I wait for a boat:

It is you talking just as much as myself . . . I act as the tongue of you,
It was tied in your mouth . . . in mine it begins to be loosened.

I swear I will never mention love or death inside a house,
And I swear I never will translate myself at all, only to him or her who privately stays with me in the open air.

The eleven other poems have each distinct purposes, curiously veiled. Theirs is no writer to be gone through with in a day or a month. Rather it is his pleasure to elude you and provoke you for deliberate purposes of his own.

Doubtless in the scheme this man has built for himself, the writing of poems is but a proportionate part of the whole. It is plain that public and private performance, politics, love, friendship, behavior, the art of conversation, science, society, the American people, the reception of the great novelties of city and country, all have their equal call upon him, and receive equal attention. In politics he could enter with the freedom and reality he shows in poetry. His scope of life is the amplest of any yet in philosophy. He is the true spiritualist. He recognizes no annihilation, or death, or loss of identity. He is the largest lover and sympathizer that has appeared in literature. He loves the earth and sun and the animals. He does not separate the learned from the unlearned, the northerner from the southerner, the white from the black, or the native from the immigrant just landed at the wharf. Every one, he seems to say, appears excellent to me; every employment is adorned, and every male and female glorious.

The press of my foot to the earth springs a hundred affections,
They scorn the best I can do to relate them.

I am enamoured of growing outdoors,
Of men that live among cattle, or taste of the ocean or woods,
Of the builders and steerers of ships, of the wielders of axes and mauls, of the drivers of horses,
I can eat and sleep with them week in and week out.

What is commonest, and cheapest, and easiest, is me,
Me going in for my chances, spending for vast returns,
Adorning myself to bestow myself on the first that will take me,
Not asking the sky to come down to my goodwill,
Scattering it freely forever.

If health were not his distinguishing attribute, this poet would be the very harlot of persons. Right and left he flings his arms, drawing men and women with undeniable love to his close embrace, loving the clasp of their hands, the touch of their necks and breasts, and the sound of their voice. All else seems to burn up under his fierce affection for persons. Politics, religions, institutions, art, quickly fall aside before them. In the whole universe, he says, I see nothing more divine than human souls.

When the psalm sings instead of the singer,
When the script preaches instead of the preacher,
When the pulpit descends and goes, instead of the carver that carved the supporting desk,
When the sacred vessels or the bits of the eucharist, or the lath and plast, procreate as effectually as the young silversmiths or bakers, or the masons in their overalls,
When a university course convinces like a slumbering woman and child convince,
When the minted gold in the vault smiles like the night-watchman's daughter,
When warrantee deeds loafe in chairs opposite and are my friendly companions,
I intend to reach them my hand and make as much of them as I make of men and women.

Who then is that insolent unknown? Who is it, praising himself as if others were not fit to do it, and coming rough and unbidden among writers, to unsettle what was settled, and to revolutionize in fact our modern civilization? Walt Whitman was born on Long Island, on the hills about thirty miles from the greatest American city, on the last day of May, 1819, and has grown up in Brooklyn and New York to be thirty-six years old, to enjoy perfect health, and to understand his country and its spirit.

Interrogations more than this, and that will not be put off unanswered, spring continually through the perusal of *Leaves of Grass*:

Must not the true American poet indeed absorb all others, and present a new and far more ample and vigorous type?

Has not the time arrived for a school of live writing and tuition consistent with the principles of these poems? consistent with the free spirit of this age, and with the American truths of politics? consistent with geology, and astronomy, and phrenology, and human physiology? consistent with the sublimity of immortality and the directness of common sense?

If in this poem the United States have found their poetic voice and taken measure and form, is it any more than a beginning? Walt Whitman himself disclaims singularity in his work, and announces the coming after him of great successions of poets, and that he but lifts his finger to give the signal.

Was he not needed? Has not literature been bred in-and-in long enough? Has it not become unbearably artificial?

Shall a man of faith and practice in the simplicity of real things be called eccentric, while every disciple of the fictitious school writes without question?

Shall it still be the amazement of the light and dark that freshness of expression is the rarest quality of all?

You have come in good time, Walt Whitman! In opinions, in manners, in costumes, in books, in the aims and occupancy of life, in associates, in poems, conformity, to all unnatural and tainted customs passes without remark, while perfect naturalness, health, faith, self-reliance, and all primal expressions of the manliest love and friendship, subject one to the stare and controversy of the world.

(*b*) Unsigned review, *American Phrenological Journal* (1856). Included in *Imprints*, pp. 38–41. In this review, entitled 'An English and an American Poet', Whitman contrasts Tennyson's *Maud, and Other Poems* (1855) with his own *Leaves of Grass* (1st edition, 1855). (See Introduction, p. 14): It is always reserved for second-rate poems immediately to gratify. As first-rate or natural objects, in their perfect simplicity and proportion, do not startle or strike, but appear no more than matters of course, so probably natural poetry does not, for all its being the rarest, and telling of the longest and largest work. The artist or writer whose talent is to please the connoisseurs of his time, may obey the laws of his time, and achieve the intense and elaborated beauty of parts. The perfect poet cannot afford any special beauty of parts, or to limit himself by any laws less than those universal ones of the great masters, which include all times, and all men and women, and the living and the dead. For from the study of the universe is drawn this irrefragable truth, that the law of the requisites of a grand poem, or any other complete workmanship, is originality, and the average and superb beauty of the ensemble. Possessed with this law, the fitness of aim, time, persons, places, surely follows. Possessed with this law, and doing justice to it, no poet or any one else will make anything ungraceful or mean, any more than any emanation of nature is.

The poetry of England, by the many rich geniuses of that wonderful little island, has grown out of the facts of the English race, the monarchy and aristocracy prominent over the rest, and conforms to the spirit of them. No nation ever did or ever will receive with national affection any poets except those born of its national blood. Of these, the writings express the finest infusions of government, traditions, faith, and the dependence or independence of a people, and even the good or bad physiognomy, and the ample or small geography. Thus what very properly fits a subject of the British crown may fit very ill an American freeman. No fine romance, no inimitable delineation of character, no grace of delicate illustrations, no rare picture of shore or mountain or sky, no deep thought of the intellect, is so important to a man as his opinion of himself is; everything receives its tinge from that. In the verse of all those undoubtedly great writers, Shakspeare just as much as the rest, there is the air which to America is the air of death. The mass of the people, the laborers and all who serve, are slag, refuse. The countenances of kings and great lords are beautiful; the countenances of mechanics are ridiculous and deformed. What play of Shakspeare, represented in America, is not an insult to America, to the marrow in its bones? How can the tone never silent in their plots and characters be applauded, unless Washington should have been caught and hung, and Jefferson was the most enormous of liars, and common persons, north and south, should bow low to their betters, and to organic superiority of blood? Sure as the heavens envelop the earth, if the Americans want a race of bards worthy of 1855, and of the stern reality of this republic, they must cast around for men essentially different from the old poets, and from the modern successions of jinglers and snivellers and fops.

English versification is full of these danglers, and America follows after them. Every body writes poetry, and yet there is not a single poet. An age greater than the proudest of the past is swiftly slipping away, without one lyric voice to seize its greatness, and speak it as an encouragement and onward lesson. We have heard, by many grand announcements, that he was to come, but will he come?

> A mighty Poet whom this age shall choose
> To be its spokesman to all coming times.
> In the ripe full-blown season of his soul,
> He shall go forward in his spirit's strength,
> And grapple with the questions of all time,
> And wring from them their meanings. As King Saul

Called up the buried prophet from his grave
To speak his doom, so shall this Poet-king
Call up the dread past from its awful grave
To tell him of our future. As the air
Doth sphere the world, so shall his heart of love—
Loving mankind, not peoples. As the lake
Reflects the flower, tree, rock, and bending heaven,
Shall he reflect our great humanity;
And as the young Spring breathes with living breath
On a dead branch, till it sprouts fragrantly
Green leaves and sunny flowers, shall he breathe life
Through every theme he touch, making all Beauty
And Poetry forever like the stars. (*Alexander Smith.*)

The best of the school of poets at present received in Great Britain and America is Alfred Tennyson. He is the bard of ennui and of the aristocracy, and their combination into love. This love is the old stock love of playwrights and romancers, Shakspeare the same as the rest. It is possessed of the same unnatural and shocking passion for some girl or woman, that wrenches it from its manhood, emasculated and impotent, without strength to hold the rest of the objects and goods of life in their proper positions. It seeks nature for sickly uses. It goes screaming and weeping after the facts of the universe, in their calm beauty and equanimity, to note the occurrence of itself, and to sound the news, in connection with the charms of the neck, hair, or complexion of a particular female.

Poetry, to Tennyson and his British and American eleves, is a gentleman of the first degree, boating, fishing, and shooting genteelly through nature, admiring the ladies, and talking to them, in company, with that elaborate half-choked deference that is to be made up by the terrible license of men among themselves. The spirit of the burnished society of upper-class England fills this writer and his effusions from top to toe. Like that, he does not ignore courage and the superior qualities of men, but all is to show forth through dandified forms. He meets the nobility and gentry half-way. The models are the same both to the poet and the parlors. Both have the same supercilious elegance, both love the reminiscences which extol caste, both agree on the topics proper for mention and discussion, both hold the same undertone of church and state, both have the same languishing melancholy and irony, both indulge largely in persiflage, both are marked by the contour of high blood and a constitutional aversion to anything cowardly and mean, both accept the love depicted in romances as the great business of a life as a poem, both seem unconscious of the mighty truths of eternity and immortality, both are silent on the presumptions of liberty and equality, and both devour themselves in solitary lassitude. Whatever may be said of all this, it harmonizes and represents facts. The present phases of high-life in Great Britain are as natural a growth there, as Tennyson and his poems are a natural growth of those phases. It remains to be distinctly admitted that this man is a real first-class poet, infused amid all that ennui and aristocracy.

Meanwhile a strange voice parts others aside and demands for its owner that position that is only allowed after the seal of many returning years has stamped with approving stamp the claims of the loftiest leading genius. Do you think the best honors of the earth are won so easily, Walt Whitman? Do you think city and country are to fall before the vehement egotism of your recitative of yourself?

I am the poet of the body,
And I am the poet of the soul.

The pleasures of heaven are with me, and the pains of hell are with me,
The first I graft and increase upon myself, the latter I translate into a new tongue.

I am the poet of the woman the same as the man,
And I say it is as great to be a woman as to be a man,
And I say there is nothing greater than the mother of men.

I chant a new chant of dilation or pride,
We have had ducking and deprecating about enough.
I show that size is only development.

It is indeed a strange voice! Critics and lovers and readers of poetry as hitherto written, may well be excused the chilly and unpleasant shudders which will assuredly run through them, to their very blood and bones, when they first read Walt Whitman's poems. If this is poetry, where must its foregoers stand? And what is at once to become of the ranks of rhymesters, melancholy and swallow-tailed, and of all the confectioners and upholsterers of verse, if the tan-faced man here advancing and claiming to speak for America and the nineteenth hundred of the Christian list of years, typifies indeed the natural and proper bard?

The theory and practice of poets have hitherto been to select certain ideas or events or personages, and then describe them in the best manner they could, always with as much ornament as the case allowed. Such are not the theory and practice of the new poet. He never presents for perusal a poem ready-made on the old models, and ending when you come to the end of it; but every sentence and every passage tells of an interior not always seen, and exudes an impalpable something which sticks to him that reads, and pervades and provokes him to tread the half-invisible road where the poet, like an apparition, is striding fearlessly before. If Walt Whitman's premises are true, then there is a subtler range of poetry than that of the grandeur of acts and events, as in Homer, or of characters, as in Shakspeare—poetry to which all other writing is subservient, and which confronts the very meanings of the works of nature and competes with them. It is the direct bringing of occurrences and persons and things to bear on the listener or beholder, to re-appear through him or her; and it offers the best way of making them a part of him and her as the right aim of the greatest poet.

Of the spirit of life in visible forms—of the spirit of the seed growing out of the ground—of the spirit of the resistless motion of the globe passing unsuspected but quick as lightning along its orbit—of them is the spirit of this man's poetry. Like them it eludes and mocks criticism, and appears unerringly in results. Things, facts, events, persons, days, ages, qualities, tumble pell-mell, exhaustless and copious, with what appear to be the same disregard of parts, and the same absence of special purpose, as in nature. But the voice of the few rare and controlling critics, and the voice of more than one generation of men, or two generations of men, must speak for the inexpressible purposes of nature, and for this haughtiest of writers that has ever yet written and printed a book. He is to prove either the most lamentable of failures or the most glorious of triumphs, in the known history of literature. And after all we have written we confess our brain-felt and heart-felt inability to decide which we think it is likely to be.

(*c*) Unsigned review, *Brooklyn Daily Times* (1856). Included in *Imprints*, pp. 30–2. (See Introduction, p. 14): To give judgment on real poems, one needs an account of the poet himself. Very devilish to some, and very divine to some, will appear the poet of these new poems, the *Leaves of Grass*; an attempt, as they are, of a naïve, masculine, affectionate, contemplative, sensual, imperious person, to cast into literature not only his own grit and arrogance, but his own flesh and form, undraped, regardless of models, regardless of modesty or law, and ignorant or silently scornful, as at first appears, of all except his own presence and experience, and all outside the fiercely loved land of his birth and the birth of his parents, and their parents for several generations before him. Politeness this man has none, and regulation he has none. A rude child of the people!—No imitation—No foreigner—but a growth and idiom of America. No discontented—a careless slouch, enjoying to-day. No dilettante democrat—a man who is art-and-part with the commonalty, and with immediate life—loves the streets—loves the docks—loves the free rasping talk of men—likes to be called by his given name, and nobody at all need Mr. him—can laugh with laughers—likes the ungenteel ways of laborers—is not prejudiced one mite against the Irish—talks readily with them—talks readily with niggers—does not make a stand on being a gentleman, nor on learning or manners—eats cheap fare, likes the strong flavored coffee of the coffee-stands in the market, at sunrise—likes a supper of oysters fresh from the oyster-smack—likes to make one at the crowded table among sailors and work-people—would leave a select soiree of elegant people any time to go with tumultuous men, roughs, receive their caresses and welcome, listen to their noise, oaths, smut, fluency, laughter, repartee—and can preserve his presence perfectly among these, and the like of these. The effects he produces in his poems are no effects of artists or the arts, but effects of the original eye or arm, or the actual atmosphere, or tree, or bird. You may feel the unconscious teaching of a fine brute, but will never feel the artificial teaching of a fine writer or speaker.

Other poets celebrate great events, personages, romances, wars, loves, passions, the victories and power of their country, or some real or imagined incident—and polish their work, and come to conclusions, and satisfy the reader. This poet celebrates natural propensities in himself; and that is the way he celebrates all. He comes to no conclusions, and does not satisfy the reader. He certainly leaves him what the serpent left the woman and the man, the taste of the Paradisaic tree of the knowledge of good and evil, never to be erased again.

What good is it to argue about egotism? There can be no two thoughts on Walt Whitman's egotism. That is avowedly what he steps out of the crowd and turns and faces them for. Mark, critics! Otherwise is not used for you the key that leads to the use of the other keys to this well-enveloped man. His whole work, his life, manners, friendships, writings, all have among their leading purposes an evident purpose to stamp a new type of character, namely his own, and indelibly fix it and publish it, not for a model but an illustration, for the present and future of American letters and American young men, for the south the same as the north, and for the Pacific and Mississippi country, and Wisconsin and Texas and Kansas and Canada and Havana and Nicaragua, just as much as New York and Boston. Whatever is needed toward this achievement he puts his hand to, and lets imputations take their time to die.

First be yourself what you would show in your poem—such seems to be this man's example and inferred rebuke to the schools of poets. He makes no allusions to books or writers; their spirits do not seem to have touched him; he has not a word to say for or against them, or their theories or ways. He never offers others; what he continually offers is the man whom our Brooklynites know so well. Of pure American breed, large and lusty—age thirty-six years (1855)—never once using medicine—never dressed in black, always dressed freely and clean in strong clothes—neck open, shirt-collar flat and broad, countenance tawny transparent red, beard well-mottled with white, hair like hay after it has been mowed in the field and lies tossed and streaked—his physiology corroborating a rugged phrenology*—a person singularly beloved and looked toward, especially by young men and the illiterate—one who has firm attachments there, and associates there—one who does not associate with literary people—a man never called upon to make speeches at public dinners—never on platforms amid the crowds of clergymen, or professors, or aldermen, or congressmen—rather down in the bay with pilots in their pilot-boat—or off on a cruise with fishers in a fishing-smack—or riding on a Broadway omnibus, side by side with the driver—or with a band of loungers over the open grounds of the country—fond of New York and Brooklyn—fond of the life of the great ferries—one whom, if you

* *Phrenological Notes on W. Whitman*, by L. N. Fowler, *July*, 1849.—Size of head large, 23 inches. Leading traits appear to be Friendship, Sympathy, Sublimity, and Self-Esteem, and markedly among his combinations the dangerous faults of Indolence, a tendency to the pleasures of Voluptuousness and Alimentiveness, and a certain reckless swing of animal will.

Amativeness large,* 6; Philoprogenitiveness, 6; Adhesiveness, 6; Inhabitiveness, 6; Concentrativeness, 4; Combativeness, 6; Destructiveness, 5 to 6; Alimentiveness, 6; Acquisitiveness, 4; Secretiveness, 3; Cautiousness, 6; Approbativeness, 4; Self-Esteem, 6 to 7; Firmness, 6 to 7; Conscientiousness, 6; Hope, 4; Marvellousness, 3; Veneration, 4; Benevolence, 6 to 7; Constructiveness, 5; Ideality, 5 to 6; Sublimity, 6 to 7; Imitation, 5; Mirthfulness, 5; Individuality, 6; Form, 6; Size, 6; Weight, 6; Color, 3; Order, 5; Calculation, 5; Locality, 6; Eventuality, 6; Time, 3; Tune, 4; Language, 5; Causality, 5 to 6; Comparison, 6; Suavitiveness, 4; Intuitiveness, or Human Nature, 6.

* The organs are marked by figures from 1 to 7, indicating their degree of development, 1 meaning very small, 2 small, 3 moderate, 4 average, 5 full, 6 large, and 7 very large.

should meet, you need not expect to meet an extraordinary person—one in whom you will see the singularity which consists in no singularity—whose contact is no dazzle or fascination, nor requires any deference, but has the easy fascination of what is homely and accustomed—as of something you knew before, and was waiting for—there you have Walt Whitman, the begetter of a new offspring out of literature, taking with easy nonchalance the chances of its present reception, and, through all misunderstandings and distrusts, the chances of its future reception—preferring always to speak for himself rather than have others speak for him.

8. Edward Everett Hale on Whitman

1856

Unsigned review, *North American Review*, LXXXII, 170 (January 1856), pp. 275–7.

Edward Everett Hale (1822–1909) is best remembered for his story 'The Man Without A Country', which was written in 1863 and is credited with doing much to strengthen the Northern cause during the Civil War. It is interesting that Hale's recognition is extended first of all to Whitman as a proud and self-conscious American.

Everything about the external arrangement of this book was odd and out of the way. The author printed it himself, and it seems to have been left to the winds of heaven to publish it. So it happened that we had not discovered it before our last number, although we believe the sheets had then passed the press. It bears no publisher's name, and, if the reader goes to a bookstore for it, he may expect to be told at first, as we were, that there is no such book, and has not been. Nevertheless, there is such a book, and it is well worth going twice to the bookstore to buy it. Walter Whitman, an American—one of the roughs—no sentimentalist,—no stander above men and women, or apart from them,—no more modest than immodest,—has tried to write down here, in a sort of prose poetry, a good deal of what he has seen, felt, and guessed at in a pilgrimage of some thirty-five years. He has a horror of conventional language of any kind. His theory of expression is, that, 'to speak in literature with the perfect rectitude and *insouciance* of the movements of animals, is the flawless triumph of art.' Now a great many men have said this before. But generally it is the introduction to something more artistic than ever,—more conventional and strained. Antony began by saying he was no orator, but none the less did an oration follow. In this book, however, the prophecy is fairly fulfilled in the accomplishment. 'What I experience or portray shall go from my composition without a shred of my composition. You shall stand by my side and look in the mirror with me.'

So truly accomplished is this promise,—which anywhere else would be a flourish of trumpets,—that this thin quarto deserves its name. That is to say, one reads and enjoys the freshness, simplicity, and reality of what he reads, just as the tired man, lying on the hill-side in summer, enjoys the leaves of grass around him,—enjoys the shadow,—enjoys the flecks of sunshine,—not for what they 'suggest to him,' but for what they are.

So completely does the author's remarkable power rest in his simplicity, that the preface to the book—which does not even have large letters at the beginning of the lines, as the rest has—is perhaps the very best thing in it. We find more to the point in the following analysis of the 'genius of the United States', than we have found in many more pretentious studies of it.

Other states indicate themselves in their deputies, but the genius of the United States is not best or most in its executive or legislatures, nor in its ambassadors or authors or colleges or churches or parlors, nor even in its newspapers or inventors;—but always most in the common people. Their manners, speech, dress, friendships;—the freshness and candor of their physiognomy, the picturesque looseness of their carriage, their deathless attachment to freedom, their aversion to everything indecorous or soft or mean, the practical acknowledgment of the citizens of one State by the citizens of all other States, the fierceness of their roused resentment, their curiosity and welcome of novelty, their self-esteem and wonderful sympathy, their susceptibility to a slight, the air they have of persons who never knew how it felt to stand in the presence of superiors, the fluency of their speech, their delight in music (the sure symptom of manly tenderness and native elegance of soul), their good temper and open-handedness, the terrible significance of their elections, the President's taking off his hat to them, not they to him,—these too are unrhymed poetry. It awaits the gigantic and generous treatment worthy of it.

The book is divided into a dozen or more sections, and in each one of these some thread of connection may be traced, now with ease, now with difficulty,—each being a string of verses, which claim to be written without effort and with entire *abandon*. So the book is a collection of observations, speculations, memories, and prophecies, clad in the simplest, truest, and often the most nervous English,—in the midst of which the reader comes upon something as much out of place as a piece of rotten wood would be among leaves of grass in the meadow, if the meadow had no object but to furnish a child's couch. So slender is the connection, that we hardly injure the following scraps by extracting them.

I am the teacher of Athletes;
He that by me spreads a wider breast than my own, proves the width of my own;
He most honors my style who learns under it to destroy the teacher;
The boy I love, the same becomes a man, not through derived power, but in his own right,
Wicked rather than virtuous out of conformity or fear,
Fond of his sweetheart, relishing well his steak,
Unrequited love, or a slight, cutting him worse than a wound cuts,
First-rate to ride, to fight, to hit the bull's-eye, to sail a skiff, to sing a song, or to play on the banjo,
Preferring scars, and faces pitted with small-pox, over all latherers and those that keep out of the sun.

Here is the story of the gallant seaman who rescued the passengers on the San Francisco:—

I understand the large heart of heroes,
The courage of present times and all times;
How the skipper saw the crowded and rudderless wreck of the steamship, and death chasing it up and down the storm,
How he knuckled tight, and gave not back one inch, and was faithful of days and faithful of nights,
And chalked in large letters on a board, 'Be of good cheer, we will not desert you';
How he saved the drifting company at last,

How the lank, loose-gowned women looked when boated from the side of
their prepared graves,
How the silent old-faced infants, and the lifted sick, and the sharp-lipped,
unshaved men;
All this I swallowed, and it tastes good; I like it well, and it becomes mine:
I am the man, I suffered, I was there.

Claiming in this way a personal interest in every thing that has ever happened in the world, and, by the wonderful sharpness and distinctness of his imagination, making the claim effective and reasonable, Mr. 'Walt. Whitman' leaves it a matter of doubt where he has been in this world, and where not. It is very clear, that with him, as with most other effective writers, a keen, absolute memory, which takes in and holds every detail of the past,—as they say the exaggerated power of the memory does when a man is drowning,—is a gift of his organization as remarkable as his vivid imagination. What he has seen once, he has seen for ever. And thus there are in this curious book little thumb-nail sketches of life in the prairie, life in California, life at school, life in the nursery,—life, indeed, we know not where not,—which, as they are unfolded one after another, strike us as real,—so real that we wonder how they came on paper.

For the purpose of showing that he is above every conventionalism, Mr. Whitman puts into the book one or two lines which he would not address to a woman nor to a company of men. There is not anything, perhaps, which modern usage would stamp as more indelicate than are some passages in Homer. There is not a word in it meant to attract readers by its grossness, as there is in half the literature of the last century, which holds its place unchallenged on the tables of our drawing-rooms. For all that, it is a pity that a book where everything else is natural should go out of the way to avoid the suspicion of being prudish.

9. Extracts from an unsigned notice

1856

Unsigned review, the *Crayon* (New York, January 1856). Included in *Imprints*, pp. 14–20.

The interest of this piece lies in its comparison between Tennyson and Whitman. Whitman undoubtedly respected Tennyson's abilities above those of any of his poetic contemporaries. At his last birthday party, he is reported to have toasted Tennyson as 'the Boss of us all'. Tennyson, to some extent, reciprocated this regard, though he appears to have sympathized with Whitman the man rather than fully appreciated the poet. He did, nevertheless, invite Whitman to visit him and to stay with him at his home on the Isle of Wight, an invitation which Whitman might have accepted had not his paralytic stroke intervened to prevent him.

THE ASSEMBLY OF EXTREMES.—A subtle old proverb says, 'extremes meet,' and science, art, and even morality, sometimes testify to the truth of the proverb; and there are some curious problems involved in the demonstration of it. The loftiest attainment of the wisdom and worth of age only reaches to the simplicity and fervor of childhood; from which we all start, and returning to which we are blessed. Art makes the same voyage round its sphere, holding ever westward its way into new and unexplored regions, until it, doing what Columbus would have done, had his faith and self-denial been greater, reaches the east again. If the individual, Columbus, failed to accomplish the destiny, the class, Columbus, fails never. And so, in art, what no one does, the many accomplish, and finally, the cycle is filled.

We see this most forcibly in the comparison of two late poems, as unlike, at first thought, as two could be, and yet in which the most striking likenesses prevail, *Maud*,* and *Leaves of Grass*;† the one as

* *Maud and other Poems*, by Alfred Tennyson. Ticknor & Fields, Boston.

† *Leaves of Grass*. Brooklyn, N. Y.

refined in its art as the most refined, delicate in its structure, and consummate in its subtlety of expression; the other rude and rough, and heedless in its forms—*nonchalant* in everything but its essential ideas. The one comes from the last stage of cultivation of the Old World, and shows evidence of morbid, luxurious waste of power, and contempt of mental wealth, from inability longer to appreciate the propriety of subjects on which to expend it; as, to one who has overlived, all values are the same, because nothing, and indifferent; while the other, from among the 'roughs,' is morbid from overgrowth, and likewise prodigal of its thought-treasure, because it has so much that it can afford to throw it away on everything, and considers all things that are, as equally worth gilding. The subject of *Maud* is nothing—a mere common-place incident, but artistically dealt with—a blanched, decayed sea-shell, around which the amber has gathered; and that of the newer poem is equally nothing, blades of sea-grass amber-cemented. Both are characterized by the extreme of affectation of suggestiveness—piers of thought being given, over which the reader must throw his own arches. Both are bold, defiant of laws which attempt to regulate forms, and of those which *should* regulate essences. *Maud* is irreligious through mental disease, produced by excess of sentimental action—*Leaves of Grass*, through irregularly-developed mental action and insufficiency of sentiment. A calmer perception of Nature would have corrected in Tennyson that feeling which looks upon sorrow as the only thing poetic, and serenity and holy trust as things to which love has no alliance; while a higher seeing of nature would have shown Walt Whitman that all things in nature are not alike beautiful, or to be loved and honored by song.

Although it is mainly with the art of the two poems that we have to deal, the form rather than the motive, yet so entirely does the former arise from the latter, that the criticism passed on the one must lie upon the other. In the mere versification, for instance, of both, see what indifference to the dignity of verse (while there is still the extorted homage to its forms), arising in both cases, it would seem, from an overweening confidence in the value of what is said, as in the following passages:

> Long have I sighed for a calm; God grant I may find it at last!
> It will never be broken by Maud, she has neither savor nor salt,
> But a cold, clear, cut face, as I found when her carriage past,
> Perfectly beautiful: let it be granted her: where is the fault?
>
> *Maud*, Sec. ii., St. I.

C

Do you suspect death? If I were to suspect death, I should die now.
Do you think I could walk pleasantly and well-suited toward annihilation?

Pleasantly and well-suited I walk,
Whither I walk I cannot define, but I know it is good.
The whole universe indicates that it is good,
The past and present indicate that it is good.

Leaves of Grass, p. 69.

All Tennyson's exquisite care over his lines produces no other impression than that which Walt Whitman's carelessness arrives at; viz., nonchalance with regard to forms. In either case, it is an imperfection, we are bold to say, since we do not love beauty and perfection of form for nothing, nor can the measure of poetic feeling be full when we do not care for the highest grace and symmetry of construction. It is an impertinence which says to us, 'my ideas are so fine that they need no dressing up,' even greater than that which says, 'mine are so fine that they cannot be dressed as well as they deserve.' The child-like instinct demands perfect melody as an essential to perfect poetry, and more than that, the melodious thought will work out its just and adequate form by the essential law of its spiritual organization—when the heart sings, the feet will move to its music. An unjust measure in verse is *prima facie* evidence of a jarring note in the soul of the poem, and studied or permitted irregularity of form proves an arrogant self-estimation or irreverence in the poet; and both these poems are irreverent, irreligious, in fact.

10. An English reaction

1856

Unsigned review, the *Critic* (London, 1 April 1856).

The singling out of Whitman's description of himself as 'a Kosmos' suggests that this reviewer may have seen the notice by Charles Eliot Norton in *Putnam's Monthly*. Evidently this reviewer felt that the most appropriate reaction to what he took to be a display of indecency was a refined form of billingsgate. His abuse at times has a certain vivacity, as in the sentence: 'Walt Whitman is as unacquainted with art as a hog is with mathematics.' The passage on p. 79 of the 1855 edition of the *Leaves*, which the Victorian reviewer alludes to tantalizingly though he does not dare to quote it (contenting himself with the observation that it 'deserves nothing so richly as the public executioner's whip'), consists, no doubt, of the following lines:

This is the female form,
A divine nimbus exhales from it from head to foot,
It attracts with fierce undeniable attraction,
I am drawn by its breath as if I were no more than a helpless vapor . . . all falls aside but myself and it,
Books, art, religion, time . . . the visible and solid earth . . . the atmosphere and the fringed clouds . . . what was expected of heaven or feared of hell are now consumed,
Mad filaments, ungovernable shoots play out of it . . . the response likewise ungovernable,
Hair, bosom, hips, bend of legs, negligent falling hands—all diffused . . . mine too diffused,
Ebb stung by the flow, and flow stung by the ebb . . . loveflesh swelling and deliciously aching,
Limitless limpid jets of love hot and enormous . . . quivering jelly of love . . . whiteblow and delirious juice,
Bridegroom night of love working surely and softly into the prostrate dawn,
Undulating into the willing and yielding day,
Lost in the cleave of the clasping and sweetfleshed day.

We had ceased, we imagined, to be surprised at anything that America could produce. We had become stoically indifferent to her Woolly Horses, her Mermaids, her Sea Serpents, her Barnums, and her Fanny Ferns; but the last monstrous importation from Brooklyn, New York, has scattered our indifference to the winds. Here is a thin quarto volume without an author's name on the title-page; but to atone for which we have a portrait engraved on steel of the notorious individual who is the poet presumptive. This portrait expresses all the features of the hard democrat, and none of the flexile delicacy of the civilised poet. The damaged hat, the rough beard, the naked throat, the shirt exposed to the waist, are each and all presented to show that the man to whom those articles belong scorns the delicate arts of civilisation. The man is the true impersonation of his book—rough, uncouth, vulgar. It was by the merest accident that we discovered the name of this erratic and newest wonder; but at page 29 we find that he is—

> Walt Whitman, an American, one of the roughs, a Kosmos,
> Disorderly, fleshly, and sensual.

The words 'an American' are a surplusage, 'one of the roughs' too painfully apparent; but what is intended to be conveyed by 'a Kosmos' we cannot tell, unless it means a man who thinks that the fine essence of poetry consists in writing a book which an American reviewer is compelled to declare is 'not to be read aloud to a mixed audience.' We should have passed over this book, *Leaves of Grass*, with indignant contempt, had not some few Transatlantic critics attempted to 'fix' this Walt Whitman as the poet who shall give a new and independent literature to America—who shall form a race of poets as Banquo's issue formed a line of kings. Is it possible that the most prudish nation in the world will adopt a poet whose indecencies stink in the nostrils? We hope not; and yet there is a probability, and we will show why, that this Walt Whitman will not meet with the stern rebuke which he so richly deserves. America has felt, oftener perhaps than we have declared, that she has no national poet—that each one of her children of song has relied too much on European inspiration, and clung too fervently to the old conventionalities. It is therefore not unlikely that she may believe in the dawn of a thoroughly original literature, now there has arisen a man who scorns the Hellenic deities, who has no belief in, perhaps because he has no knowledge of, Homer and Shakspere; who relies on his own rugged nature, and trusts to his own rugged language, being himself what he shows in his poems.

Once transfix him as the genesis of a new era, and the manner of the man may be forgiven or forgotten. But what claim has this Walt Whitman to be thus considered, or to be considered a poet at all? We grant freely enough that he has a strong relish for nature and freedom, just as an animal has; nay, further, that his crude mind is capable of appreciating some of nature's beauties; but it by no means follows that, because nature is excellent, therefore art is contemptible. Walt Whitman is as unacquainted with art, as a hog is with mathematics. His poems—we must call them so for convenience—twelve in number, are innocent of rhythm, and resemble nothing so much as the war-cry of the Red Indians. Indeed, Walt Whitman has had near and ample opportunities of studying the vociferations of a few amiable savages. Or rather perhaps, this Walt Whitman reminds us of Caliban flinging down his logs, and setting himself to write a poem. In fact Caliban, and not Walt Whitman, might have written this:

> I too am not a bit tamed—I too am untranslatable.
> I sound my *barbaric yawp* over the roofs of the world.

Is this man with the 'barbaric yawp' to push Longfellow into the shade, and he meanwhile to stand and 'make mouths' at the sun? The chance of this might be formidable were it not ridiculous. That object or that act which most develops the ridiculous element carries in its bosom the seeds of decay, and is wholly powerless to trample out of God's universe one spark of the beautiful. We do not, then, fear this Walt Whitman, who gives us slang in the place of melody, and rowdyism in the place of regularity. The depth of his indecencies will be the grave of his fame, or ought to be if all proper feeling is not extinct. The very nature of this man's compositions excludes us from proving by extracts the truth of our remarks; but we, who are not prudish, emphatically declare that the man who wrote page 79 of the *Leaves of Grass* deserves nothing so richly as the public executioner's whip. Walt Whitman libels the highest type of humanity, and calls his free speech the true utterance of *a man:* we, who may have been misdirected by civilisation, call it the expression of *a beast.*

The leading idea of Walt Whitman's poems is as old as the hills. It is the doctrine of universal sympathy which the first poet maintained, and which the last on earth will maintain also. He says:

> Not a mutineer walks handcuffed to the jail but I am handcuffed to him and walk by his side,
> Not a cholera patient lies at the last gasp but I also lie at the last gasp.

To show this sympathy he instances a thousand paltry, frivolous, and obscene circumstances. Herein we may behold the difference between a great and a contemptible poet. What Shakspere—mighty shade of the mightiest bard, forgive us the comparison!—expressed in a single line,

> One touch of nature makes the whole world kin,

this Walt Whitman has tortured into scores of pages. A single extract will show what we mean. This miserable spinner of words declares that the earth has 'no themes, or hints, or provokers,' and never had, if you cannot find such themes, or hints, or provokers in

> The veneer and gluepot . . . the confectioner's ornaments . . . the decanter and glasses . . . the shears and flatiron;
> The awl and kneestrap . . . the pint measure and quart measure . . . the counter and stool . . . the writingpen of quill or metal;
> Billiards and tenpins . . . the ladders and hanging ropes of the gymnasium, and the manly exercises;
> The designs for wallpapers or oilcloths or carpets . . . the fancies for goods for women . . . the bookbinder's stamps;
> Leatherdressing, coachmaking, boilermaking, ropetwisting, distilling, sign-painting, limeburning, coopering, cottonpicking,
> The walkingbeam of the steam engine . . . the throttle and governors, and the up and down rods,
> Stavemachines and plainingmachines . . . the cart of the carman . . . the omnibus . . . the ponderous dray;
> The snowplough and two engines pushing it . . . the ride in the express train of only one car . . . the swift go through a howling storm:
> The bearhunt or coonhunt . . . the bonfire of shavings in the open lot in the city . . . the crowd of children watching;
> The blows of the fighting-man . . . the upper cut and one-two-three;
> The shopwindows . . . the coffins in the sexton's wareroom . . . the fruit on the fruitstand . . . the beef on the butcher's stall,
> The bread and cakes in the bakery . . . the white and red pork in the pork-store;
> The milliner's ribbons . . . the dressmaker's patterns . . . the tea-table . . . the home-made sweetmeats:
> The columns of wants in the one-cent paper . . . the news by telegraph . . . the amusements and operas and shows:
> The cotton and woollen and linen you wear . . . the money you make and spend;
> Your room and bedroom . . . your piano-forte . . . the stove and cookpans,
> The house you live in . . . the rent . . . the other tenants . . . the deposits in the savings-bank . . . the trade at the grocery,
> The pay on Saturday night . . . the going home, and the purchases;

Can it be possible that its author intended this as a portion of a poem? Is it not more reasonable to suppose that Walt Whitman has been learning to write, and that the compositor has got hold of his copy-book? The American critics are, in the main, pleased with this man because he is self-reliant, and because he assumes all the attributes of his country. If Walt Whitman has really assumed those attributes, America should hasten to repudiate them, be they what they may. The critics are pleased also because he talks like a man unaware that there was ever such a production as a book, or ever such a being as a writer. This in the present day is a qualification exceedingly rare, and *may* be valuable, so we wish those gentlemen joy of their GREAT UNTAMED.

We must not neglect to quote an unusual passage, which may be suggestive to writers of the Old World. To silence our incredulous readers, we assure them that the passage may be found at page 92:—

Is it wonderful that I should be immortal? As every one is immortal, I know it is wonderful; but my eyesight is equally wonderful, and how I was conceived in my mother's womb is equally wonderful.
And how I was not palpable once but am now, and was born on the last day of May 1819, and passed from a babe in the creeping trance of three summers and three winters to articulate and walk, are all equally wonderful.
And that I grew six feet high, and that I have become a man thirty-six years old in 1855, and that I am here anyhow, are all equally wonderful.

The transformation and the ethereal nature of Walt Whitman is marvellous to us, but perhaps not so to a nation from which the spirit-rappers sprung.

I depart as air, I shake my white locks at the runaway sun;
I effuse my flesh in eddies, and drift it in lacy jags;
I bequeath myself to the dirt, to grow from the grass I love.
If you want me again, look for me under your boot-soles.

Here is also a sample of the man's slang and vulgarity:

This hour I tell things in confidence.
I might not tell everybody, but I will tell you.
Who goes there! hankering, gross, mystical, nude?
How is it I extract strength from the beef I eat?
What is a man anyhow! What am I? and what are you?
All I mark as my own you shall offset it with your own,
Else it were time lost listening to me.
I do not snivel that snivel the world over,
That months are vacuums and the ground but wallow and filth,

That life is a suck and a sell, and nothing remains at the end but threadbare crape and tears.

And here a spice of his republican insolence, his rank Yankeedom, and his audacious trifling with death:

I rose this morning early to get betimes in Boston town.
Here's a good place at the corner. I must stand and see the show.
I love to look on the stars and stripes. I hope the fifes will play Yankee Doodle.
I will whisper it to the mayor, he shall send a committee to England?
They shall get a grant from the Parliament, and go with a cart to the royal vault.
Dig out King George's coffin, unwrap him quick from the grave-clothes, box up his bones for a journey.
Find a swift Yankee clipper: here is freight for you, blackbellied clipper.
Up with your anchor! shake out your sails, steer straight towards Boston Bay.
The committee open the box and set up the regal ribs, and glue those that will not stay,
And clap the skull on top of the ribs, and clap a crown on top of the skull.
You have got your revenge, Old Buster!

We will neither weary nor insult our readers with more extracts from this notable book. Emerson *has praised it*, and called it the 'most extraordinary piece of wit and wisdom America has yet contributed.' Because Emerson has grasped substantial fame, he can afford to be generous; but Emerson's generosity must not be mistaken for justice. If this work is really a work of genius—if the principles of those poems, their free language, their amazing and audacious egotism, their animal vigour, be real poetry and the divinest evidence of the true poet—then our studies have been in vain, and vainer still the homage which we have paid the monarchs of Saxon intellect, Shakspere, and Milton, and Byron. This Walt Whitman holds that his claim to be a poet lies in his robust and rude health. He is, in fact, as he declares, 'the poet of the body.' Adopt this theory, and Walt Whitman is a Titan; Shelley and Keats the merest pigmies. If we had commenced a notice of *Leaves of Grass* in anger, we could not but dismiss it in grief, for its author, we have just discovered, is conscious of his affliction. He says, at page 33,

I am given up by traitors;
I talk wildly, I am mad.

11. An American echo

1856

Unsigned review, *Boston Intelligencer* (3 May 1856). Printed in an Appendix, titled 'The Opinions, 1855–6,' to the second edition of *Leaves of Grass*.

The suggestion that Whitman's effrontery is worthy of 'the lash' may be an indication that the reviewer had just read the preceding review, newly arrived from London, in which it had been proposed to put the author under 'the public executioner's whip'.

We were attracted by the very singular title of this work, to seek the work itself, and what we thought ridiculous in the title is eclipsed in the pages of this heterogeneous mass of bombast, egotism, vulgarity and nonsense. The beastliness of the author is set forth in his own description of himself, and we can conceive no better reward than the lash for such a violation of decency as we have before us. The *Criterion* says: 'It is impossible to imagine how any man's fancy could have conceived it, unless he were possessed of the soul of a sentimental donkey that had died of disappointed love.'

This book should find no place where humanity urges any claim to respect, and the author should be kicked from all decent society as below the level of a brute. There is neither wit nor method in his disjointed babbling, and it seems to us he must be some escaped lunatic, raving in pitiable delirium.

12. 'impious and obscene'

1856

Unsigned review, *Christian Examiner* (Boston, June 1856). Included in *Imprints*, pp. 6–7.

So, then, these rank *Leaves* have sprouted afresh, and in still greater abundance. We hoped that they had dropped, and we should hear no more of them. But since they thrust themselves upon us again, with a pertinacity that is proverbial of noxious weeds, and since these thirty-two poems (!) threaten to become 'several hundred,—perhaps a thousand,'—we can no longer refrain from speaking of them as we think they deserve. For here is not a question of literary opinion principally, but of the very essence of religion and morality. The book might pass for merely hectoring and ludicrous, if it were not something a great deal more offensive. We are bound in conscience to call it impious and obscene. *Punch* made sarcastic allusion to it some time ago, as a specimen of American literature. We regard it as one of its worst disgraces. Whether or not the author really bears the name he assumes,—whether or not the strange figure opposite the title-page resembles him, or is even intended for his likeness—whether or not he is considered among his friends to be of a sane mind,—whether he is in earnest, or only playing off some disgusting burlesque,—we are hardly sure yet. We know only, that, in point of style, the book is an impertinence towards the English language; and in point of sentiment, an affront upon the recognized morality of respectable people. Both its language and thought seem to have just broken out of Bedlam. It sets off upon a sort of distracted philosophy, and openly deifies the bodily organs, senses, and appetites, in terms that admit of no double sense. To its pantheism and libidinousness it adds the most ridiculous swell of self-applause; for the author is 'one of the roughs, a kosmos, disorderly, fleshy, sensual, divine inside and out. This head more than churches or bibles or creeds. The scent of these arm-pits an aroma finer than prayer. If I worship any particular thing, it shall be some of the spread of my body.' He leaves 'washes and razors for foofoos;' thinks the talk 'about virtue and about vice' only 'blurt,' he being above and indifferent to both of them; and he himself, 'speaking the pass-word primeval, By God! will accept nothing which all cannot have the counterpart of on the same terms.' These quotations are made with cautious delicacy. We pick our way as cleanly as we can between other passages which are more detestable.

A friend whispers as we write, that there is nevertheless a vein of benevolence running through all this vagabondism and riot. Yes; there is plenty of that philanthropy, which cares as little for social rights as for the laws of God. This Titan in his own esteem is perfectly willing that all the rest of the world should be as frantic as himself. In fact, he has no objection to any persons whatever, unless they wear good clothes, or keep themselves tidy. Perhaps it is not judicious to call any attention to such a prodigious impudence. Dante's guide through the infernal regions bade him, on one occasion, Look and pass on. It would be a still better direction sometimes, when in neighborhoods of defilement and death, to pass on without looking. Indeed, we should even now hardly be tempted to make the slightest allusion to this crazy outbreak of conceit and vulgarity, if a sister Review had not praised it, and even undertaken to set up a plea in apology for its indecencies. We must be allowed to say, that it is not good to confound the blots upon great compositions with the compositions that are nothing but a blot. It is not good to confound the occasional ebullitions of too loose a fancy or too wanton a wit, with a profession and 'illustrated' doctrine of licentiousness. And furthermore, it is specially desirable to be able to discern the difference between the nudity of a statue and the gestures of a satyr; between the plain language of a simple state of society, and the lewd talk of the opposite state, which a worse than heathen lawlessness has corrupted; between the '*εὐνῇ καὶ φιλότητι*,' or '*φιλότητι καὶ εὐνῇ μιγῆναι*,' of the Iliad and Odyssey, and an ithyphallic audacity that insults what is most sacred and decent among men.[1]

There is one feature connected with the second edition of this foul work to which we cannot feel that we do otherwise than right in making a marked reference, because it involves the grossest violation of literary comity and courtesy that ever passed under our notice. Mr. Emerson had written a letter of greeting to the author on the perusal of the first edition, the warmth and eulogium of which amaze

[1] These Greek phrases may be rendered as 'in love and marriage' and 'to join in love and intercourse'.

us. But 'Walt Whitman' has taken the most emphatic sentence of praise from this letter, and had it stamped in gold, signed 'R. W. Emerson,' upon the back of his *second* edition. This *second* edition contains some additional pieces, which in their loathsomeness exceed any of the contents of the first. Thus the honored name of Emerson, which has never before been associated with anything save refinement and delicacy in speech and writing, is made to indorse a work that teems with abominations.

13. Bronson Alcott on Whitman

1856

The Journals of Bronson Alcott (Boston, 1938), selected and edited by Odell Shepard.

(a) Entry for 4 October 1856, pp. 286–7: P. M. To Brooklyn, and see Walt Whitman. I pass a couple of hours, and find him to be an extraordinary person, full of brute power, certainly of genius and audacity, and likely to make his mark on Young America—he affirming himself to be its representative man and poet. I must meet him again, and more than once, to mete his merits and place in this Pantheon of the West. He gives me his book of poems, the *Leaves of Grass*, 2nd Edition, with new verses, and asks me to write to him if I have any more to say about him or his master, Emerson.

A nondescript, he is not so easily described, nor seen to be described. Broad-shouldered, rouge-fleshed, Bacchus-browed, bearded like a satyr, and rank, he wears his man-Bloomer in defiance of everybody, having these as every thing else after his own fashion, and for example to all men hereafter. Red flannel undershirt, open-breasted, exposing his brawny neck; striped calico jacket over this, the collar Byroneal, with coarse cloth overalls buttoned to it; cowhide boots; a heavy round-about, with huge outside pockets and buttons to match; and a slouched hat, for house and street alike. Eyes gray, unimaginative, cautious yet melting. When talking will recline upon the couch at length, pillowing his head upon his bended arm, and informing you naively how lazy he is, and slow. Listens well; asks you to repeat what he has failed to catch at once, yet hesitates in speaking often, or gives over as if fearing to come short of the sharp, full, concrete meaning of his thought. Inquisitive, very; over-curious even; inviting criticism on himself, on his poems—pronouncing it 'pomes.'—In fine, an egotist, incapable of omitting, or suffering any one long to omit, noting Walt Whitman in discourse. Swaggy in his walk, burying both hands in his outside pockets. Has never been sick, he says, nor taken medicine, nor sinned; and so is quite innocent of repentance and man's fall. A bachelor, he professes great respect for women. Of Scotch descent by his father; by his mother, German. Age 38, and Long Island born.

(b) Entry for 10 November 1856, p. 290: This morning we call on Whitman, Mrs. Tyndall accompanying us to whet her curiosity on the demigod. He receives us kindly, yet awkwardly, and takes us up two narrow flights of stairs to sit or stand as we might in his attic study—also the bedroom of himself and his feeble brother, the pressure of whose bodies was still apparent in the unmade bed standing in one corner, and the vessel scarcely hidden underneath. A few books were piled disorderly over the mantel-piece, and some characteristic pictures—a Hercules, a Bacchus, and a satyr—were pasted, unframed, upon the rude walls.

There was a rough table in the room, and but a single window, fronting Ellison Avenue, upon which he lives, his being the middle tenement of a single block of three private dwellings and far out on Myrtle Avenue, in the very suburbs of the city of Brooklyn.

He took occasion to inform us three, while surveying his premises aloft, of his bathing daily through the midwinter; said he rode sometimes a-top of an omnibus up and down Broadway from morning till night beside the driver, and dined afterwards with the whipsters, frequented the opera during the season, and 'lived to make pomes,' and for nothing else particularly.

He had told me on my former visit of his being a house-builder, but I learned from his mother that his brother was the house-builder, and not Walt, who, she said, had no business but going out and coming in to eat, drink, write, and sleep. And she told how all the common folks loved him. He had his faults, she knew, and was not a perfect man, but meant us to understand that she thought him an extraordinary son of a fond mother.

I said, while looking at the pictures in his study: 'Which, now, of the three, particularly, is the new poet here—this Hercules, the Bacchus, or the satyr?' On which he begged me not to put my questions too close, meaning to take, as I inferred, the virtues of the three to himself unreservedly. And I think he might fairly, being himself the modern Pantheon—satyr, Silenus, and him of the twelve labours—combined.

He is very curious of criticism on himself or his book, inviting it from all quarters, nor suffering the conversation to stray very wide away from Walt's godhead without recalling it to that high mark. I hoped to put him in communication direct with Thoreau, and tried my hand a little after we came down stairs and sat in the parlour below; but each seemed planted fast in reserves, surveying the other curiously,—like two beasts, each wondering what the other would do, whether to snap or run; and it came to no more than cold compliments between them. Whether Thoreau was meditating the possibility of Walt's stealing away his 'out-of-doors' for some sinister ends, poetic or pecuniary, I could not well divine, nor was very curious to know; or whether Walt suspected or not that he had here, for once, and for the first time, found his match and more at smelling out 'all Nature,' a sagacity potent, penetrating and peerless as his own, if indeed not more piercing and profound, finer and more formidable. I cannot say. At all events, our stay was not long, and we left the voluminous Mrs. Tyndall . . . with the savage sovereign of the flesh, he making an appointment to meet me at the International tomorrow and deliver himself further, if the mood favored and the place.

(c) Entry for 12 December 1856, pp. 293–4: Today fair and sunny, and I walk for two hours in the Park. Walt Whitman comes, and we dine at Taylor's Saloon, discussing America, its men and institutions. Walt thinks the best thing it has done is the growing of Emerson, the only man there is in it—unless it be himself. Alcott, he fancies, may be somebody, perhaps, to be named by way of courtesy in a country so crude and so pregnant with coming great men and women. He tells me he is going presently to Washington City to see and smell of, or at, the pigmies assembled there at the Capitol, whom he will show up in his letters from there in some of the newspapers, and will send me samples of his work by mail to me at Walpole. It will be curious to see what he will make of Congress and the Society at the Capitol. Walt has been editor of a paper once, at Brooklyn, and a contributor to the magazines sometimes. If a broader and finer intercourse with men serves to cure something of his arrogance and take out his egotism, good may come, and great things, of him.

14. Thoreau on Whitman

1856

Letter from Henry David Thoreau to Harrison Blake, 7 December 1856. Published in *Letters to Various Persons* (Boston, 1865), by Henry David Thoreau, pp. 146–8.

That Walt Whitman, of whom I wrote you, is the most interesting fact to me at present. I have just read his second edition (which he gave me), and it has done me more good than any reading for a long time. Perhaps I remember best the poem of Walt Whitman, an American, and the Sun-Down Poem. There are two or three pieces in the book which are disagreeable, to say the least; simply sensual. He does not celebrate love at all. It is as if the beasts spoke. I think that men have not been ashamed of themselves without reason. No doubt there have always been dens where such deeds were unblushingly recited, and it is no merit to compete with the inhabitants. But even on this side he has spoken more truth than any American or modern that I know. I have found his poem exhilarating, encouraging. As for its sensuality,—and it may turn out to be less sensual than it appears,—I do not so much wish that those parts were not written, as that men and women were so pure, that they could read them without harm, that is, without understanding them. One woman told me that no woman could read it,—as if a man could read what a woman could not. Of course Walt Whitman can communicate to us no experience, and if we are shocked, whose experience is it that we are reminded of?

On the whole, it sounds to me very brave and American, after whatever deductions. I do not believe that all the sermons, so called, that have been preached in this land put together are equal to it for preaching.

We ought to rejoice greatly in him. He occasionally suggests something a little more than human. You can't confound him with the other inhabitants of Brooklyn or New York. How they must shudder when they read him! He is awfully good.

To be sure I sometimes feel a little imposed on. By his heartiness and broad generalities he puts me into a liberal frame of mind prepared to see wonders,—as it were, sets me upon a hill or in the midst of a plain,—stirs me well up, and then—throws in a thousand of brick. Though rude and sometimes ineffectual, it is a great primitive poem,—an alarum or trumpet-note ringing through the American camp. Wonderfully like the Orientals, too, considering that when I asked him if he had read them, he answered, 'No: tell me about them.'

I did not get far in conversation with him,—two more being present,—and among the few things which I chanced to say, I remember that one was, in answer to him as representing America, that I did not think much of America or of politics, and so on, which may have been somewhat of a damper to him.

Since I have seen him, I find that I am not disturbed by any brag or egoism in his book. He may turn out the least braggart of all, having a better right to be confident.

He is a great fellow.

15. 'It is a lie to . . . review . . . one's own book'

1856

Unsigned review, *New York Daily Times* (1856). Included in *Imprints*, pp. 20–7.

What Centaur have we here, half man, half beast, neighing defiance to all the world? What conglomerate of thought is this before us, with insolence, philosophy, tenderness, blasphemy, beauty and gross indecency tumbling in drunken confusion through the pages? Who is this arrogant young man who proclaims himself the Poet of the Time, and who roots like a pig among a rotten garbage of licentious thoughts? Who is this flushed and full-blooded lover of Nature who studies her so affectionately, and who sometimes utters her teachings with a lofty tongue? This mass of extraordinary contradictions, this fool and this wise man, this lover of beauty and this sunken sensualist, this original thinker and blind egotist, is Mr. WALT WHITMAN, author of *Leaves of Grass*, and, according to his own account, 'a Kosmos.'

Some time since there was left at the office of this paper a thin quarto volume bound in green and gold. On opening the book we first beheld, as a frontispiece, the picture of a man in his shirt sleeves, wearing an expression of settled arrogance upon his countenance. We next arrived at a title page of magnificent proportions, with letter-press at least an inch and a half in length. From this title page we learned that the book was entitled *Leaves of Grass*, and was printed at Brooklyn in the year 1855. This inspected, we passed on to what seemed to be a sort of preface, only that it had no beginning, was remarkable for a singular sparseness in the punctuation, and was broken up in a confusing manner by frequent rows of dots separating the paragraphs. To this succeeded eighty-two pages of what appeared at the first glance to be a number of prose sentences printed somewhat after a biblical fashion. Almost at the first page we opened we lighted upon the confession that the author was

> WALT WHITMAN, an American, one of the roughs,
> a Kosmos,
> Disorderly, fleshy and sensual. . . .

This was sufficient basis for a theory. We accordingly arrived at the conclusion that the insolent-looking young man on the frontispiece was this same WALT WHITMAN, and author of the *Leaves of Grass*.

Then returning to the fore-part of the book, we found proof slips of certain review articles about the *Leaves of Grass*. One of these purported to be extracted from a periodical entitled the *United States Review*, the other was headed 'From the *American Phrenological Journal*.' These were accompanied by a printed copy of an extravagant letter of praise addressed by Mr. RALPH WALDO EMERSON to Mr. WALT WHITMAN, complimenting him on the benefaction conferred on society in the present volume. On subsequently comparing the critiques from the *United States Review* and the *Phrenological Journal* with the preface of the *Leaves of Grass*, we discovered unmistakable internal evidence that Mr. WALT WHITMAN, true to his character as a Kosmos, was not content with writing a book, but was also determined to review it; so Mr. WALT WHITMAN, had concocted both those criticisms of his own work, treating it we need not say how favorably. This little discovery of our 'disorderly' acquaintance's mode of proceeding rather damped any enthusiasm with which Mr. EMERSON's extravagant letter may have inspired us. We reflected, here is a man who sets himself up as the poet and teacher of his time; who professes a scorn of everything mean and dastardly and double-faced, who hisses with scorn as he passes one in the street whom he suspects of the taint, hypocrisy—yet this self-contained teacher, this rough-and-ready scorner of dishonesty, this rowdy knight-errant who tilts against all lies and shams, himself perpetrates a lie and a sham at the very outset of his career. It is a lie to write a review of one's own book, then extract it from the work in which it appeared and send it out to the world as an impartial editorial utterance. It is an act that the most degraded helot of literature might blush to commit. It is a dishonesty committed against one's own nature, and all the world. Mr. WALT WHITMAN in one of his candid rhapsodies announces that he is 'no more modest than immodest.' Perhaps in literary matters he carries the theory farther, and is no more honest than dishonest. He likewise says in his preface: 'The great poets are known by the absence in them of tricks, and by the justification of perfect personal candor.' Where, then, can we place Mr. WALT WHITMAN's claims upon immortality?

We confess we turn from Mr. WHITMAN as Critic, to Mr. WHITMAN as Poet, with considerable pleasure. We prefer occupying that independent position which Mr. WHITMAN claims for man, and forming our own opinions, rather than swallowing those ready-made. This gentleman begins his poetic life with a coarse and bitter scorn of the past. We have been living stale and unprofitable lives; we have been surfeited with luxury and high living, and are grown lethargic and dull; the age is fast decaying ,when, lo! the trump of the Angel Whitman brings the dead to life, and animates the slumbering world. If we obey the dictates of that trumpet, we will do many strange things. We will fling off all moral clothing and walk naked over the earth. We will disembarrass our language of all the proprieties of speech, and talk indecency broadcast. We will act in short as if the Millenium were arrived in this our present day, when the absence of all vice would no longer necessitate a virtuous discretion. We fear much, Mr. WALT WHITMAN, that the time is not yet come for the nakedness of purity. We are not yet virtuous enough to be able to read your poetry aloud to our children and our wives. What might be pastoral simplicity five hundred years hence, would perhaps be stigmatized as the coarsest indecency now, and—we regret to think that you have spoken too soon.

The adoration of the 'Me,' the 'Ego,' the 'eternal and universal I,' to use the jargon of the Boston Oracle, is the prevailing motive of *Leaves of Grass*. Man embraces and comprehends the whole. He is everything, and everything is him. All nature ebbs and flows through him in ceaseless tides. He is 'his own God and his own Devil,' and everything that he does is good. He rejoices with all who rejoice; suffers with all who suffer. This doctrine is exemplified in the book by a panorama as it were of pictures, each of which is shared in by the author, who belongs to the universe, as the universe belongs to him. In detailing these pictures he hangs here and there shreds and tassels of his wild philosophy, till his work, like a maniac's robe, is bedizened with fluttering tags of a thousand colors. With all his follies, insolence, and indecency, no modern poet that we know of has presented finer descriptive passages than Mr. WALT WHITMAN. His phrasing, and the strength and completeness of his epithets, are truly wonderful. He paints in a single line with marvellous power and comprehensiveness. The following rhapsody will illustrate his fulness of epithet:

I am he that walks with the tender and growing night;
I call to the earth and sea, half held by the night.

Press close bare-bosomed night! Press close magnetic, nourishing night!
Night of South winds! Night of the large few stars!
Still nodding night! Mad, naked, Summer night!

Smile, O voluptuous cool-breathed earth!
Earth of the slumbering and liquid trees!
Earth of departed sunset! Earth of the mountains misty-topt!
Earth of the vitreous pour of the full moon just tinged with blue!
Earth of shine and dark, mottling the tide of the river!
Earth of the limpid gray of clouds brighter and clearer for my sake!
Far-swooping elbowed earth! Rich apple-blossomed earth!
Smile, for your lover comes!

You sea! I resign myself to you also . . . I guess what you mean,
I behold from the beach your crooked inviting fingers,
I believe you refuse to go back without feeling of me;
We must have a turn together . . . I undress . . . hurry me out of sight of the land.
Cushion me soft . . . *rock me in billowy drowse,*
Dash me with amorous wet . . . I can repay you.

Sea of stretched ground-swells!
Sea, breathing broad and convulsive breaths!
Sea of the brine of life! *Sea of unshovelled and always ready graves!*
Howler and scooper of storms! Capricious and dainty sea!
I am integral with you . . . I too am of one phase and of all phases.

Here are fine expressions well placed. Mr. WHITMAN's study of nature has been close and intense. He had expressed certain things better than any other man who has gone before him. He talks well, and largely, and tenderly of sea and sky, and men and trees, and women and children. His observation and his imagination are both large and well-developed. Take this picture; how pathetic, how tenderly touched!

Agonies are one of my changes of garments;
I do not ask the wounded person how he feels . . . I myself become the wounded person,
My hurt turns livid upon me as I lean on a cane and observe.

I am the mashed fireman with breast-bone broken . . . tumbling walls buried me in their debris.
Heat and smoke I inspired . . . I heard the yelling shouts of my comrades,
I heard the distant click of their picks and shovels;
They have cleared the beams away . . . they tenderly lift me forth.

I lie in the night air in my red shirt . . . the pervading hush is for my sake,
Painless after all I lie, exhausted but not so unhappy.

White and beautiful are the faces around me . . . the heads are bared of their fire-caps.
The kneeling crowd fades with the light of the torches.

If it were permitted to us to outrage all precedent, and print that which should not be printed, we could cull some passages from the *Leaves of Grass*, and place them in strange contrast with the extracts we have already made. If being a Kosmos is to set no limits to one's imagination; to use coarse epithets when coarseness is not needful; to roam like a drunken satyr, with inflamed blood, through every field of lascivious thought; to return time after time with a seemingly exhaustless prurient pleasure to the same licentious phrases and ideas, and to jumble all this up with bits of marvellously beautiful description, exquisite touches of nature, fragments of savagely uttered truth, shreds of unleavened philosophy; if to do all this is to be a Kosmos, then indeed we cede to Mr. WALT WHITMAN his arrogated title. Yet it seems to us that one may be profound without being beastly; one may teach philosophy without clothing it in slang; one may be a great poet without using a language which shall outlaw the minstrel from every decent hearth. Mr. WALT WHITMAN does not think so. He tears the veil from all that society by a well-ordered law shrouds in a decent mystery. He is proud of his nakedness of speech; he glories in his savage scorn of decorum. Like the priests of Belus, he wreathes around his brow the emblems of the Phallic worship.

With all this muck of abomination soiling the pages, there is a wondrous, unaccountable fascination about the *Leaves of Grass*. As we read it again and again, and we will confess that we have returned to it often, a singular order seems to arise out of its chaotic verses. Out of the mire and slough edged thoughts and keen philosophy start suddenly, as the men of Cadmus sprang from the muddy loam. A lofty purpose still dominates the uncleanness and the ridiculous self-conceit in which the author, led astray by ignorance, indulges. He gives token everywhere that he is a huge uncultivated thinker. No country save this could have given birth to the man. His mind is Western—brawny, rough, and original. Wholly uncultivated, and beyond his associates, he has begotten within him the egotism of intellectual solitude. Had he mingled with scholars and men of intellect, those effete beings whom he so despises, he would have learned much that would have been beneficial. When we have none of our own size to measure ourselves with, we are apt to fancy ourselves broader and taller than we are. The poet of the little country town, who has reigned for years the Virgil or

Anacreon of fifty square miles, finds, when he comes into the great metropolis, that he has not had all the thinking to himself. There he finds hundreds of men who have thought the same things as himself, and uttered them more fully. He is astonished to discover that his intellectual language is limited, when he thought that he had fathomed expression. He finds his verse unpolished, his structure defective, his best thoughts said before. He enters into the strife, clashes with his fellows, measures swords with this one, gives thrust for thrust with the other, until his muscles harden and his frame swells. He looks back upon his provincial intellectual existence with a smile; he laughs at his country arrogance and ignorant faith in himself. Now we gather from Mr. WHITMAN'S own admissions—admissions that assume the form of boasts—that he has mingled but little with intellectual men. The love of the physical—which is the key-note of his entire book—has as yet altogether satisfied him. To mix with large-limbed, clean-skinned men, to look on ruddy, fair-proportioned women, is his highest social gratification. This love of the beautiful is by him largely and superbly expressed in many places, and it does one good to read those passages pulsating with the pure blood of animal life. But those associates, though manly and handsome, help but little to a man's inner appreciation of himself. Perhaps our author among his comrades had no equal in intellectual force. He reigned triumphantly in an unquestioning circle of admirers. How easy, then, to fancy one's self a wonderful being! How easy to look around and say, 'There are none like me here. I am the coming man!' It may be said that books will teach such a man the existence of other powerful minds, but this will not do. Such communion is abstract, and has but little force. It is only in the actual combat of mind striving with mind that a man comes properly to estimate himself. Mr. WHITMAN has grown up in an intellectual isolation which has fully developed all the eccentricities of his nature. He has made some foolish theory that to be rough is to be original. Now, external softness of manner is in no degree incompatible with muscularity of intellect; and one thinks no more of a man's brains for his treading on one's toes without an apology, or his swearing in the presence of women. When Mr. WHITMAN shall have learned that a proper worship of the individual man need not be expressed so as to seem insolence, and that men are not to be bullied into receiving as a Messiah every man who sneers at them in his portrait, and disgusts them in his writings, we have no doubt that in some chastened mood of mind he will produce moving and powerful books. We select some passages exhibiting the different phases of Mr. WHITMAN's character. We do so more readily as, from the many indecencies contained in *Leaves of Grass*, we do not believe it will find its way into many families.

A MODEST PROFESSION OF FAITH.

Nothing, not God, is greater to one than one's self is,
And whoever walks a furlong without sympathy, walks to his own funeral,
Dressed in his shroud.

A FINE LANDSCAPE.

The turbid pool that lies in the Autumn forest.
The moon that descends the steeps of the soughing twilight,
Toss, sparkles of day and dusk . . . toss on the black stems that decay in the muck;
Toss to the moaning gibberish of the dry limbs.

A TRUTH.

I, too, am not a bit tamed . . . I, too, am untranslatable;
I sound my barbaric yawp over the roofs of the world.

A DEATH-BED.

When the dull nights are over, and the dull days also;
When the soreness of lying so much in bed is over,
When the physician, after long putting off, gives the silent and terrible look for an answer;
When the children come hurried and weeping, and the brothers and sisters have been sent for;
When medicines stand unused on the shelf, and the camphor-smell has pervaded the rooms;
When the faithful hand of the living does not desert the hand of the dying;
When the twitching lips press lightly on the forehead of the dying;
When the breath ceases, and the pulse of the heart ceases;
Then the corpse limbs stretch on the bed, and the living look upon them,
They are palpable as the living are palpable.
The living look upon the corpse with their eye-sight,
But without eye-sight lingers a different living and looks curiously on the corpse.

IMMORTALITY.

If maggots and rats ended us, then suspicion, and treachery and death.
Do you suspect death? If I were to suspect death I should die now.
Do you think I could walk pleasantly and well-suited towards annihilation?

THE REVOLUTION OF 1848.

Yet behind all, lo, a shape.
Vague as the night, draped interminably, head, front and form in scarlet folds,

Whose face and eyes none may see,
Out of its robes only this . . . the red robes lifted by the arm,
One finger pointed high over the top, like the head of a snake appears.

Meanwhile corpses lie in new-made graves . . . bloody corpses of young men:
The rope of the gibbet, hangs heavily . . . the bullets of princes are flying . . . the creatures of power laugh aloud.
And all these things bear fruits . . . and they are good.

Those corpses of young men,
Those martyrs that hang from the gibbets . . . those hearts pierced by the gray lead,
Cold and motionless as they seem . . . live elsewhere with unslaughtered vitality.

They live in other young men, O Kings,
They live in brothers again ready to defy you;
They were purified by death . . . they were taught and exalted.

Not a grave of the murdered for freedom but sows seed for freedom . . . in its turn to bear seed,
Which the winds carry afar and resow, and the rains and the snows nourish;
Not a disembodied spirit can the weapons of tyrant let loose,
But it stalks invisibly o'er the earth . . . whispering, counselling, cautioning.

Since the foregoing was written—and it has been awaiting its turn at the printing press some months—Mr. WALT WHITMAN has published an enlarged edition of his works, from which it is fair to infer that his first has had a ready sale. From twelve poems, of which the original book was composed, he has brought the number up to thirty, all characterized by the same wonderful amalgamation of beauty and indecency. He has, however been in his new edition guilty of a fresh immodesty. He has not alone printed Mr. EMERSON's private letter in an appendix, but he has absolutely printed a passage of that gentleman's note, 'I greet you at the beginning of a great career,' in gold letters on the back, and affixed the name of the writer. Now, Mr. EMERSON wrote a not very wise letter to Mr. WHITMAN on the publication of the first twelve poems—indorsing them; and so there might be some excuse for the poet's anxiety to let the public know that his first edition was commended from such a quarter. But with the additional poems, Mr. EMERSON has certainly nothing whatever to do; nevertheless, the same note that indorsed the twelve is used by Mr. WHITMAN in the coolest manner to indorse the thirty-two. This is making a private letter go very far indeed. It is as if after a man signed a deed, the person interested should introduce a number of additional clauses, making the original signature still cover them. It is a literary fraud, and Mr. WHITMAN ought to be ashamed of himself.

Still, this man has brave stuff in him. He is truly astonishing. The originality of his philosophy is of little account, for if it is truth, it must be ever the same, whether uttered by his lips or PLATO'S. In manner only can we be novel, and truly Mr. WHITMAN is novelty itself. Since the greater portion of this review was written, we confess to having been attracted again and again to *Leaves of Grass*. It has a singular electric attraction. Its manly vigor, its brawny health, seem to incite and satisfy. We look forward with curious anticipation to Mr. WALT WHITMAN'S future works.

16. A favourable English reaction

1856

Unsigned review by William Howitt or William J. Fox, *London Weekly Dispatch* (1856). Included in *Imprints*, pp. 29–30.

The attribution of this unsigned favourable review is of some interest. Unfortunately authorities equally eminent in Whitman studies disagree about it. The attribution to William Howitt is made by Gay Wilson Allen on p. 176 of his book *The Solitary Singer*, and he in turn bases this upon the volume *New York Dissected*, edited by Emory Holloway and Ralph Adimari and published in New York in 1936. Professor Harold Boldgett, on p. 14 in his excellent study *Walt Whitman in England* (Ithaca, New York, 1934), attributes the review to the lesser known critic William J. Fox.

Although it is difficult to pin down the attribution of this brief, interesting notice with complete certainty, the balance of the evidence seems to favour the authorship of William J. Fox (1786–1864). The review appeared around the middle of March, 1856 in the *Weekly Dispatch*. The attribution by Allen, Holloway and Adimari is based upon the reprint of it in Fowler and Wells' *Life Illustrated* on 19 April 1856. Fowler and Wells had an interest in the success of *Leaves of Grass*, the second edition of which they were to bring out two months later. What makes the Howitt authorship of this review unlikely is that he appears to have written a review of the *Leaves* in the *Spiritual Magazine*, of January 1870. This was a review of the Rossetti Selections from Whitman, published in London two years earlier. This latter review is quoted in Carl Ray Woodring's *Victorian Sampler: William and Mary Howitt* (University of Kansas Press, Lawrence, Kansas, 1952). Although it has some favourable things to say about Whitman, it is altogether more critical of his accomplishment ('. . . frequently oppressive') than this review. Fox, on the other hand, as we learn from the biography of him by Richard Garnett (London, 1910), was a regular contributor to the *Weekly Dispatch* from 1846 to 1856 and his contributions, according to Garnett, 'are practically a chronicle of Radical thought of the day'. There is no evidence to support Howitt's discovery of Whitman much earlier than the appearance of his review in 1870.

We have before us one of the most extraordinary specimens of Yankee intelligence and American eccentricity in authorship it is possible to conceive. It is of a *genus* so peculiar as to embarass us, and has an air at once so novel, so audacious, and so strange, as to verge upon absurdity, and yet it would be an injustice to pronounce it so, as the work is saved from this extreme by a certain mastery over diction not very easy of definition. What Emerson has pronounced to be good must not be lightly treated, and before we pronounce upon the merits of this performance it is but right to examine them. We have, then, a series of pithy prose sentences strung together—forming twelve grand divisions in all, but which, having a rude rhythmical cadence about them, admit of the designation poetical being applied. They are destitute of rhyme, measure of feet, and the like, every condition under which poetry is generally understood to exist being absent; but in their strength of expression, their fervor, hearty wholesomeness, their originality, mannerism, and freshness, one finds in them a singular harmony and flow, as if by reading they gradually formed themselves into melody, and adopted characteristics peculiar and appropriate to themselves alone. If, however, some sentences be fine, there are others altogether laughable; nevertheless, in the bare strength, the unhesitating frankness of a man who 'believes in the flesh and the appetites,' and who dares to call simplest things by their plainest names, conveying also a large sense of the beautiful, and with an emphasis which gives a clearer conception of what manly modesty really is than any thing we have, in all conventional forms of word, deed, or act so far known of, that we rid ourselves, little by little, of the strangeness with which we greet this bluff new-comer, and beginning to understand him better, appreciate him in proportion as he becomes more known. He will soon make his way into the confidence of his readers, and his poems in time will become a pregnant text-book, out of which quotations as sterling as the minted gold will be taken and applied to every form and phrase of the 'inner' or the 'outer' life; and we express our pleasure in making the acquaintance of Walt Whitman, hoping to know more of him in time to come.

17. 'His style is everywhere graphic'

1856

Unsigned review, *Christian Spiritualist* (1856). Included in *Imprints*, pp. 32–6.

Carlyle represents a contemporary reviewer taking leave of the Belles-Lettres department somewhat in this abrupt manner:

> The end having come, it is fit that we end—Poetry having ceased to be read, or published, or written, how can it continue to be reviewed? With your Lake Schools, and Border-Thief Schools, and Cockney and Satanic Schools, there has been enough to do; and now, all these Schools having burnt or smouldered themselves out, and left nothing but a wide-spread wreck of ashes, dust, and cinders—or perhaps dying embers, kicked to and fro under the feet of innumerable women and children in the magazines, and at best blown here and there into transient sputters, what remains but to adjust ourselves to circumstances? Urge me not, [continues this desperate *litterateur*] with considerations that Poetry, as the inward Voice of Life, must be perennial; only dead in one form to become alive in another; that this still abundant deluge of Metre, seeing there must needs be fractions of Poetry floating, scattered in it, ought still to be net-fished; at all events, surveyed and taken note of. The survey of English metre, at this epoch, perhaps transcends the human faculties; to hire out the reading of it by estimate, at a remunerative rate per page, would, in a few quarters, reduce the cash-box of any extant review to the verge of insolvency.

Such is the humorous but essentially truthful picture of the condition and product of the creative faculties during the second quarter of the present century. The great poets, Byron, Shelley, Wordsworth, Goethe, and Schiller, had fulfilled their tasks and gone to other spheres; and all that remained with few exceptions, were weak and feeble echoes of their dying strains, caught up and repeated by numerous imitators and pretenders. And so has it ever been; the visions and perceptions of one man become the creed and superficial life-element of other minds. Swedenborg is worthy to be enrolled among the master minds of the world, because he entered for himself into the Arcana of the profoundest mysteries that can concern human intelligences; his greatest thoughts are revolved, quoted and represented in all 'New Church' publications, but very rarely digested and assimilated by those who claim to be his followers. Still more rare is it to find any receiver of 'the heavenly doctrines' determined to enter for himself into the very interiors of all that Swedenborg taught—to see, not the mighty reflections that Swedenborg was able to give of interior realities, but their originals as they stand constellated in the heavens!

But Divine Providence, leading forth the race, as a father the tottering steps of his children, causes the outward form, on which all men are prone to rely, to be forever changing and passing away before their eyes. The seeds of death are ever found lurking in the fairest external appearances, till those externals become the mere correspondences and representatives of interior realities, and then, though enduring as the fadeless garments of the blest, they are ever-varying, as those robes of light change with each changing state. The Coming Age will recognize the profoundest truths in the internal thought of the Swedish sage, while his most tenacious adherents will be forced to admit that, in externals, he often erred, and was not unfrequently deceived. But the discovered error will not only wean them from a blind and bigoted reliance upon frail man, but confirm the sincere lovers of truth in loyalty to her standard. So also, the Spiritualists are being taught a severe but salutary lesson, that if they will penetrate into the heavenly Arcana of the Inner Life, they must do so by purifying and elevating their own minds, and not by 'sitting in circles' or ransacking town and country to find the most 'reliable Mediums.' Still no step in human progress and development is in vain; even the falls of the child are essential to its discipline. The mistakes and errors of men are needful while in their present imperfect state. They are to the seekers of truth what trials and losses are to those in the pursuit of wealth; they but enhance the value of the prize, and confirm the devotion of the true aspirant as frowns rekindle the ardor of lovers.

Moreover, as man must ever enter into the kingdom of a new unfolding truth with the simplicity and teachableness of little children, it is well that the outer form of the old disappear, that the new may stand alone in its place. It seems also to be a Law that when a change entire and universal is to be outwrought, the means preparatory to its introduction shall be equally widespread, and ultimated to the lowest possible plane. Hence the Spiritual manifestations meet the most external minds; and allow even the unregenerate to know by experience the fact and process of Spiritual inspiration; so that scepticism becomes impossible to the candid and living mind. The second step will be, after such have been convinced that Spiritual intercourse is possible, that they learn that it is worse than useless for the purpose of attaining anything desirable, beyond this conviction—except so far as is orderly and directed, not by the will of man, but of God. But as the old form of poetic inspiration died out with Byron and Shelley, Wordsworth and Goethe, and as the miscellaneous Spirit-intercourse itself also as quickly passes away, there will, we apprehend, spring up forms of mediatorial inspiration, of which there will be two permanent types. The first and highest, as it seems to us, will be the opening of the interiors to direct influx to the inspiring sources of love and wisdom. The heavens will flow down into the hearts and lives, into the thought and speech of harmonic natures, as the silent dews impregnate the patient earth. Men will live in heaven, hence they must be inspired by that breath of life that fills its ethereal expanse. A second class of Media will be used for the ultimation, for ends of use and in accordance with Laws of Order, of the creative thoughts and hymns, the Epics and Lyrics, of individual Spirits and societies of Spirits. These will be to the former Media as the youthful artist who copies the work of a master, to the Angelos and Raphaels, who both design and execute their plans, though they themselves, in their deepest interiors, are instructed and sustained from above.

But in the transition period in which we now are, many varieties of Mediumship must be expected. There are those who stand in rapport with the diseased mentalities of the past and present and pour forth as Divine Revelations the froth and scum of a receding age; they are the sponges who absorb the waste and impurities of humanity. They are also like running sores that gather the corrupt humors and drain the body of its most noxious fluids. There are others who come in contact with the outmost portion of the Spirit-life. These give crude, and in themselves, false notions of the state of man after death; yet they prepare the way for more truthful disclosures; if in no other way by stimulating the appetite for more substantial nourishment. There are those who are lifted by genial inspirations to receive influxes from the upper mind-sphere of the age. They stand, as it were, on clear mountains of intellectual elevation, and with keenest perception discern the purer forms of new unfolding truths ere they become sufficiently embodied to be manifest to the grosser minds of the race. Of these Ralph Waldo Emerson is the highest-type. He sees the future of truths as our Spirit-seers discern the future of man; he welcomes those impalpable forms, as Spiritualists receive with gladdened minds the returning hosts of Spirit-friends.

There are other mediatorial natures who are in mental and heart-sympathy with man, as he now is, struggling to free himself from the tyranny of the old and effete, and to grasp and retain the new life flowing down from the heavens. And as the kindling rays at first produce more smoke than fire, so their lay is one of promise rather than performance. Such we conceive to be the interior condition of the author of *Leaves of Grass*. He accepts man as he is as to his whole nature, and all men as his own brothers. The lambent flame of his genius encircles the world—nor does he clearly discern between that which is to be preserved, and that which is but as fuel for the purification of the ore from its dross. There is a wild strength, a Spartan simplicity about the man, and he stalks among the dapper gentlemen of this generation, like a drunken Hercules amid the dainty dancers. That his song is highly mediatorial he himself asserts, though probably he is unacquainted with the Spiritual developments of the age.

> Through me [he sings] many long dumb voices,
> Voices of the interminable generations of slaves,
> Voices of the diseased and despairing.
> Voices of the cycles of preparation and accretion,
> And of threads that connect the stars,
> And of the rights of them the others are down upon.
> Through me forbidden voices—voices veiled,
> Voices indecent, by me clarified and transfigured.

We omit much even in this short extract, for the book abounds in passages that cannot be quoted in drawing-rooms, and expressions that fall upon the tympanums of ears polite, with a terrible dissonance. His very gait, as he walks through the world, makes dainty people nervous; and conservatives regard him as a social revolution. His style is everywhere graphic and strong, and he sings many things before untouched in prose or rhyme in an idiom that is neither prose nor rhyme, nor yet orthodox blank verse. But it serves his purpose well. He wears his strange garb, cut and made by himself, as gracefully as a South American cavalier his poncho. We will continue our quotations.

[Extract of several pages.]

Such are the graphic pictures which this new world-painter flings from his easel and dashes upon the moving panorama of life. His night-thoughts are not less striking, as, borne by the Muse, he looks into every chamber, and hears the quiet breathing of slumbering humanity.

As the volume advances towards its conclusion, the Spirit of the poet becomes calmer and more serenely elevated. But everywhere his sympathy is with *man*, and not with conventionalisms.

We cannot take leave of this remarkable volume without advising our friends who are not too delicately nerved, to study the work as a sign of the times, written, as we perceive, under powerful influxes; a prophecy and promise of much that awaits all who are entering with us into the opening doors of a new era. A portion of that thought which broods over the American nation, is here seized and bodied forth by a son of the people, rudely, wildly, and with some perversions, yet strongly and genuinely, according to the perception of this bold writer. He is the young Hercules who has seized the serpents that would make him and us their prey; but instead of strangling, he would change them to winged and beautiful forms, who shall become the servants of mankind.

18. 'full of beauties and blemishes'

1856

Unsigned review, *Brooklyn Daily Eagle* (1856). Included in *Imprints*, pp. 52–4.

Here we have a book which fairly staggers us. It sets all the ordinary rules of criticism at defiance. It is one of the strangest compounds of transcendentalism, bombast, philosophy, folly, wisdom, wit, and dulness which it ever entered into the heart of man to conceive. Its author is Walt Whitman, and the book is a reproduction of the author. His name is not on the frontispiece, but his portrait, half length, is. The contents of the book form a daguerreotype of his inner being, and the title page bears a representation of its physical tabernacle. It is a poem; but it conforms to none of the rules by which poetry has ever been judged. It is not an epic, nor an ode, nor a lyric; nor does its verse move with the measured pace of poetical feet—of iambic, trochaic, or anapestic, nor seek the aid of amphibrach, of dactyl, or spondee, nor of final or cesural pause, except by accident. But we had better give Walt's own conception of what a poet of the age and country should be. We quote from the preface:

> His spirit responds to his country's spirit: he incarnates its geography and natural life, and rivers and lakes. Mississippi with annual freshets and changing chutes—Missouri, and Columbia, and Ohio, and the beautiful masculine Hudson, do not embouchure where they spend themselves more than they embouchure into him. The blue breadth over the inland sea of Virginia and Maryland, and the sea off Massachusetts and Maine, and over Manhattan Bay, over Champlain and Erie, and over Ontario and Huron, and Michigan and Superior, and over the Texan, and Mexican, and Floridian, and Cuban seas, and over the seas off California and Oregon—is not tallied by the blue breadth of the waters below, more than the breadth of above and below is tallied by him.
>
> . . . To him enter the essences of the real things, and past and present events —of the enormous diversity of temperature, and agriculture, and mines— the tribes of red aborigines—the weather-beaten vessels entering new ports or making landings on rocky coasts—the first settlement North and South—the rapid stature and muscle—the haughty defiance of '76 and the war, and peace, and formation of the constitution—the Union always surrounded by blatherers, and always calm and impregnable—the immigrants—the wharf-hemmed cities and superior marine—the unsurveyed interior—the log houses, and clearings, and wild animals, and hunters, and trappers—the free commerce, the fishing, and whaling, and gold digging—the endless gestation of new States—the convening of Congress every December, the members duly coming up from all climates and the uttermost parts—the noble character of the young mechanics, and of all free American workmen and workwomen—the general ardor, and friendliness, and enterprise—the perfect equality of the female with the male —the large amativeness—the fluid movement of the population, &c. . . . For such the expression of the American poet is to be transcendent and new.

And the poem seems to accord with the ideas here laid down. No drawing-room poet is the author of the *Leaves of Grass*; he prates not of guitar-thrumming under ladies windows, nor deals in the extravagances of sentimentalism; no pretty conceits or polished fancies are tacked together 'like orient pearls at random strung;' but we have the free utterance of an untrammelled spirit without the slightest regard to established models or fixed standards of taste. His scenery presents no shaven lawns or neatly trimmed arbors; no hothouse conservatory, where delicate exotics odorize the air and enchant the eye. If we follow the poet we must scale unknown precipices and climb untrodden mountains; or we boat on nameless lakes, encountering probably rapids and waterfalls, and start wild fowls, never classified by Wilson or Audubon: or we wander among primeval forests, now pressing the yielding surface of velvet moss, and anon caught among thickets and brambles. He believes in the ancient philosophy that there is no more real beauty or merit in one particle of matter than another; he appreciates all; everything is right that is in its place, and everything is wrong that is not in its place. He is guilty, not only of breaches of conventional decorum, but treats with nonchalant defiance what goes by the name of refinement and delicacy of feeling and expression. Whatever is natural he takes to his heart; whatever is artificial—in the frivolous sense—he makes of no account. The following description of himself is more truthful than many self-drawn pictures:

> Apart from the pulling and hauling, stands what I am,
> Stands amused, complacent, compassionating, idle, unitary,
> Looks down, is erect, bends an arm on an impalpable certain rest,
> Looks with its side-curved head, curious what will come next,
> Both in and out of the game, and watching and wondering at it.

As a poetic interpretation of nature, we believe the following is not surpassed in the range of poetry:

A child said, What is the grass? fetching it to me with full hands;
How could I answer the child? I do not know what it is any more than he.

I guess it is the handkerchief of the Lord,
A scented gift and remembrancer designedly dropped,
Bearing the owner's name someway in the corners, that we may see and remark, and say, Whose?

We are afforded glimpses of half-formed pictures to tease and tantalize with their indistinctness; like a crimson cheek and flashing eye looking on us through the leaves of an arbor—mocking us for a moment, but vanishing before we can reach them. Here is an example:

> Twenty-eight young men bathe by the shore,
> Twenty-eight young men and all so friendly;
> Twenty-eight years of womanly life and all so lonesome.

She owns the fine house by the rise of the bank;
She hides handsome and richly drest aft the blinds of the window.

Which of the young men does she like the best?
Ah, the homeliest of them is beautiful to her.

Dancing and laughing along the beach came the twenty-ninth bather;
The rest did not see her, but she saw them, [&c.]

Well, did the lady fall in love with the twenty-ninth bather, or *vice versa?* Our author scorns to gratify such puerile curiosity; the denouement which novel readers would expect is not hinted at.

In his philosophy justice attains its proper dimensions:

I play not a march for victors only: I play great marches for conquered and slain persons.

Have you heard that it was good to gain the day?
I also say that it is good to fall—battles are lost in the same spirit in which they are won;
I sound triumphal drums for the dead—I fling thro' my embouchures the loudest and gayest music for them.

Vivas to those who have failed and to those whose war vessels sank in the sea,
And to those themselves who sank into the sea,
And to all generals that lost engagements, and all overcome heroes, and the numberless unknown heroes, equal to the greatest heroes known.

The triumphs of victors had been duly celebrated, but surely a poet was needed to sing the praises of the defeated whose cause was righteous, and the heroes who had been trampled under the hoofs of iniquity's onward march.

He does not pick and choose sentiments and expressions fit for general circulation—he gives a voice to whatever *is*, whatever we see, and hear, and think, and feel. He descends to grossness, which debars the poem from being read aloud in any mixed circle. We have said that the work defies criticism; we pronounce no judgment upon it; it is a work that will satisfy few upon a first perusal; it must be read again and again, and then it will be to many unaccountable. All who read it will agree that it is an extraordinary book, full of beauties and blemishes, such as Nature is to those who have only a half-formed acquaintance with her mysteries.

19. Lincoln and *Leaves of Grass*

1857 (?)

Excerpt from Henry B. Rankin, *Personal Recollections of Abraham Lincoln* (1916), pp. 124–7.

Rankin claimed to have been a law clerk in Lincoln's office, and this passage describes events which presumably occurred in 1857. Rankin's reminiscence is accepted as authentic by Thomas B. Mosher in *A Facsimile of 1855 Edition of Leaves of Grass* and by Gay Wilson Allen in *The Solitary Singer* (1955). It is seriously questioned, however, by William E. Barton in *Abraham Lincoln and Walt Whitman* (1928), pp. 92–4, on grounds which appear to be compelling.

No part of Lincoln's life has suffered more in history from false colouring and belittling sensationalism than that of the earlier years he lived in Springfield; and especially is this true in respect to his mental and literary activities of that period. While I knew Lincoln in office life then every new book that appeared on the table had his attention, and was taken up by him on entering to glance through more or less thoroughly. I can say the same of the books in Bateman's office adjoining the law-office. Walt Whitman's *Leaves of Grass*, then just published, I recall as one of the few new books of poetry that interested him, and which, after reading aloud a dozen or more pages in his amusing way, he took home with him. He brought it back the next morning, laying it on Bateman's table and remarking in a grim way that he 'had barely saved it from being purified in fire by the women.'

Readers of this day hardly comprehended the shock Whitman's first book gave the public. Lincoln, from the first, appreciated Whitman's peculiar poetic genius, but he lamented his rude, coarse naturalness. It may be worth while to relate the office scene when Lincoln first read Whitman's poetry. It was exceptional for Lincoln to read aloud in the office anything but a newspaper extract. Only books that had a peculiar and unusual charm for him in their ideas, or form of expression, tempted him to read aloud while in the office,—and this only when the office family were alone present. It was quite usual and expected by us at such times, when he would become absorbed in reading some favourite author, as Burns's poems, or one of Shakespeare's plays, for him to begin reading aloud, if some choice character or principle had appealed to him, and he would then continue on to the end of the act, and sometimes to the end of the play or poem.

When Walt Whitman's *Leaves of Grass* was first published it was placed on the office table by Herndon. It had been read by several of us and, one day, discussions hot and extreme had sprung up between office students and Mr. Herndon concerning its poetic merit, in which Dr. Bateman engaged with us, having entered from his adjoining office. Later, quite a surprise occurred when we found that the Whitman poetry and our discussions had been engaging Lincoln's silent attention. After the rest of us had finished our criticism of some peculiar verses and of Whitman in general, as well as of each other's literary taste and morals in particular, and had resumed our usual duties or had departed, Lincoln, who during the criticisms had been apparently in the unapproachable depths of one of his glum moods of meditative silence,—referred to elsewhere,—took up *Leaves of Grass* for his first reading of it. After half an hour or more devoted to it he turned back to the first pages, and to our general surprise, began to read aloud. Other office work was discontinued by us all while he read with sympathetic emphasis verse after verse. His rendering revealed a charm of new life in Whitman's versification. Save for a few comments on some broad allusions that Lincoln suggested could have been veiled, or left out, he commended the new poet's verses for their virility, freshness, unconventional sentiments, and unique forms of expression, and claimed that Whitman gave promise of a new school of poetry.

At his request, the book was left by Herndon on the office table. Time and again when Lincoln came in, or was leaving, he would pick it up as if to glance at it for only a moment, but instead he would often settle down in a chair and never stop without reading aloud such verses or pages as he fancied. His estimate of the poetry differed from any brought out in the office discussions. He foretold correctly the place the future would assign to Whitman's poems, and that *Leaves of Grass* would be followed by other and greater work. A few years later, immediately following the tragedy of Lincoln's assassination, Whitman wrote that immortal elegy, 'O Captain! My Captain!' which became the nation's—aye, the world's—funeral dirge of our First American. When I first read this requiem its thrilling lines revived in my memory that quiet afternoon in the Springfield law-office, and Lincoln's first reading and comments on *Leaves of Grass*. That scene was so vividly recalled then as to become more firmly fixed in my memory than any other of the incidents at the Lincoln and Herndon office, and this is my apology for giving space for rehearsing it so fully here.

20. 'a wild Tupper of the West'

1857

Unsigned review, *Examiner* (London, 1857). Included in *Imprints*, pp. 45–7.

The interest of this review lies perhaps principally in the comparison between Whitman and Martin Tupper (1810–89), the author of *Proverbial Philosophy*. But the reviewer also appears to feel that he has scored 'a very palpable hit' in his satire of Whitman's 'catalogues'.

We have too long overlooked in this country the great poet who has recently arisen in America, of whom some of his countrymen speak in connection with Bacon and Shakespeare; whom others compare with Tennyson—much to the disadvantage of our excellent laureate—and to whom Mr. Emerson writes that he finds in his book 'incomparable things, said incomparably well.' The book he pronounces 'the most extraordinary piece of wit and wisdom that America has yet contributed;' at which, indeed, says Mr. Emerson in the printed letter sent to us—'I rubbed my eyes a little, to see if this sunbeam were no illusion.'

No illusion truly is Walt Whitman, the new American prodigy, who, as he is himself candid enough to intimate, sounds his barbaric yawp over the roofs of the world. He is described by one of his own local papers as 'a tenderly affectionate, rowdyish, contemplative, sensual, moral, susceptible, and imperious person,' who aspires to cast some of his own grit, whatever that may be, into literature. We have ourselves been disposed to think there is in literature grit enough, according to the ordinary sense, but decidedly Walt Whitman tosses in some more. The author describes himself as 'one of the roughs, a kosmos;' indeed, he seems to be very much impressed with the fact that he is a kosmos, and repeats it frequently. A kosmos we may define, from the portrait of it on the front of the book, is a gentleman in his shirt-sleeves, with one hand in a pocket of his pantaloons, and his wide-awake cocked with a damme-sir air over his forehead.

On the other hand, according to an American review that flatters Walt Whitman, this kosmos is a 'compound of the New England transcendentalist and New York rowdy.'

But as such terms of compliment may not be quite clear to English readers, we must be content, in simpler fashion, to describe to them this Brooklyn boy as a wild Tupper of the West. We can describe him perfectly by a few suppositions. Suppose that Mr. Tupper had been brought up to the business of an auctioneer, then banished to the backwoods, compelled to live for a long time as a backwoodsman, and thus contracting a passion for the reading of Emerson and Carlyle; suppose him maddened by this course of reading, and fancying himself not only an Emerson but a Carlyle and an American Shakespeare to boot, when the fits come on, and putting forth his notion of that combination in his own self-satisfied way, and in his own wonderful cadences? In that state he would write a book exactly like Walt Whitman's *Leaves of Grass.*

[Extracts and interlineated remarks.]

We must be just to Walt Whitman in allowing that he has one positive merit. His verse has a purpose. He desires to assert the pleasure that a man has in himself, his body and its sympathies, his mind (in a lesser degree, however) and its sympathies. He asserts man's right to express his delight in animal enjoyment, and the harmony in which he should stand, body and soul, with fellow-men and the whole universe. To express this, and to declare that the poet is the highest manifestation of this, generally also to suppress shame, is the purport of these *Leaves of Grass.* Perhaps it might have been done as well, however, without being always so purposely obscene, and intentionally foul-mouthed, as Walt Whitman is.

[Extracts and interlineations.]

In the construction of our artificial Whitman, we began with the requirement that a certain philosopher should have been bred to the business of an auctioneer. We must add now, to complete the imitation of Walt Whitman, that the wild philosopher and poet, as conceived by us, should be perpetually haunted by the delusion that he has a catalogue to make. Threefourths of Walt Whitman's book is poetry as catalogues of auctioneers are poems. Whenever any general term is used, off the mind wanders on this fatal track, and an attempt is made to specify all lots included under it. Does Walt Whitman speak of a town, he is at once ready with pages of town lots. Does he mention the American country, he feels bound thereupon to draw up a list of barns, wagons, wilds, mountains, animals, trees, people, 'a Hoosier, a Badger, a Buckeye, a Louisianian or Georgian, a poke-easy from sand-hills and pines,' &c., &c. We will give an illustration of this form of lunacy. The subject from which the patient starts off is equivalent to things in general, and we can spare room only for half the catalogue. It will be enough, however, to show how there arises catalogue within catalogue, and how sorely the paroxysm is aggravated by the incidental mention of any one particular that is itself again capable of subdivision into lots.

The usual routine, the workshop, factory, yard, office, store, or desk;
The jaunt of hunting or fishing, or the life of hunting or fishing.
Pasture-life, foddering, milking and herding, and all the personnel and usages;
The plum-orchard and apple-orchard, gardening, seedlings, cuttings, flowers and vines,
Grains and manures, marl, clay, loam, the subsoil plough, the shovel and pick and rake and hoe, irrigation and draining:
The currycomb, the horse-cloth, the halter and bridle and bits, the very wisps of straw,
The barn and barn-yard, the bins and mangers, the mows and racks;
Manufactures, commerce, engineering, the building of cities, and every trade carried on there, and the implements of every trade.

[Extract continued.]

Now let us compare with this a real auctioneer's catalogue. We will take that of Goldsmith's chambers, by way of departing as little as we can from the poetical. For, as Walt Whitman would say (and here we quote quite literally, prefixing only a verse of our own, from 'A Catalogue of the Household Furniture with the select collection of scarce, curious, and valuable books of Dr. Goldsmith, deceased, which by order of the adm^{r}, will be sold by auction,' &c., &c.)

[The Examiner's burlesque of Walt Whitman.]

Surely the house of a poet is a poem, and behold a poet in the auctioneer who tells you the whole lot of it—
The bath stone, compass front, open border, fender, shovel, tongs, and poker,
The blue moreen festoon window-curtain, the mahogany dining-table on the floor,
The six ditto hollow seat chairs covered with blue moreen,
Covered with blue moreen and finished with a double row of brass nails and check cases,
The Wilton carpet, sun shade, line and pulleys, the deal sideboard stained,
The teapot, five coffee cups, sugar basin and cover, four saucers and six cups,
Two quart decanters and stoppers, one plain ditto, eleven glasses, one wine and water glass,
A pair of bellows and a brush, a footman, copper tea-kettle and coal-scuttle,
Two pairs of plated candlesticks,
A mahogany teaboard, a pet bordered ditto, a large round japanned ditto and two waiters,
The Tragic Muse in a gold frame.

After all, we are not sure whether the poetry of that excellent Mr. Good, the auctioneer who, at his Great Room, No. 121 Fleet Street, sold the household furniture of Oliver Goldsmith in the summer of 1774, does not transcend in wisdom and in wit, 'the most extraordinary piece of wit and wisdom that' (according to Mr. Emerson) 'America has yet contributed.'

21. Praise and blame

1857

Unsigned review, *London Leader* (1857). Included in *Imprints*, pp. 48–9.

For reason to think that this review may have been written by G. H. Lewes, see Dowden, p. 240. Dowden quotes a letter to him written by W. M. Rossetti in 1884 in which he notes that Lewes was the editor of the (*London*) *Leader* at the time of the appearance of *Leaves of Grass* and remembers his having written 'something discerning' about Whitman. Rossetti assured Dowden that though the notice was unsigned, it was generally attributed to Lewes. Dowden adds: 'This article I have not seen.' George Eliot, who quotes some lines from *Leaves of Grass* as an epigraph to book 4, chapter 29, of her novel *Daniel Deronda*, may have had her attention first directed to the poet by Lewes, though Buxton Forman many years later claimed credit for urging her to read Whitman again after she had told him in conversation that *Leaves of Grass* had 'no message for her soul'.

Lewes, George Henry (1817–78), British philosopher and literary critic, wrote essays on drama which were collected into several volumes. He had married in 1840, but in 1851 he became acquainted with Marian Evans (George Eliot) and in 1854 left his wife. His best known work is his *Life of Goethe* (1855).

'Latter-day poetry' in America is of a very different character from the same manifestation in the old country. Here it is occupied for the most part with dreams of the middle ages, of the old knightly and religious times; in America it is employed chiefly with the present, except when it travels out into the undiscovered future. Here our latter-day poets are apt to whine over the times, as if heaven were perpetually betraying the earth with a show of progress that is in fact retrogression, like the backward advance of crabs; there, the minstrels of the stars and stripes blow a loud note of exultation before the grand new epoch, and think the Greeks and Romans, the early Oriental races, and the later men of the middle centuries, of small account before the onward tramping of these present generations. Of this latter sect is a certain phenomenon who has recently started up in Brooklyn, New York—one Walt Whitman, author of *Leaves of Grass*, who has been received by a section of his countrymen as a sort of prophet, and by Englishmen as a kind of fool. For ourselves, we are not disposed to accept him as the one, having less faith in latter-day prophets than in latter-day poets; but assuredly we cannot regard him as the other. Walt is one of the most amazing, one of the most startling, one of the most perplexing creations of the modern American mind; but he is no fool, though abundantly eccentric, nor is his book mere food for laughter, though undoubtedly containing much that may easily and fairly be turned into ridicule.

The singularity of the author's mind—his utter disregard of ordinary forms and modes—appears in the very title-page and frontispiece of his work. Not only is there no author's name, (which in itself would not be singular,) but there is no publisher's name—that of the English bookseller being a London addition. Fronting the title is a portrait of a bearded gentleman in his shirt-sleeves and a Spanish hat, with an all-pervading atmosphere of Yankee-doodle about him; but again there is no patronymic, and we can only infer that this roystering blade is the author of the book. Then follows a long prose treatise by way of preface (and here once more the anonymous system is carried out, the treatise having no heading whatever;) and after that we have the poem, in the course of which a short autobiographical discourse reveals to us the name of the author.

(Extracted from Preface.)

The poem is written in wild, irregular, unrhymed, almost unmetrical 'lengths,' like the measured prose of Mr. Martin Farquhar Tupper's *Proverbial Philosophy*, or some of the Oriental writings. The external form, therefore, is startling and by no means seductive to English ears, accustomed to the sumptuous music of ordinary metre; and the central principle of the poem is equally staggering. It seems to resolve itself into an all-attracting egotism—an eternal presence of the individual soul of Walt Whitman in all things, yet in such wise that this one soul shall be presented as a type of all human souls whatsoever. He goes forth into the world, this rough, devil-may-care Yankee; passionately identifies himself with all forms of being, sentient or inanimate;

sympathizes deeply with humanity; riots with a kind of Bacchanal fury in the force and fervor of his own sensations; will not have the most vicious or abandoned shut out from final comfort and reconciliation; is delighted with Broadway, New York, and equally in love with the desolate backwoods, and the long stretch of the uninhabited prairie, where the wild beasts wallow in the reeds, and the wilder birds start upward from their nests among the grass; perceives a divine mystery wherever his feet conduct, or his thoughts transport him; and beholds all things tending toward the central and sovereign Me. Such, as we conceive, is the key to this strange, grotesque, and bewildering book; yet we are far from saying that the key will unlock all the quirks and oddities of the volume. Much remains of which we confess we can make nothing; much that seems to us purely fantastical and preposterous; much that appears to our muddy vision gratuitously prosaic, needlessly plain-speaking, disgusting without purpose, and singular without result. There are so many evidences of a noble soul in Whitman's pages that we regret these aberrations, which only have the effect of discrediting what is genuine by the show of something false; and especially do we deplore the unnecessary openness with which Walt reveals to us matters which ought rather to remain in sacred silence. It is good not to be ashamed of Nature; it is good to have an all-inclusive charity; but it is also good, sometimes, to leave the veil across the Temple.

22. 'It is the healthiest book, morally'

1859

Excerpt from a book identified only as *Fourteen Thousand Miles Afoot* (1859). Included in *Imprints*, pp. 51–2.

Nothing can more clearly demonstrate the innate vulgarity of our American people, their radical immodesty, their internal licentiousness, their unchastity of heart, their foulness of feeling, than the tabooing of Walt Whitman's *Leaves of Grass*. It is quite impossible to find a publisher for the new edition which has long since been ready for the press, so measureless is the depravity of public taste. There is not an indecent word, an immodest expression, in the entire volume; not a suggestion which is not purity itself; and yet it is rejected on account of its indecency! So much do I think of this work by the healthiest and most original poet America has produced, so valuable a means is it of rightly estimating character, that I have been accustomed to try with it of what quality was the virtue my friends possessed. How few stood the test I shall not say. Some did, and praised it beyond measure. These I set down without hesitation as radically pure, as 'born again,' and fitted for the society of heaven and the angels. And this test I would recommend to every one. Would you, reader, male or female, ascertain if you be actually modest, innocent, pure-minded? read the *Leaves of Grass*. If you find nothing improper there, you are one of the virtuous and pure. If, on the contrary, you find your sense of decency shocked, then is that sense of decency an exceedingly foul one, and you, man or woman, a very vulgar, dirty person.

The atmosphere of the *Leaves of Grass* is as sweet as that of a hayfield. Its pages exhale the fragrance of nature. It takes you back to man's pristine state of innocence in Paradise, and lifts you Godwards. It is the healthiest book, morally, this century has produced: and if it were reprinted in the form of a cheap tract, and scattered broadcast over the land, put into the hands of youth, and into the hands of men and women everywhere, it would do more towards elevating our nature, towards eradicating this foul, vulgar, licentious, sham modesty, which so degrades our people now, than any other means within my knowledge. What we want is not outward, but inward modesty, not external, but internal virtue, not silk and broad-cloth decency, but a decency infused into every organ of the body and faculty of the soul. Is modesty a virtue? Is it then worn in clothes? Does it hang over the shoulders, or does it live and breathe in the heart? Our modesty is a Jewish phylactery, sewed up in the padding of a coat, and stitched into a woman's stays.

23. Three views of 1860

These three brief notices suggest the span of Whitman's contemporary reception—(a) whimsically cautious, (b) contemptuous and (c) admiring.

(a) Unsigned notice, *Boston Saturday Evening Gazette*, 21 April 1860; included in *Imprints*, p. 65: WALT WHITMAN IN BOSTON.—The poet of *Leaves of Grass*, (who hails from New York) has been spending the last four weeks in Boston, busy in the overseeing of a much larger and superior collection of his tantalizing *Leaves*, which, after running the gauntlet of the United States and Great Britain, and receiving divers specimens of about the tallest kind of indignant as well as favorable criticism, seem to have arrived at a position where they can read their title clear to be considered *something*, at any rate. Whether good, better, or best,—or bad, worse, or worst—we shall be better able to tell when we get the new volume.

(b) Excerpt from unsigned notice, *Literary Gazette* (London, 7 July 1860); reprinted in Bucke, p. 202: Of all the writers we have ever perused Walt Whitman is the most silly, the most blasphemous, and the most disgusting. If we can think of any stronger epithets we will print them in a second edition.

(c) Unsigned notice, *Brooklyn City News* (1860); included in *Imprints*, pp. 60–1. The poem referred to here is 'Out of the Cradle Endlessly Rocking' (see No. 26): Admirers of Walt Whitman's *Leaves of Grass* will find a curious ballad, a new poem, after the same rude and mystical type of versification in the issue of that literary paper, the New York Saturday Press, for to-day. The piece we allude to, 'A Child's Reminiscence,' has for its locale, this island of ours, under its old aboriginal name of Paumanok. The plot is a simple one, founded on the advent here, as occasionally happens on 'the south side,' in the breeding season, of a pair of southern mocking-birds,

Two guests from Alabama—two together,

Whose nest by the sea-shore, the boy-poet cautiously watches. The gay and wild notes of the he-bird are translated, until his mate disappears. Now the song turns into sadness; for

Thenceforth, all that Spring,
And all that Summer, in the sound of the sea,
And at night, under the full of the moon, in calmer weather,
Over the hoarse surging of the sea,
Or flitting from brier to brier by day,
I saw, I heard at intervals, the remaining one, the he-bird,
The solitary guest from Alabama.

We will not follow the poet's rendering of the bird's warble; indeed the whole poem needs to be read in its entirety—and several times at that. We will, however, give one detached stanza, as a specimen of Walt Whitman's versification. It follows the bird's plaintive notes. It brings rapidly and artistically together, in the moonlit midnight, the three leading characters, if we may call them so, of the poem—the Barefoot boy, the Mocking-bird, and the Sea, (the 'Savage Old Mother:')

The aria sinking,
All else continuing—the stars shining,
The winds blowing—the notes of the wondrous bird echoing,
With angry moans, the fierce old mother yet, as ever, incessantly moaning,
On the sands of Paumanok's shore gray and rustling,
The yellow half-moon, enlarged, sagging down, drooping, the face of the sea almost touching.
The boy ecstatic—with his bare feet the waves, with his hair the atmosphere dallying.
The love in the heart pent, now loose, now at last tumultuously bursting,

The aria's meaning, the ears, the soul swiftly depositing,
The strange tears down the cheeks coursing,
The colloquy there—the trio—each uttering,
The undertone—the savage old mother, incessantly crying.
To the boy's soul's questions sullenly timing—some drowned secret hissing,
To the outsetting bard of love.

24. 'the primordial music of nature'

1860

Unsigned review, *New York Illustrated News* (5 May 1860). Included in *Imprints*, p.65.

Thayer & Eldridge, of Boston, advertise as nearly ready the redoubtable poems of Walt Whitman,—a new and enlarged edition of the *Leaves of Grass*,—which made so much astonishment in literary and other circles, when it was first flung pell-mell at the heads of the reading public some eight years ago. We shall have something to say about it when it comes to us in the due time and season of publication. In the mean while we warn our readers who may know nothing about this poet and his works, that strange as his speech is,—wild, rude, and barbaric as they will find it at first,—that there is the genuine stuff in this man, and that his sentences resound with the primordial music of nature, and are in harmony with the mountains and seas, and with the songs of the morning stars. Captious, flippant, and foolish people, who are also smart and brilliant, affect already, and will continue to affect, to despise these poems, and adjudge them to the trunk maker. But they are not to be disposed of thus. The 'Court as of Angels,' who, according to Emerson, make up the final verdict about every book, will dispose of it in quite another and far different manner. We find in it all sorts of marvellous insights and truths; the broadest intellectual and moral recognitions and suggestions; and a culture which is up to the high-water mark to which the age has risen. In our judgment,—without of course indorsing either the phraseology or the sentiments of particular passages,—it is the first true word which has been spoken of America—its people, institutions, laws, customs, its physical and moral portraitures—by an American. The genius of this continent and of this wonderful civilization speaks through his pen; and his sentences will one day become the Mosaics of the literature, and be woven into the common speech of the people of America. We know all this is treason at present, in the estimation of poodles and the snobs of literature and of society; but Whitman can afford to wait for the judgment of the 'Court as of Angels,' and smile at poodledom.

25. More puzzling than Swedenborg

1860

Extract from unsigned review, *Boston Post* (1860). Reprinted in Bucke, p. 201.

We have alluded just now to our incapability of comprehending the writings of Swedenborg, but still more, in some parts, do we acknowledge ourselves nonplussed and puzzled by these *Leaves of Grass*. It would be more correct, however, to say how utterly at a loss we are to understand by what motive or impulse so eminent a lecturer and writer, and, as we have always understood, with all his crotchety ideas and pantheistic prattlings, so pure-minded a man as R. Waldo Emerson could have written that eulogy of the *Leaves*, which certainly acted as our chief inducement for inspecting their structure.

Grass is the gift of God for the healthy sustenance of his creatures, and its name ought not to be desecrated by being so improperly bestowed upon these foul and rank leaves of the poison-plants of egotism, irreverence, and of lust run rampant and holding high level in its shame!

We see that the volume arrogantly assumes to itself the claim of founding an original and independent American Literature. Woe and shame for the Land of Liberty if its literature's stream is thus to flow from the filthy fountains of licentious corruption! Little fear, however, should we have of such an issue from the *Leaves* themselves. The pure and elevated moral sense of America would leave them to decay and perish amid their own putridity. But there is danger of their corrupting influences being diffused and extended to the great injury of society, when leaders of our literature, like Emerson, are so infatuated in judgment, and so untrue to the most solemn responsibilities of their position, as to indorse such a prurient and polluted work;— to address its author in such terms as these, 'I give you joy of your free and brave thought—I have great joy in it—I wish to see my benefactor.'

The most charitable conclusion at which we can arrive is, that both Whitman's *Leaves* and Emerson's laudation had a common origin in temporary insanity.

It in no degree shakes our judgement to find more than one eminent Review coinciding more or less in the praise of this work, to which we ourselves by no means deny the possession of much originality of thought and vigor of expression. No amount, however, of such merits can in the judgment of sound and honest criticism,—whose bounden duty it is to endeavor to guide the mind of the nation in a healthy, moral course—atone for the exalting audacity of Priapus worshipping obscenity, which marks a large portion of the volume. Its vaunted manliness and independence, tested by the standard of a truthful judgment, is nothing but the deification of Self, and defiance of the Deity;—its liberty is the wildest license; its love the essence of the lowest lust!

26. 'the *Leaves* . . . resemble the Hebrew Scriptures'

1860

Extract from unsigned review, the *Cosmopolite* (Boston, 4 August 1860. Reprinted in Bucke, p. 200.

In no other modern poems do we find such a lavish outpouring of wealth. It is as if, in the midst of a crowd of literati bringing handfuls of jewels, a few of pure metal elaborately wrought, but the rest merely pretty specimens of pinchbeck, suddenly a herculean fellow should come along with an entire gold mine. Right and left he scatters the glittering dust,—and it is but dust in the eyes of those who look only for pleasing trinkets. Out of his deep California sacks, mingled with native quartz and sand, he empties the yellow ore,—sufficient to set up fifty small practical jewellers dealing in galvanized ware, if they were not too much alarmed at the miner's rough garb to approach and help themselves. Down from his capacious pockets tumble astonishing nuggets,—but we, who are accustomed to see the stuff never in its rude state, but only in fashionable shapes of breastpins, or caneheads, start back with affright, and scream for our toes.

It is much to be regretted that treasures of such rare value are lost to the age through the strange form and manner in which they are presented. But it is time lost blaming the miner. Perhaps he could have done differently, perhaps not; at all events, we must take him as he is, and if we are wise, make the best of him.

The first and greatest objection brought against Walt Whitman and his *Leaves of Grass* is their indecency. Nature is treated here without fig-leaves; things are called by their names, without any apparent sense of modesty or shame. Of this peculiarity—so shocking in an artificial era—the dainty reader should be especially warned. But it is a mistake to infer that the book is on this account necessarily immoral. It is the poet's design, not to entice to the perversion of Nature, which is vice, but to lead us back to Nature, which in his theory is the only virtue.

His theory may be wrong, and the manner in which he carried it out repulsive, but no one who reads and understands him will question the sincerity of his motives, however much may be doubted the wisdom of attempting in this way to restore mankind to the days of undraped innocence.

In respect of plain speaking, and in most respects, the *Leaves* more resemble the Hebrew Scriptures than do any other modern writings. The style is wonderfully idiomatic and graphic. The commonest daily objects and the most exalted truths of the soul, this bard of Nature touches with the ease and freedom of a great master. He wonders at all things, he sympathizes with all things and with all men. The nameless something which makes the power and spirit of music, of poetry, of all art, throbs and whirls under and through his verse, affecting us we know not how, agitating and ravishing the soul. And this springs so genuinely from the inmost nature of the man, that it always appears singularly in keeping even with that extravagant egotism, and with those surprisingly quaint or common expressions, at which readers are at first inclined only to laugh. In his frenzy, in the fire of his inspiration, are fused and poured out together elements hitherto considered antagonistic in poetry—passion, arrogance, animality, philosophy, brag, humility, rowdyism, spirituality, laughter, tears, together with the most ardent and tender love, the most comprehensive human sympathy which ever radiated its divine glow through the pages of poems.

27. 'a curious warble'?

1860

Unsigned review, *Cincinnati Commercial* (1860). Included in *Imprints*, pp. 57–60.

The poem discussed here was revised and in 1871 was given its present title, 'Out of the Cradle Endlessly Rocking'. For an admiring notice of the same poem, see No. 22(c).

The author of *Leaves of Grass* has perpetrated another 'poem.' The N. Y. Saturday Press, in whose columns, we regret to say, it appears, calls it 'a curious warble.' Curious, it may be; but warble it is not, in any sense of that mellifluous word. It is a shade less heavy and vulgar than the *Leaves of Grass*, whose unmitigated badness seemed to cap the climax of poetic nuisances. But the present performance has all the emptiness, without half the grossness, of the author's former efforts.

How in the name of all the Muses this so-called 'poem' ever got into the columns of the Saturday Press, passes our poor comprehension. We had come to look upon that journal as the prince of literary weeklies, the *arbiter elegantiarum* of dramatic and poetic taste, into whose well-filled columns nothing stupid or inferior could intrude. The numerous delicious poems; the sparkling *bon mots;* the puns, juicy and classical, which almost redeemed that vicious practice, and raised it to the rank of a fine art; the crisp criticisms, and delicate dramatic humors of 'Personne,' and the charming piquancies of the *spirituelle* Ada Clare—all united to make up a paper of rare excellence. And it is into this gentle garden of the Muses that that unclean cub of the wilderness, Walt Whitman, has been suffered to intrude, trampling with his vulgar and profane hoofs among the delicate flowers which bloom there, and soiling the spotless white of its fair columns with lines of stupid and meaningless twaddle.

Perhaps our readers are blissfully ignorant of the history and achievements of Mr. Walt Whitman. Be it known, then, that he is a native and resident of Brooklyn, Long Island, born and bred in an obscurity from which it were well he never had emerged. A person of coarse nature, and strong, rude passions, he has passed his life in cultivating, not the amenities, but the rudenesses of character; and instead of tempering his native ferocity with the delicate influences of art and refined literature, he has studied to exaggerate his deformities, and to thrust into his composition all the brute force he could muster from a capacity not naturally sterile in the elements of strength. He has undertaken to be an artist, without learning the first principle of art, and has presumed to put forth 'poems,' without possessing a spark of the poetic faculty. He affects swagger and independence, and blurts out his vulgar impertinence under a full assurance of 'originality.'

In his very first performance, this truculent tone was manifested. He exaggerated every sentiment, and piled up with endless repetition every epithet, till the reader grew weary, even to nausea, of his unmeaning rant. He announces himself to the world as a new and striking thinker, who had something to reveal. His *Leaves of Grass* were a revelation from the Kingdom of Nature. Thus he screams to a gaping universe:

> I, Walt Whitman, an American, one of the roughs, a Cosmos; I shout my voice high and clear over the waves; I send my barbaric yawp over the roofs of the world!

Such was the style of his performance, only it was disfigured by far worse sins of morality than of taste. Never, since the days of Rabelais, was there such literature of uncleanness as some portions of this volume exhibited. All that is beautiful and sacred in love was dragged down to the brutal plane of animal passion, and the writer appeared to revel in language fit only for the lips of the Priapus of the old mythology.

We had hoped that the small reception accorded to his first performance had deterred Mr. Whitman from fresh trespasses in the realms of literature. Several years had passed away; his worse than worthless book had been forgotten, and we hoped that this Apollo of the Brooklyn marshes had returned to his native mud. But we grieve to say he revived last week, and although somewhat changed, changed very little for the better. We do not find so much that is offensive, but we do find a vast amount of irreclaimable drivel and inexplicable nonsense.

We have searched this 'poem' through with the serious and deliberate endeavour to find out the reason of its being written; to discover some clue to the mystery of so vast an expenditure of words. But we honestly confess our utter inability to solve the problem. It is destitute of all the elements which are commonly desiderated in poetical composition; it has neither rhythm nor melody, rhyme nor reason, metre nor sense. We do solemnly assert, that there is not to be discovered, throughout the whole performance, so much as the glimmering ghost of an idea. Here is the poem, which the author, out of his characteristic perversity, insists upon calling the *Pre-verse:*

Out of the rocked cradle,
Out of the mocking-bird's throat, the musical shuttle,
Out of the boy's mother's womb, and from the nipples of her breasts,
Out of the Ninth-Month midnight,
Over the sterile sea-sands, and the fields beyond, where the child, leaving his bed, wandered alone, bareheaded, barefoot,
Down from the showered halo and the moonbeams,
Up from the mystic play of shadows twining and twisting as if they were alive,
Out from the patches of briers and blackberries,
From the memories of the bird that chanted to me,
From your memories, sad brother—from the fitful risings and fallings I heard,
From that night, infantile, under the yellow half-moon, late risen, and swollen as if with tears,
From those beginning notes of sickness and love, there in the mist,
From the thousand responses in my heart, never to cease,
From the myriad thence-aroused words,
From the word stronger and more delicious than any,
From such, as now they start, the scene revisiting,
As a flock, twittering, rising, or overhead passing,
Borne hither—ere all eludes me, hurriedly,
A man—yet by these tears a little boy again,
Throwing myself on the sand, I,
Confronting the waves, sing.

This is like nothing we ever heard of in literature unless it be the following lucid and entertaining composition:

Once there was an old woman went into the garden to get some cabbage to make an apple pie. Just then a great she-bear comes up and pops his head into the shop. 'What, no soap!' So he died, and she married the barber; and there was present at the wedding the Jicaninies and the Piccaninies, and the Grand Panjandrum himself, with the little round button at the top; and they all fell to playing the game of catch as catch can, till the gunpowder ran out of the heels of their boots.

The 'poem' goes on, after the same maudlin manner, for a hundred lines or more, in which the interjection 'O' is employed about five-and thirty times, until we reach the following gem:

Never again leave me to be the peaceful child I was before what there in the night,
By the sea, under the yellow and sagging moon,
The dusky demon aroused, the fire, the sweet hell within,
The unknown want, the destiny of me.

O, but this is bitter bad!

O give me some clue!
O if I am to have so much, let me have more!
O a word! O what is my destination?
O I fear it is henceforth chaos!

There is no doubt of it, we do assure you! And, what is more, it never was anything else. Now, what earthly object can there be in writing and printing such unmixed and hopeless drivel as that? If there were any relief to the unmeaning monotony, some glimpse of fine fancy, some oasis of sense, some spark of 'the vision and the faculty divine,' we would not say a word. But we do protest, in the name of the sanity of the human intellect, against being invited to read such stuff as this, by its publication in the columns of a highly respectable literary journal. What is the comment of the Saturday Press itself on the 'poem'? It says:

Like the *Leaves of Grass*, the purport of this wild and plaintive song, well enveloped, and eluding definition, is positive and unquestionable, like the effect of music. The piece will bear reading many times—perhaps, indeed, only comes forth, as from recesses, by many repetitions.

Well, Heaven help us, then, for as we are a living man, we would not read that poem 'many times' for all the poetry that was ever perpetrated since the morning stars sang together. 'Well enveloped, and eluding definition.' Indeed! We should think so. For our part, we hope it will remain 'well enveloped' till doomsday; and as for 'definition,' all we can do in that direction is to declare that either that 'poem' is nonsense, or we are a lunatic.

If any of the tuneful Nine have ever descended upon Mr. Walt Whitman, it must have been long before that gentleman reached the present sphere of existence. His amorphous productions clearly belong to that school which it is said that neither gods nor men can endure.

There is no meaning discoverable in his writings, and if there were, it would most certainly not be worth the finding out. He is the laureate of the empty deep of the incomprehensible; over that immortal limbo described by Milton, he has stretched the drag-net of his genius; and as he has no precedent and no rival, so we venture to hope that he will never have an imitator.

1865–92

28. Henry James on Whitman

1865

Unsigned review of *Drum-Taps* in the *Nation* (16 November 1865).

For a much later and more approving statement by James, see No. 55 (and see Introduction, pp. 9–10).

It has been a melancholy task to read this book; and it is a still more melancholy one to write about it. Perhaps since the day of Mr. Tupper's *Philosophy* there has been no more difficult reading of the poetic sort. It exhibits the effort of an essentially prosaic mind to lift itself, by a prolonged muscular strain, into poetry. Like hundreds of other good patriots, during the last four years, Mr. Walt Whitman has imagined that a certain amount of violent sympathy with the great deeds and sufferings of our soldiers, and of admiration for our national energy, together with a ready command of picturesque language, are sufficient inspiration for a poet. If this were the case we had been a nation of poets. The constant developments of the war moved us continually to strong feeling and to strong expression of it. But in those cases in which these expressions were written out and printed with all due regard to prosody, they failed to make poetry, as anyone may see by consulting now in cold blood the back volumes of the 'Rebellion Record'.[1] *Of course* the city of Manhattan, as Mr. Whitman delights to call it, when regiments poured through it in the first months of the war, and its own sole god, to borrow the words of a real poet, ceased for a while to be the millionaire, was a noble spectacle, and a poetical statement to this effect is possible. *Of course* the tumult of a battle is

[1] A series of twelve volumes edited by Frank Moore and published between 1862 and 1868 in New York. It is a compilation of official papers, editorials, military records and verse inspired by the American Civil War.

grand, the results of a battle tragic, and the untimely deaths of young men a theme for elegies. But he is not a poet who merely reiterates these plain facts *ore rotundo*. He only sings them worthily who views them from a height. Every tragic event collects about it a number of persons who delight to dwell upon its superficial points—of minds which are bullied by the *accidents* of the affair. The temper of such minds seems to us to be the reverse of the poetic temper; for the poet, although he incidentally masters, grasps, and uses the superficial traits of his theme, is really a poet only in so far as he extracts its latent meaning and holds it up to common eyes. And yet from such minds most of our war-verses have come, and Mr. Whitman's utterances, much as the assertion may surprise his friends, are in this respect no exception to general fashion. They are an exception, however, in that they openly pretend to be something better; and this it is that makes them melancholy reading. Mr. Whitman is very fond of blowing his own trumpet, and he has made very explicit claims for his book. 'Shut not your doors,' he exclaims at the outset—

> Shut not your doors to me, proud libraries,
> For that which was lacking among you all, yet needed most, I bring;
> A book I have made for your dear sake, O soldiers,
> And for you, O soul of man, and you, love of comrades;
> The words of my book nothing, the life of it everything;
> A book separate, not link'd with the rest, nor felt by the intellect;
> But you will feel every word, O Libertad! arm'd Libertad!
> It shall pass by the intellect to swim the sea, the air,
> With joy with you, O soul of man.

These are great pretensions, but it seems to us that the following are even greater:

From Paumanok starting, I fly like a bird,
Around and around to soar, to sing the idea of all;
To the north betaking myself, to sing there arctic songs,
To Kanada, 'till I absorb Kanada in myself—to Michigan then,
To Wisconsin, Iowa, Minnesota, to sing their songs (they are inimitable);
Then to Ohio and Indiana, to sing theirs—to Missouri and Kansas and Arkansas to sing theirs,
To Tennessee and Kentucky—to the Carolinas and Georgia, to sing theirs,
To Texas, and so along up toward California, to roam accepted everywhere;
To sing first (to the tap of the war-drum, if need be)
The idea of all—of the western world, one and inseparable,
And then the song of each member of these States.

Mr. Whitman's primary purpose is to celebrate the greatness of our armies; his secondary purpose is to celebrate the greatness of the city of New York. He pursues these objects through a hundred pages of matter which remind us irresistibly of the story of the college professor who, on a venturesome youth's bringing him a theme done in blank verse, reminded him that it was not customary in writing prose to begin each line with a capital. The frequent capitals are the only marks of verse in Mr. Whitman's writing. There is, fortunately, but one attempt at rhyme. We say fortunately, for if the inequality of Mr. Whitman's lines were self-registering, as it would be in the case of an anticipated syllable at their close, the effect would be painful in the extreme. As the case stands, each line starts off by itself, in resolute independence of its companions, without a visible goal. But if Mr. Whitman does not write verse, he does not write ordinary prose. The reader has seen that liberty is 'libertad.' In like manner, comrade is 'camerado'; Americans are 'Americanos'; a pavement is a 'trottoir,' and Mr. Whitman himself is a 'chansonnier.' If there is one thing that Mr. Whitman is not, it is this, for Béranger was a *chansonnier*. To appreciate the force of our conjunction, the reader should compare his military lyrics with Mr. Whitman's declamations. Our author's novelty, however, is not in his words, but in the form of his writing. As we have said, it begins for all the world like verse and turns out to be arrant prose. It is more like Mr. Tupper's proverbs than anything we have met. But what if, in form it *is* prose? it may be asked. Very good poetry has come out of prose before this. To this we would reply that it must first have gone into it. Prose, in order to be good poetry, must first be good prose. As a general principle, we know of no circumstance more likely to impugn a writer's earnestness than the adoption of an anomalous style. He must have something very original to say if none of the old vehicles will carry his thoughts. Of course he *may* be surprisingly original. Still, presumption is against him. If on an examination the matter of his discourse proves very valuable, it justifies, or at any rate excuses, his literary innovation.

But if, on the other hand, it is of a common quality, with nothing new about it but its manners, the public will judge the writer harshly. The most that can be said of Mr. Whitman's vaticinations is, that, cast in a fluent and familiar manner, the average substance of them might escape unchallenged. But we have seen that Mr. Whitman prides himself especially on the substance—the life—of his poetry. It may be rough, it may be grim, it may be clumsy—such we take to be the author's argument—but it is sincere, it is sublime, it appeals to the soul of man, it is the voice of a people. He tells us, in the lines quoted, that the words of his book are nothing. To our perception they are everything, and very little at that. A great deal of verse that is nothing but words has, during the war, been sympathetically sighed over and cut out of newspaper corners, because it has possessed a certain simple melody. But Mr. Whitman's verse, we are confident, would have failed even of this triumph, for the simple reason that no triumph, however small, is won but through the exercise of art, and that this volume is an offense against art. It is not enough to be grim and rough and careless; common sense is also necessary, for it is by common sense that we are judged. There exists in even the commonest minds, in literary matters, a certain precise instinct of conservatism, which is very shrewd in detecting wanton eccentricities. To this instinct Mr. Whitman's attitude seems monstrous. It is monstrous because it pretends to persuade the soul while it slights the intellect; because it pretends to gratify the feelings while it outrages the taste. The point is that it does this *on theory*, wilfully, consciously, arrogantly. It is the little nursery game of 'open your mouth and shut your eyes.' Our hearts are often touched through a compromise with the artistic sense, but never in direct violation of it. Mr. Whitman sits down at the outset and counts out the intelligence. This were indeed a wise precaution on his part if the intelligence were only submissive! But when she is deliberately insulted, she takes her revenge by simply standing erect and open-eyed. This is assuredly the best she can do. And if she could find a voice she would probably address Mr. Whitman as follows:

You came to woo my sister, the human soul. Instead of giving me a kick as you approach, you should either greet me courteously, or, at least, steal in unobserved. But now you have me on your hands. Your chances are poor. What the human heart desires above all is sincerity, and you do not appear to me sincere. For a lover you talk entirely too much about yourself. In one place you threaten to absorb Kanada. In another you call upon the city of New York to incarnate you, as you have incarnated it. In another you inform us that neither youth pertains to you nor 'delicatesse,' that you are awkward in the parlor, that you do not dance, and that you have neither bearing, beauty, knowledge, nor fortune. In another place, by an allusion to your 'little songs,' you seem to identify yourself with the third person of the Trinity. For a poet who claims to sing 'the idea of all,' this is tolerably egotistical. We look in vain, however, through your book for a single idea. We find nothing but flashy imitations of ideas. We find a medley of extravagances and commonplaces.

We find art, measure, grace, sense sneered at on every page, and nothing positive given us in their stead. To be positive one must have something to say; to be positive requires reason, labor, and art; and art requires, above all things, a suppression of one's self, a subordination of one's self to an idea. This will never do for you, whose plan is to adapt the scheme of the universe to your own limitations. You cannot entertain and exhibit ideas; but, as we have seen, you are prepared to incarnate them. It is for this reason, doubtless, that when once you have planted yourself squarely before the public, and in view of the great service you have done to the ideal, have become, as you say, 'accepted everywhere,' you can afford to deal exclusively in words. What would be bald nonsense and dreary platitudes in anyone else becomes sublimity in you. But all this is a mistake. To become adopted as a national poet, it is not enough to discard everything in particular and to accept everything in general, to amass crudity upon crudity, to discharge the undigested contents of your blotting-book into the lap of the public. You must respect the public which you address; for it has taste, if you have not. It delights in the grand, the heroic, and the masculine; but it delights to see these conceptions cast into worthy form. It is indifferent to brute sublimity. It will never do for you to thrust your hands into your pockets and cry out that, as the research of form is an intolerable bore, the shortest and most economical way for the public to embrace its idols —for the nation to realize its genius—is in your own person. This democratic, liberty-loving, American populace, this stern and war-tried people, is a great civilizer. It is devoted to refinement. If it has sustained a monstrous war, and practiced human nature's best in so many ways for the last five years, it is not to put up with spurious poetry afterwards. To sing aright our battles and our glories it is not enough to have served in a hospital (however praiseworthy the task in itself), to be aggressively careless, inelegant, and ignorant, and to be constantly preoccupied with yourself. It is not enough to be rude, lugubrious, and grim. You must also be serious. You must forget yourself in your ideas. Your personal qualities—the vigor of your temperament, the manly independence of your nature, the tenderness of your heart—these facts are impertinent. You must be *possessed*, and you must strive to possess your possession. If in your striving you break into divine eloquence, then you are a poet. If the idea which possesses you is the idea of your country's greatness, then you are a national poet, and not otherwise.

29. William Douglas O'Connor on Whitman

1866

Extracts from *The Good Gray Poet: A Vindication* (dated 2 September 1865; published 1866), pp. 3–12, 44–6.

William Douglas O'Connor, an ardent abolitionist author whom Whitman had first met in Boston, was employed in Washington as a clerk in the Treasury Department during the Civil War. He was, as Allen's biography of Whitman indicates, very helpful in getting Whitman a clerkship in the Interior Department at $1,200 a year. It was from this job that Whitman was dismissed by Secretary Harlan, as told in O'Connor's pamphlet. It may be remarked parenthetically that no great financial harm to Whitman ensued, since he was merely transferred to the Department of Justice, where O'Connor's friend, who had got the job for Whitman originally worked. The dismissal, in fact, worked out to Whitman's benefit by inspiring O'Connor's irate pamphlet. Its title, suggested by a line in Tennyson, soon became synonymous with Whitman's name, and he is still occasionally referred to, even in our own day, as 'the good gray poet'.

William Sloane Kennedy in *The Fight of a Book for the World* (1926) writes of O'Connor's work that it is 'full of hyperbole, to be sure, but also of the flaming lava of invective and of ripest culture. . . . Wendell Philips spoke of it as "the most brilliant piece of controversial literature issued during the nineteenth century." Even the hostile Richard H. Stoddard called it "one of the most extraordinary things we ever encountered".' A few years later, O'Connor published a war story *The Carpenter* in which the hero, under a thin disguise, is an idealized version of Walt Whitman. In *The Good Gray Poet*, his plan is to meet an *ad hominem* attack with an *ad hominem* defence. Its idea is Whitman's that in some mystic and ultimate sense, the poem and the poet are one; he who touched his book touched a man as well.

O'Connor's effusion is not in any sense comparable in literary worth to Emerson's famous letter of a decade before but, by making Whitman into a literary martyr, the document played a vital role in the history of the widespread public recognition of the validity of claims made on his behalf as a poet.

Nine weeks have elapsed since the commission of an outrage, to which I have not till now been able to give my attention, but which, in the interest of the sacred cause of free letters, and in that alone, I never meant should pass without its proper and enduring brand.

For years past, thousands of people in New York, in Brooklyn, in Boston, in New Orleans, and latterly in Washington, have seen, even as I saw two hours ago, tallying, one might say, the streets of our American cities, and fit to have for his background and accessories, their streaming populations and ample and rich façades, a man of striking masculine beauty—a poet—powerful and venerable in appearance; large, calm, superbly formed; oftenest clad in the careless, rough, and always picturesque costume of the common people; resembling, and generally taken by strangers for, some great mechanic, or stevedore, or seaman, or grand laborer of one kind or another; and passing slowly in this guise, with nonchalant and haughty step along the pavement, with the sunlight and shadows falling around him. The dark sombrero he usually wears was, when I saw him just now, the day being warm, held for the moment in his hand; rich light an artist would have chosen, lay upon his uncovered head, majestic, large, Homeric, and set upon his strong shoulders with the grandeur of ancient sculpture; I marked the countenance, serene, proud, cheerful, florid, grave; the brow seamed with noble wrinkles; the features, massive and handsome, with firm blue eyes; the eybrows and eyelids especially showing that fullness of arch seldom seen save in the antique busts; the flowing hair and fleecy beard, both very gray, and tempering with a look of age the youthful aspect of one who is but forty-five; the simplicity and purity of his dress, cheap and plain, but spotless, from snowy falling collar to burnished boot, and exhaling faint fragrance; the whole form surrounded with manliness, as with a nimbus, and breathing, in its perfect health and vigor, the august charm of the strong. We who have looked upon this figure, or listened to that clear, cheerful, vibrating voice, might thrill to think, could we but transcend our age, that we had been thus near to one of the greatest of the sons of men. But Dante stirs no deep pulse, unless it be of hate, as he walks the streets of Florence; that shabby, one-armed soldier, just out of jail and hardly noticed, though he has amused Europe, is Michael Cervantes; that son of a vine-dresser, whom Athens laughs at as an eccentric genius, before it is thought worth while to roar him into exile, is the century-shaking Æschylus; that phantom whom the wits of the seventeenth century think not worth extraordinary notice, and the wits of the eighteenth century, spluttering with laughter, call a barbarian, is Shakespeare; that earth-soiled, vice-stained ploughman, with the noble heart and sweet, bright eyes, whom the good abominate and the gentry patronize—subject now of anniversary banquets by gentlemen who, could they wander backward from those annual hiccups into Time, would never help his life or keep his company—is Robert Burns; and this man, whose grave, perhaps, the next century will cover with passionate and splendid honors, goes regarded with careless curiosity or phlegmatic composure by his own age. Yet, perhaps, in a few hearts he has waked that deep thrill due to the passage of the sublime. I heard lately, with sad pleasure, of the letter introducing a friend, filled with noble courtesy, and dictated by the reverence for genius, which a distinguished English nobleman, a stranger, sent to this American bard. Nothing deepens my respect for the beautiful intellect of the scholar Alcott, like the bold sentence, 'Greater than Plato,' which he once uttered upon him. I hold it the surest proof of Thoreau's insight, that after a conversation, seeing how he incarnated the immense and new spirit of the age, and was the compend of America, he came away to speak the electric sentence, 'He is Democracy!' I treasure to my latest hour, with swelling heart and springing tears, the remembrance that Abraham Lincoln, seeing him for the first time from the window of the East Room of the White House as he passed slowly by, and gazing at him long with that deep eye which read men, said, in the quaint, sweet tone which those who have spoken with him will remember, and with a significant emphasis which the type can hardly convey—'Well, *he* looks like A MAN!' Sublime tributes, great words; but none too high for their object, the author of *Leaves of Grass*, Walt Whitman, of Brooklyn.

On the 30th of June last, this true American man and author was dismissed, under circumstances of peculiar wrong, from a clerkship he had held for six months in the Department of the Interior. His dismissal was the act of the Hon. James Harlan, the Secretary of the

Department, formerly a Methodist clergyman, and President of a Western college.

Upon the interrogation of an eminent officer of the Government, at whose instance the appointment had, under a former Secretary, been made, Mr. Harlan averred that Walt Whitman had been in no way remiss in the discharge of his duties, but that, on the contrary, so far as he could learn, his conduct had been most exemplary. Indeed, during the few months of his tenure of office, he had been promoted. The sole and only cause of his dismissal, Mr. Harlan said, was that he had written the book of poetry entitled *Leaves of Grass*. This book Mr. Harlan characterized as 'full of indecent passages.' The author, he said, was 'a very bad man,' a 'Free-Lover.' Argument being had upon these propositions, Mr. Harlan was, as regards the book, utterly unable to maintain his assertions; and, as regards the author, was forced to own that his opinions of him had been changed. Nevertheless, after this substantial admission of his injustice, he absolutely refused to revoke his action. Of course, under no circumstances would Walt Whitman, the proudest man that lives, have consented to again enter into office under Mr. Harlan: but the demand for his reinstatement was as honorable to the gentleman who made it, as the refusal to accede to it was discreditable to the Secretary.

The closing feature of this transaction, and one which was a direct consequence of Mr. Harlan's course, was its remission to the scurrilous, and in some instances libellous, comment of a portion of the press. To sum up, an author, solely and only for the publication, ten years ago, of an honest book, which no intelligent and candid person can regard as hurtful to morality, was expelled from office by the Secretary, and held up to public contumely by the newspapers. It remains only to be added here, that the Hon. James Harlan is the gentleman who, upon assuming the control of the Department, published a manifesto, announcing that it was thenceforth to be governed upon the principles of Christian civilization.

This act of expulsion, and all that it encloses, is the outrage to which I referred in the opening sentence of this letter.

I have had the honor, which I esteem a very high one, to know Walt Whitman intimately for several years, and am perfectly conversant with the details of his life and history. Scores and scores of persons, who know him well, can confirm my own report of him, and I have therefore no hesitation in saying that the scandalous assertions of Mr. Harlan, derived from whom I know not, as to his being a bad man, a Free-Lover, &c., belong to the category of those calumnies at which, as Napoleon said, innocence itself is confounded. A better man in all respects, or one more irreproachable in his relation to the other sex, lives not upon this earth. His is the great goodness, the great chastity of spiritual strength and sanity. I do not believe that from the hour of his infancy, when Lafayette held him in his arms, to the present hour, in which he bends over the last wounded and dying of the war, that any one can say aught of him that does not consort with the largest and truest manliness. I am perfectly aware of the miserable lies which have been put into circulation respecting him, of which the story of his dishonoring an invitation to dine with Emerson, by appearing at the table of the Astor House in a red shirt, and with the manners of a rowdy, is a mild specimen. I know, too, the inferences drawn by wretched fools, who, because they have seen him riding upon the top of an omnibus; or at Pfaff's restaurant; or dressed in rough clothes suitable for his purposes, and only remarkable because the wearer was a man of genius; or mixing freely and lovingly, like Lucretius, like Rabelais, like Francis Bacon, like Rembrandt, like all great students of the world, with low and equivocal and dissolute persons, as well as with those of a different character must needs set him down as a brute, a scallawag, and a criminal. Mr. Harlan's allegations are of a piece with these. If I could associate the title with a really great person, or if the name of man were not radically superior, I should say that for solid nobleness of character, for native elegance and delicacy of soul, for a courtesy which is the very passion of thoughtful kindness and forbearance, for his tender and paternal respect and manly honor for women, for love and heroism carried into the pettiest details of life, and for a large and homely beauty of manners, which makes the civilities of parlors fantastic and puerile in comparison, Walt Whitman deserves to be considered the grandest gentleman that treads this continent. I know well the habits and tendencies of his life. They are all simple, sane, domestic; worthy of him as one of an estimable family and a member of society. He is a tender and faithful son, a good brother, a loyal friend, an ardent and devoted citizen. He has been a laborer, working successively as a farmer, a carpenter, a printer. He has been a stalwart editor of the Republican party, and often, in that powerful and nervous prose of which he is master, done yeoman's service for the great cause of human liberty and the imperial conception of the indivisible Union. He has been a visitor of prisons; a protector of fugitive slaves; a constant voluntary nurse, night and day, at the hospitals, from the beginning of the war to the present time; a brother and friend through life to the neglected and the forgotten, the poor, the degraded, the criminal, the outcast; turning away from no man for his guilt, nor woman for her vileness. His is the strongest and truest compassion I have ever known. I remember here the anecdote told me by a witness, of his meeting in a by-street in Boston a poor ruffian, one whom he had known well as an innocent child, now a full-grown youth, vicious far beyond his years, flying to Canada from the pursuit of the police, his sin-trampled features bearing marks of the recent bloody brawl in New York in which, as he supposed, he had killed some one; and having heard his hurried story, freely confided to him, Walt Whitman, separated not from the bad even by his own goodness, with well I know what tender and tranquil feeling for this ruined being, and with a love which makes me think of that love of God which deserts not any creature, quietly at parting, after assisting him from his means, held him for a moment, with his arm around his neck, and, bending to the face, horrible and battered and prematurely old, kissed him on the cheek; and the poor hunted wretch, perhaps for the first time in his low life, receiving a token of love and compassion ike a touch from beyond the sun, hastened away in deep dejection, sobbing and in tears. It reminds me of the anecdotes Victor Hugo, in his portraiture of Bishop Myriel, tells, under a thin veil of fiction, of Charles Miolles, the good bishop of Rennes.—I know not what talisman Walt Whitman carries, unless it be an unexcluding friendliness and goodness which is felt upon his approach like magnetism; but I know that in the subterranean life of cities, among the worst roughs, he goes safely; and I could recite instances where hands that, in mere wantonness of ferocity, assault anybody, raised against him, have of their own accord been lowered almost as quickly, or, in some cases, been dragged promptly down by others; this, too, I mean, when he and the assaulting gang were mutual strangers. I have seen singular evidence of the mysterious quality which not only guards him, but draws to him with intuition, rapid as light, simple and rude people, as to their natural mate and friend. I remember, as I passed the White House with him one evening, the startled feeling with which I saw the soldier on guard there—a stranger to us both, and with something in his action that curiously proved that he was a stranger—suddenly bring his musket to the 'present,' in military salute to him, quickly mingling with this respect due to his colonel, a gesture of greeting with the right hand as to a comrade; grinning, meanwhile, good fellow, with shy, spontaneous affection and deference; his ruddy, broad face glowing in the flare of the lampions. I remember, on another occasion, as I crossed the street with him, the driver of a street car, a stranger, stopping the conveyance, and inviting him to get on and ride with him. Adventures of this kind are frequent, and, 'I took a fancy to you,' or, 'You look like one of my style,' is the common explanation he gets upon their occurrence. It would be impossible to exaggerate the personal adhesion and strong, simple affection given him, in numerous instances on sight, by multitudes of plain persons—sailors, mechanics, drivers, soldiers, farmers, sempstresses, old people of the past generation, mothers of families—those powerful, unlettered persons, among whom as he says in his book, he has gone freely, and who never in most cases even suspect as an author him whom they love as a man, and who loves them in return.—His intellectual influence upon many young men and women—spirits of the morning sort, not willing to belong to that intellectual colony of Great Britain which our literary classes compose, nor helplessly tied like them to the old forms—I note as kindred to that of Socrates upon the youth of ancient Attica, or Raleigh upon the gallant young England of his day. It is a power at once liberating, instructing, and inspiring.—His conversation is a university. Those who have heard him in some roused hour, when the full afflatus of his spirit moved him, will agree with me that the grandeur of talk was accomplished. He is known as a passionate lover and powerful critic of the great music and of art. He is deeply cultured by some of the best books, especially the Bible, which he prefers above all other great literature; but principally by contact and communion with things themselves, which literature can only mirror and celebrate. He has travelled through most of the United States, intent on comprehending and absorbing the genius and meaning of his country, that he might do his best to start a literature worthy of her, sprung from her own polity, and tallying her own unexampled magnificence among the nations. To the same end, he has been a long, patient, and laborious student of life, mixing intimately with all varieties of experience and men, with curiosity and with love. He has given his thought, his life, to this beautiful ambition, and, still young, he has grown gray in its service. He has never married; like Giordano Bruno, he has made Thought in the service of his fellow-creatures his *bella donna*, his best beloved, his bride. His patriotism is boundless. It is no intellectual sentiment; it is a personal passion. He performs with scrupulous fidelity and zeal, the duties of a citizen. For eighteen years, not missing once, his ballot has dropped on every national and local election day, and his influence has been ardently given, for the good cause. Of all men I know, his life is most in the life of the nation. I remember, when the first draft was ordered, at a time when he was already performing an arduous and perilous duty as a volunteer attendant upon the wounded in the field—a duty which cost him the only illness he ever had in his life, and a very severe and dangerous illness it was, the result of poison absorbed in his devotion to the worst cases of the hospital gangrene; and when it would have been the easiest thing in the world to evade duty, for though then only forty-two or three years old, and subject to the draft, he looked a hale sixty, and no enrolling officer would have paused for an instant before his gray hair—I remember, I say, how anxious and careful he was to get his name put on the enrolment lists, that he might stand his chance for martial service. This, too, at a time when so many gentlemen were skulking, dodging, agonizing for substitutes, and practising every conceivable device to escape military duty. What music of speech, though Cicero's own—what scarlet and gold superlatives could adorn or dignify this simple antique trait of private heroism?—I recall his love for little children, for the young, and for very old persons, as if the dawn and the evening twilight of life awakened his deepest tenderness. I recall the affection for him of numbers of young men, and invariably of all good women. Who, knowing him, does not regard him as a man of the highest spiritual culture? I have never known one of greater and deeper religious feeling. To call one like him good, seems an impertinence. In our sweet country phrase, he is one of God's men. And as I write these hurried and broken memoranda—as his strength and sweetness of nature, his moral health, his rich humor, his gentleness, his serenity, his charity, his simple-heartedness, his courage, his deep and varied knowledge of life and men, his calm wisdom, his singular and beautiful boy-innocence, his personal majesty, his rough scorn of mean actions, his magnetic and exterminating anger on due occasions—all that I have seen and heard of him, the testimony of associates, the anecdotes of friends, the remembrance of hours with him that should be immortal, the traits, lineaments, incidents of his life and being—as they come crowding into memory—his seems to me a character which only the heroic pen of Plutarch could record, and which Socrates himself might emulate or envy.

This is the man whom Mr. Harlan charges with having written a bad book. I might ask, How long is it since bad books have been the flower of good lives? How long is it since grape-vines produced thorns or fig-trees thistles? But, Mr. Harlan says the book is bad because it is 'full of indecent passages.' This allegation has been brought against *Leaves of Grass* before. It has been sounded loud and strong by many of the literary journals of both continents. As criticism it is legitimate. I may contemn the mind or deplore the moral life in which such a criticism has its source; still, as criticism it has a right to existence. But Mr. Harlan, passing the limits of opinion, inaugurates punishment. He joins the band of the hostile verdict; he incarnates their judgment; then, detaching himself, he proceeds to a solitary and signal vengeance. As far as he can have it so, this author, for having written his book shall starve. He shall starve, and his name shall receive a brand. This is the essence of Mr. Harlan's action. It is a dark and serious step to take. Upon what grounds is it taken?

I have carefully counted out from Walt Whitman's poetry the lines, perfectly moral to me, whether viewed in themselves or in the light of their sublime intentions and purport, but upon which ignorant and indecent persons of respectability base their sweeping condemnation of the whole work. Taking *Leaves of Grass*, and the recent small volume, *Drum-Taps* (which was in Mr. Harlan's possession), there are in the whole about nine thousand lines or verses. From these, including matter which I can hardly imagine objectionable to any one, but counting everything which the most malignant virtue could shrink from, I have culled eighty lines. Eighty lines out of nine thousand! It is a less proportion than one finds in Shakespeare. Upon this so slender basis, rests the whole crazy fabric of American and European slander, and the brutal lever of the Secretary. . . .

So let me leave him. And if there be any who think this tribute in bad taste, even to a poet so great, a person so unusual, a man so heroic and loving, I answer, that when on grounds of taste foes withhold detraction, friends may withhold eulogy; and that at any rate I recognize no reason for keeping back just words of love and reverence when, as in this case, they must glow upon the sullen foil of the printed hatreds of ten years. To that long record of hostility, I am only glad and proud to be able to oppose this record of affection.—And, with respect to the crowning enmity of the Secretary of the Interior, let no person misjudge the motives upon which I denounce it. Personally, apart from this act, I have nothing against Mr. Harlan. He is of my own party; and my politics have been from my youth essentially the same as his own. I do not know him; I have never even seen him; I criticise no attitude nor action of his life but this; and I criticise this with as little personality as I can give to an action so personal. I withhold, too, as far as I can, every expression of resentment; and no one who knew all I know of this matter could fail to credit me with singular and great moderation. For, behind what I have related, there is another history, every incident of which I have recovered from the obscurity to which it was confided; and, as I think of it, it is with difficulty that I restrain my just indignation. Instead of my comparatively cold and sober treatment, this transaction deserves rather the pitiless exposure and the measureless, stern anger and red-hot steel scourge of Juvenal. But I leave untold its darkest details; and, waiving every other consideration, I rest solely and squarely on the general indignity and injury this action offers to intellectual liberty. I claim that to expel an author from a public office and subject him to public contumely, solely because he has published a book which no one can declare immoral without declaring all the grand books immoral, is to affix a penalty to thought, and to obstruct the freedom of letters. I declare this act the audacious captain of a series of acts and a style of opinions whose tendency and effect throughout Christendom is to dwarf and degrade literature, and to make great books impossible, except under pains of martyrdom. As such, I arraign it before every liberal and thoughtful mind. I denounce it as a sinister precedent; as a ban upon the free action of genius; as a logical insult to all commanding literature; and as in every way a most serious and heinous wrong. Difference of opinion there may and must be upon the topics which in this letter I have grouped around it, but upon the act itself there can be none. As I drag it up here into the sight of the world, I call upon every scholar, every man of letters, every editor, every good fellow everywhere who wields the pen, to make common cause with me in rousing upon it the full tempest of reprobation it deserves. I remember Tennyson, a spirit of vengeance over the desecrated grave of Moore; I think of Scott rolling back the tide of obloquy from Byron; I see Addison gilding the blackening fame of Swift; I mark Southampton befriending Shakespeare; I recall Du Bellay enshielding Rabelais; I behold Hutten fortressing Luther; here is Boccaccio lifting the darkness from Dante, and scattering flame on his foes in Florence; this is Bembo protecting Pomponatius; that is Grostête enfolding Roger Bacon from the monkish fury; there, covered with light, is Aristophanes defending Æschylus: and if there lives aught of that old chivalry of letters, which in all ages has sprung to the succor and defence of genius, I summon it to act the part of honor and duty upon a wrong which, done to a single member of the great confraternity of literature, is done to all, and which flings insult and menace upon every immortal page that dares transcend the wicked heart or the constricted brain. I send this letter to Victor Hugo, for its passport through Europe; I send it to John Stuart Mill, to Newman, and Matthew Arnold, for England; I send it to Emerson and Wendell Phillips; to Charles Summer; to every Senator and Representative in Congress; to all our journalists; to the whole American people; to every one who guards the freedom of letters and the liberty of thought throughout the civilized world. God grant that not in vain upon this outrage do I invoke the judgment of the mighty spirit of literature, and the fires of every honest heart!

30. Rossetti's London edition 1868

Extracts from *Rossetti Papers 1868–1870: A Compilation by William Michael Rossetti* (1903).

(*a*) Extract from a letter from Horace Scudder to Rossetti, 24 April 1866 (p. 181): Have you seen Walt Whitman's *Drum Taps?* It is just possible that you have not; and I will take the opportunity afforded by a friend's going to London to send you a copy, and also a brochure of a very enthusiastic friend of his—known for the author of a spasmodic anti-slavery novel, *Harrington*, published about the same time as *Leaves of Grass* by same publishers. The pamphlet will perhaps give you some information respecting Whitman: certainly I can add nothing, except to say that you will see in Thoreau's Letters an account of his visit to the poet, and the estimation in which he held him. I do not think that Mr. Lincoln's death brought out any nobler expression of the personal grief of the best natures in the country than 'O Captain, my Captain!' The *lonely* grief of the poet in the strong contrast which he presents was really that felt by all. I have but lately got the volume;

and, although I do not believe that any new American poetry is to be established on a reckless disregard of natural laws of rhythm, simply because such laws have produced conventional rules, I think that no one else has caught so rarely the most elusive elements of American civilization.

(*b*) Extract from Diary entry, 22 September 1867 (p. 240): Began writing my introduction to Whitman. Conway called, and showed me the large photograph of W[hitman] lately sent over, with his autograph. He denies that Emerson has ever turned against W[hitman], but on the contrary admires him quite as much as he ever expressed in writing: he also got Lincoln to approve W[hitman]'s going to the camp-hospitals, with no remuneration (W[hitman] stipulated there should be none) but with the ordinary camp-rations. . . .

(*c*) Extract from Diary entry, 16 November 1867 (p. 243): E. Routledge called at Somerset House, and I agreed to write for *The Broadway* articles on Ruskin and Browning. We agreed upon Houghton to illustrate the coffin-scene in my poem, though R[outledge] would have preferred Watson. Conway sends me a letter to him from Whitman concerning my Selection. He authorizes me to make such alterations in words as I may consider needful for decency. This would, I think, enable Hotten to bring out at once a modified complete edition, instead of a mere Selection.

(*d*) Extract from Diary entry, 28 November 1867 (p. 244): Conway sent me a letter he has received from O'Connor, author of *The Good Grey Poet.* He intimates that Whitman, though resigned, is not really pleased at the publication of a mere selection from his poems; while O'C[onnor] himself views it with great distaste, as practically a concession to the outcry against W[hitman]'s indecencies. O'C[onnor] has written another letter (not yet in Conway's hands) setting forth the points he would wish insisted on in any prefatory work of mine. I replied to him in cordial terms, but to the effect that the Preface and part of the Selection are now in print, and cannot well be remodelled.

(*e*) Extract from Diary entry, 16 December 1867 (p. 245): Received a most friendly and indeed affectionate letter from Whitman. Writing in reply to a (now superseded) suggestion that the London book should be made a slightly modified complete edition instead of a Selection without alterations or omissions, he expresses a strong objection to the plan; but readiness to put up with it rather than traverse any arrangements which may be actually in course of completion. I wrote back explaining that the plan of a Selection has been reverted to.

(*f*) Extract from a letter from John Burroughs to Moncure Conway, 10 August 1867 (p. 270): We were deeply impressed with Mr Rossetti's article in *The Chronicle*. It is a grand and lofty piece of criticism. It was not till the third reading that I saw the full scope and significance of it. I am sure Walt feels very grateful to him and to yourself. The article has had its effect here. *The Round Table* copied the conclusion of it, and completely reversed its verdict of a year ago. *The Nation*, *Times*, etc., copied also; and now *The Citizen* appears with the article entire. We shall circulate it well. Our cause gains fast. The leaven is working and no mistake. The Editor of *The Galaxy*, Mr Church, wrote O'Connor the other day saying he would like a poem from Walt for his Magazine, and suggested for theme the harvest which the returned soldiers have sown and gathered. The proposition was well received by Walt; and a few mornings afterward he fell to work, and in a couple of days had finished the piece. Church writes back that it is splendid, and will appear in the September number of his Magazine. It is called *A Carol of Harvest for 1867*. It is one of his grandest poems, and I think will take well.

(*g*) Letter from Whitman to Rossetti, 22 November 1867, with introductory bracketed note by Rossetti (pp. 283–4): [Mr Whitman was quite right in assuming that I had no idea of bringing out 'an expurgated edition' of his poems. I selected such poems only as could not, even in the opinion of the most punctilious persons, require any expurgation: from the prose preface alone I omitted two or three phrases. My volume did not correspond to his proposal in every minute detail: if I remember right, it was chiefly in print before I received the present letter.—'Mr Burroughs's Notes' are that able writer's *Notes on Walt Whitman as Poet and Person*.]

My dear Mr Rossetti,—I suppose Mr Conway has received, and you have read, the letter I sent over about three weeks since, assenting to the substitution of other words etc., as proposed by you, in your reprint of my book, or selections therefrom.

I suppose the reprint intends to avoid any expressed or implied character of being an expurgated edition. I hope it will simply assume the form and name of a selection from the various editions of my pieces printed here. I suggest, in the interest of that view, whether the adjoining might not be a good form of title-page:—

WALT WHITMAN'S POEMS

SELECTED FROM THE AMERICAN EDITIONS

BY

WM. M. ROSSETTI

I wish particularly not only that the little figures numbering the stanzas, but also that the larger figures dividing the pieces into separate passages or sections, be carefully followed and preserved, as in copy.

When I have my next edition brought out here, I shall change the title of the piece When lilacs last in the dooryard bloomed to *President Lincoln's Funeral-Hymn*. You are at liberty to take the latter name or the old one, at your option (that is, if you include the piece).

It is quite certain that I shall add to my next edition (carrying out my plan from the first) a brief cluster of pieces born of thoughts on the deep themes of Death and Immortality.

Allow me to send you an article I have written on *Democracy;* a hasty charcoal-sketch of a piece, but indicative, to any one interested in *Leaves of Grass*, as of the audience the book supposes, and in whose interest it is made. I shall probably send it next mail.

Allow me also to send you (as the ocean-postage law is now so easy) a copy of Mr Burroughs's *Notes*, and some papers. They go same mail with this.

And now, my dear Sir, you must just make what use (or no use at all) of anything I suggest or send as your occasions call for. Very likely some of my suggestions have been anticipated.

I remain, believe me, with friendliest feelings and wishes. . . .

(*h*) Extract from Diary entry, 29 July 1868 (p. 320): So strong is the prejudice against Whitman in America that H[otten] has not even yet succeeded in getting an American publisher for the Selection: he is expecting however to arrange soon with a Joint-stock Company.

(*i*) Extract from a letter from John Addington Symonds, Jn., to Rossetti, 15 August 1868, with introductory bracketed note by

Rossetti (pp. 363–4): [Mr Symonds (whom I had never the good fortune to know personally) was right in inferring that the two poems by Whitman first mentioned by him were omitted from my selection simply on the ground that they could not well go in without the cancelling of some phrases. As to the other poem from *Calamus*, I cannot now say anything distinct.]

May I be permitted, as a sincere admirer of Walt Whitman, to express to you my thanks for your edition of his select works—one of the most valuable of your many valuable contributions to our literature?

I should hardly have ventured thus to address you, had the readers and admirers of Whitman been a large body in England. But, as it is, there are so few who are able to understand his excellences, so many who are irritated into a kind of madness by his want of taste in details, that I feel justified in expressing to you my sympathy with all that you have said in your preface, and my admiration of the taste and judgment of your selection.

Might I ask you on what account you have omitted *Sleep-Chasings* and *A Leaf of Faces* from your volume? I have always regarded these as among Whitman's most characteristic pieces. Is it because you would not submit them to the necessary purgation for English readers? I remember that one passage in the latter poem moved Tennyson's wrath in particular when he first came across *Leaves of Grass*. I should also have liked to see the poem of *Calamus* (old edition), 'Long I thought that knowledge alone would suffice me,' in your collection —the more so perhaps because it has been omitted in the last edition by Mr Whitman himself. Do you happen to know what induced him to suppress it?

(*j*) Letter from Anne Gilchrist to Rossetti, 1 January 1870 (p. 497): (See No. 33 for Rossetti's explanation of the relationship and an article by Mrs Gilchrist.) Will you please tell Mr Whitman that he could not have devised for me a more welcome pleasure than this letter of his to you (now mine, thanks to you and him), and the picture; and that I feel grateful to you for having sent the extracts, since they have been a comfort to him.

I should like also to take this opportunity of saying (if you think I may) how much I wish, if Mr Whitman see no reason against it, that the new edition should be issued in two volumes; not lettered

Vols. I and II, but 1st Series and 2nd Series, so that they could be priced and sold separately when so desired. This simple expedient would, I think, overcome a serious difficulty. Those who are not able to receive aright all he has written might to their own infinite gain have what they *can* receive, and grow by means of that food to be capable of the whole perhaps: while Mr Whitman would stand as unflinchingly as hitherto by what he has written. I know I am glad that your Selections were put into my hands first, so that I was lifted up by them to stand firm on higher ground than I had ever stood on before, and furnished with a golden key before approaching the rest of the poems.

(*k*) Extract from a letter from Edward Dowden to Rossetti, 5 February 1870 (p. 519): I post to you to-day my article. . . . I ought to have made it clearer that I view Whitman's work by no means as supply to answer such demand as the American people makes, or is likely for some time to make; but as the utterances of a man of genius standing in the presence of a great democracy, and delivering himself with no concern for his hearers' tastes or wishes. Whitman's want of popularity therefore in his own country affords no argument against the statement that he is the poet of democracy. The Hebrew prophets, in the same way, were unpopular, yet were no less on that account the truest interpreters of the Hebrew spirit.

31. Review of the London edition

1868

Unsigned review of *Poems by Walt Whitman: Selected and Edited by William Michael Rossetti* (1868), *Saturday Review* (London, 2 May 1868), pp. 589–90.

Some years ago, when a few copies of a volume called *Leaves of Grass* found their way into this country from America, the general verdict of those who had an opportunity of examining the book was that much of it was indescribably filthy, most of it mere incoherent rhapsody, none of it what could be termed poetry in any sense of the word, and that, unless at the hands of some enterprising Holywell Street publisher, it had no chance of the honour of an English reprint. In part this opinion is already proved to have been a mistaken one, for a West-end publisher has taken compassion on the stranger, and now presents it to the British public in a comely form. It may be as well to state at the outset, that the volume published by Mr. Hotten is not precisely a reprint of the original *Leaves of Grass*. It contains much new matter written since the appearance of that work, and does *not* contain any of the pieces marked by that peculiar freedom of speech which is generally associated in men's minds with the name of Walt Whitman. For the sake of all parties, the prurient as well as the prudish, lest the one should be unnecessarily alarmed or the other led into an unremunerative venture, it is only fair to say that there is nothing in the present edition to disqualify it for decent society, not to say qualify it for a place in the *Bibliothèque bleue*. It has cost Mr. Rossetti severe pangs, so he informs us, to part with so much as, from considerations of prudence, he has been obliged to exclude. 'This peculiarly nervous age,' this 'mealy-mouthed British nineteenth century,' with its present absurd notions about decency, morality, and propriety, could not be expected to receive 'the indecencies scattered through Whitman's writings' in that aesthetic spirit in which they should be accepted; and, as he was unwilling to mutilate, 'the consequence is that the reader loses *in toto* several important poems, and some extremely fine ones—notably one of quite exceptional value and excellence, entitled *Walt Whitman*.' In one respect we are willing to admit the loss sustained in this last instance. The 'poem' here referred to is the one which contains the key to Walt Whitman's philosophy and poetic theory. It is in it that he describes himself and his qualifications for the office of poet of the future, grounding his claim upon the fact of his being 'hankering, gross, mystical, nude, one of the roughs, a kosmos, disorderly, fleshy, sensual, no more modest than immodest'; and proposing to produce poetry of corresponding qualities, a promise which we must say he most conscientiously fulfils. Its excellence may be open to question, but about its value to the reader who wishes to understand Walt Whitman there can be no doubt whatever.

The present edition is to be considered as an experiment. By excluding everything offensive, the editor hopes to induce people to reconsider the case of Walt Whitman, and reverse the verdict which has been already pronounced. This, we need scarcely observe, is rather more than they can be fairly asked to do, while the evidence which supports the gravest of the charges brought against him is suppressed. But this is not all that Mr. Rossetti expects. The present selection is so to brace and fortify the British mind that in a short time, he trusts, it will be able to relish what now in its weakness it rejects. A complete edition of Walt Whitman, with all the dirt left in, he looks forward to as 'the right and crowning result' of his labours. This is but the schoolboy's pudding, which, if we only finish it off, is to be succeeded by a full meal of the uncommonly strong meat he has in reserve for us. A fellow-countryman of the poet's, who had unsuccessfully besieged the virtue of a married lady, is said to have consoled himself with the reflection that, at any rate, he had 'lowered her moral tone some.' Though he himself had not gained his point, his labours, he thought, had diminished the difficulties in the way of the next comer. Something of this sort appears to be the modest mission of the present volume. We must confess we should very much prefer to see Mr. Rossetti employing himself on some task more worthy of his abilities. He has on many occasions done good service as a critic to literature and art, but we cannot look upon his present enterprise as one in any way beneficial to either. He desires to have Walt Whitman recognised, not merely as a great poet, but as the founder of a new school of poetic literature which is to be greater and more powerful than any the world has yet seen. He is not, it is true, entirely alone in this attempt. There have been already certain indications of a Walt Whitman movement in one or two other quarters. More than a year ago there was a paper in the *Fortnightly Review*, which, however, was not so much a criticism of his poetry as of his person, the writer having had, as well as we recollect, the privilege of reviewing him as he bathed—an important advantage, certainly, in the case of a poet whose principal theme is his own body. Then Mr. Robert Buchanan took him up in the *Broadway* magazine, and, saying nearly all that has ever been said against Walt Whitman—that he is no poet and no artist, that he is gross, monotonous, loud, obscure, prone to coarse animalism and to talking rank nonsense—nevertheless arrived at pretty much the same conclusion as Mr. Rossetti, at least as to the powerful influence he is to exercise over the literature of the future.

But of course the special charm of Walt Whitman is that he is so—what his admirers call—unconventional; that is, that he says things which other people do not say, and in language which other people do not generally use. His unconventionality, however, is of a very cheap sort. It is nothing more than the unconventionality of the man who considers clothes conventional, and goes about without them. It is true that for the present we are spared the bolder strokes of his genius in this respect, but, as has been already mentioned, it is only for the present; and besides, Walt Whitman's grossness is not accidental, but constitutional. It arises partly from an insensibility to the difference between that which is naturally offensive and that which is not, partly from his peculiar theory of poetry. As it is a fundamental principle of his to recognise no law of any kind, and to submit to no restrictions of artistic propriety, it follows that with him all subjects are equally fit for poetic treatment. As Mr. Rossetti puts it, 'he knows of no reason why what is universally seen and known, necessary and right, should not also be allowed and proclaimed in speech,' and it is just this ignorance of his which, independently of other reasons, makes any attempt to set him up as a poetic model mischievous to the interests of literary art. It is not a question of squeamishness or hyper-sensitiveness. There is no prudery in objecting to nastiness, nor is there any originality, honesty, manliness, or courage in obtruding what even instinct teaches us to avoid. We cannot say, however, that we anticipate any serious injury to English or American literature from the influence or popularity of Walt Whitman's poetry, so long at least as people are courageous enough to use their common sense, and do not allow themselves to be led away by transcendental 'high-falutin' into pretending an admiration which they do not feel.

32. Swinburne on Whitman

1868

Extract from Algernon Charles Swinburne, *William Blake* (1868). Reprinted in *The Complete Works of Swinburne* (1926), ed. Sir Edmund Gosse and Thomas James Wise, VI, pp. 342–6.

For a criticism of Swinburne's favourable comparison of Whitman with Blake, see the end of No. 43.

The points of contact and sides of likeness between William Blake and Walt Whitman are so many and so grave, as to afford some ground of reason to those who preach the transition of souls or transfusion of spirits. The great American is not a more passionate preacher of sexual or political freedom than the English artist. To each the imperishable form of a possible and universal Republic is equally requisite and adorable as the temporal and spiritual queen of ages as of men. To each all sides and shapes of life are alike acceptable or endurable. From the fresh free ground of either workman nothing is excluded that is not exclusive. The words of either strike deep and run wide and soar high. They are both full of faith and passion, competent to love and to loathe, capable of contempt and of worship. Both are spiritual, and both democratic; both by their works recall, even to so untaught and tentative a student as I am, the fragments vouchsafed to us of the Pantheistic poetry of the East. Their casual audacities of expression or speculation are in effect wellnigh identical. Their outlooks and theories are evidently the same on all points of intellectual and social life. The divine devotion and selfless love which make men martyrs and prophets are alike visible and palpable in each. It is no secret now, but a matter of public knowledge, that both these men, being poor in the sight and the sense of the world, have given what they had of time or of money, of labour or of love, to comfort and support all the suffering and sick, all the afflicted and misused, whom they had the chance or the right to succour and to serve. The noble and gentle labours of the one are known to those who live in his time; the similar deeds of the other deserve and demand a late recognition. No man so poor and so obscure as Blake appeared in the eyes of his generation ever did more good works in a more noble and simple spirit. It seems that in each of these men at their birth pity and passion, and relief and redress of wrong, became incarnate and innate. That may well be said of the one which was said of the other: that 'he looks like a man.' And in externals and details the work of these two constantly and inevitably coheres and coincides. A sound as of a sweeping wind; a prospect as over dawning continents at the fiery instant of a sudden sunrise; a splendour now of stars and now of storms; an expanse and exultation of wing across strange spaces of air and above shoreless stretches of sea: a resolute and reflective love of liberty in all times and in all things where it should be; a depth of sympathy and a height of scorn which complete and explain each other, as tender and as bitter as Dante's; a power, intense and infallible, of pictorial concentration and absorption, most rare when combined with the sense and the enjoyment of the widest and the highest things; an exquisite and lyrical excellence of form when the subject is well in keeping with the poet's tone of spirit; a strength and security of touch in small sweet sketches of colour and outline, which bring before the eyes of their student a clear glimpse of the thing designed—some little inlet of sky lighted by moon or star, some dim reach of windy water or gentle growth of meadow-land or wood; these are qualities common to the work of either. Had we place or time or wish to touch on their shortcomings and errors, it might be shown that these two are nearly akin; that their poetry has at once the melody and the laxity of a fitful storm wind; that, being oceanic, it is troubled with violent ground-swells and sudden perils of ebb and reflux, of shoal and reef, perplexing to the swimmer or the sailor; in a word, that it partakes the powers and the faults of elemental and eternal things; that it is at times noisy and barren and loose, rootless and fruitless and informal; and is in the main fruitful and delightful and noble, a necessary part of the divine mechanism of things. Any work of art of which this cannot be said is superfluous and perishable, whatever of grace or charm it may possess or assume. Whitman has seldom struck a note of thought and speech so just and so profound as Blake has now and then touched upon; but his work is generally more frank and fresh, smelling of sweeter air, and readier to expound or expose its message, than this of the 'Prophetic Books.' Nor is there among these any poem or passage of equal length so faultless and so noble as his *Voice out of the Sea*, or as his dirge over President Lincoln—the most sweet and sonorous nocturne ever chanted in the church of the world. But in breadth of outline and charm of colour, these poems recall the work of Blake; and to neither poet can a higher tribute of honest praise be paid than this.

33. Anne Gilchrist on Whitman

1870

Anne Gilchrist, 'A Woman's Estimate of Walt Whitman', the *Radical* (Boston, May 1870). Reprinted in *In Re*, pp. 41–55.

The article is accompanied by an introductory footnote by William Michael Rossetti, dated 20 November 1869;

The great satisfaction which I felt in arranging, about two years ago, the first edition (or rather selection) of Walt Whitman's poems published in England has been, in due course of time, followed by another satisfaction —and one which, rightly laid to heart, is both less mixed and more intense. A lady, whose friendship honors me, read the selection last summer, and immediately afterwards accepted from me the loan of the complete edition, and read that also. Both volumes raised in her a boundless and splendid enthusiasm, ennobling to witness. This found expression in some letters which she addressed to me at the time, and which contain (I affirm it without misgiving, and I hope not without some title to form an opinion) about the fullest, farthest-reaching and most eloquent appreciation of Whitman yet put into writing, and certainly the most valuable, whether or not I or other readers find cause for critical dissent at an item here and there. The most valuable, I say, because this is the expression of what *a woman* sees in Whitman's poems—a woman who has read and thought much, and whom to know is to respect and esteem in every relation, whether of character, intellect, or culture.

I longed that what this lady had written should be published for the benefit of English, and more especially of American readers. She has generously acceded to my request. The ensuing reflections upon Whitman's poems contain several passages reproduced verbatim from the letters in question, supplemented by others which the same lady has added so as more fully to define and convey the impression which those unparalleled and deathless writings have made upon her.

For another communication between Rossetti and Mrs Gilchrist, see No. 30(*j*).

This remarkable appreciation was written by the widow of Alexander Gilchrist, the biographer of William Blake. Anne Gilchrist brought her husband's unfinished biography of Blake to completion after his untimely death in 1860, and in doing so she made a reputation for herself which won for her the friendship of the Rossettis, Swinburne, Carlyle and Tennyson. Whitman's writings affected her so powerfully that she later quite plainly hinted her desire to marry him and came to settle with her family in Philadelphia. Whitman visited the Gilchrist home with some frequency in 1876 and the years following.

June 22, 1869.—I was calling on [Mr. Madox Brown] a fortnight ago, and he put into my hands your edition of Walt Whitman's poems. I shall not cease to thank him for that. Since I have had it, I can read no other book: it holds me entirely spell-bound, and I go through it again and again with deepening delight and wonder.

June 23.—I am very sure you are right in your estimate of Walt Whitman. There is nothing in him that I shall ever let go my hold of. For me the reading of his poems is truly a new birth of the soul.

I shall quite fearlessly accept your kind offer of the loan of a complete edition, certain that great and divinely beautiful nature has not, could not infuse any poison into the wine he has poured out for us. And as for what you specially allude to, who so well able to bear it—I will say, to judge wisely of it—as one who, having been a happy wife and mother, has learned to accept all things with tenderness, to feel a sacredness in all? Perhaps Walt Whitman has forgotten—or, through some theory in his head, has overridden—the truth that our instincts are beautiful facts of nature, as well as our bodies; and that we have a strong instinct of silence about some things.

July 11.—I think it was very manly and kind of you to put the whole of Walt Whitman's poems into my hands; and that I have no other friend who would have judged them and me so wisely and generously.

I had not dreamed that words could cease to be words, and become electric streams like these. I do assure you that, strong as I am, I feel sometimes as if I had not bodily strength to read many of these poems. In the series headed *Calamus*, for instance, in some of the 'Songs of Parting,' the 'Voice out of the Sea,' the poem beginning 'Tears, Tears,' etc., there is such a weight of emotion, such a tension of the heart, that mine refuses to beat under it—stands quite still—and I am obliged to lay the book down for a while. Or again, in the piece called 'Walt Whitman,' and one or two others of that type, I am as one hurried through stormy seas, over high mountains, dazed with sunlight, stunned with a crowd and tumult of faces and voices, till I am breathless, bewildered, half dead. Then come parts and whole poems in which there is such calm wisdom and strength of thought, such a cheerful breadth of sunshine, that the soul bathes in them renewed and strengthened. Living impulses flow out of these that make me exult in life, yet look longingly towards 'the superb vistas of Death.' Those who admire this poem, and don't care for that, and talk of formlessness, absence of meter, etc., are quite as far from any genuine recognition of Walt Whitman as his bitter detractors. Not, of course, that all the pieces are equal in power and beauty, but that all are vital; they grew—they were not made. We criticise a palace or a cathedral; but what is the good of criticising a forest? Are not the hitherto-accepted masterpieces of literature akin rather to noble architecture; built up of material rendered precious by elaboration; planned with subtle art that makes beauty go hand in hand with rule and measure, and knows where the last stone will come, before the first is laid; the result stately, fixed, yet such as might, in every particular, have been different from what it is (therefore inviting criticism), contrasting proudly with the careless freedom of nature, opposing its own rigid adherence to symmetry to her willful dallying with it? But not such is this book. Seeds brought by the winds from north, south, east and west, lying long in the earth, not resting on it like the stately building, but hid in and assimilating it, shooting upwards to be nourished by the air and the sunshine and the rain which beat idly against that,—each bough and twig and leaf growing in strength and beauty its own way, a law to itself, yet, with all this freedom of spontaneous growth, the result inevitable, unalterable (therefore setting criticism at naught), above all things vital,—that is, a source of ever-generating vitality: such are these poems.

Roots and leaves themselves alone are these,
Scents brought to men and women from the wild woods and from the pond-side,
Breast sorrel and pinks of love, fingers that wind around tighter than vines,
Gushes from the throats of birds hid in the foliage of trees as the sun is risen,
Breezes of land and love, breezes sent from living shores out to you on the living sea,—to you, O sailors!
Frost-mellowed berries and Third-month twigs, offered fresh to young persons wandering out in the fields when the winter breaks up,
Love-buds put before you and within you, whoever you are,
Buds to be unfolded on the old terms.
If you bring the warmth of the sun to them, they will open, and bring form, color, perfume, to you:

If you become the aliment and the wet, they will become flowers, fruits, tall branches and trees.

And the music takes good care of itself too. As if it *could* be otherwise! As if those 'large, melodious thoughts,' those emotions, now so stormy and wild, now of unfathomed tenderness and gentleness, could fail to vibrate through the words in strong, sweeping, long-sustained chords, with lovely melodies winding in and out fitfully amongst them! Listen, for instance, to the penetrating sweetness, set in the midst of rugged grandeur, of the passage beginning,—

I am he that walks with the tender and growing night;
I call to the earth and sea half held by the night.

I see that no counting of syllables will reveal the mechanism of the music; and that this rushing spontaneity could not stay to bind itself with the fetters of meter. But I know that the music is there, and that I would not for something change ears with those who cannot hear it. And I know that poetry must do one of two things,—either own this man as equal with her highest, completest manifestors, or stand aside, and admit that there is some thing come into the world nobler, diviner than herself, one that is free of the universe, and can tell its secrets as none before.

I do not think or believe this; but see it with the same unmistakable definiteness of perception and full consciousness that I see the sun at this moment in the noonday sky, and feel his rays glowing down upon me as I write in the open air. What more can you ask of the words of a man's mouth than that they should 'absorb into you as food and air, to appear again in your strength, gait, face,'—that they should be 'fibre and filter to your blood,' joy and gladness to your whole nature?

I am persuaded that one great source of this kindling, vitalizing power—I suppose *the* great source—is the grasp laid upon the present, the fearless and comprehensive dealing with reality. Hitherto the leaders of thought have (except in science) been men with their faces resolutely turned backwards; men who have made of the past a tyrant that beggars and scorns the present, hardly seeing any greatness but what is shrouded away in the twilight, underground past; naming the present only for disparaging comparisons, humiliating distrust that tends to create the very barrenness it complains of; bidding me warm myself at fires that went out to mortal eyes centuries ago; insisting, in religion above all, that I must either 'look through dead men's eyes,' or shut my own in helpless darkness. Poets fancying themselves so happy over the chill and faded beauty of the past, but not making me happy at all,—rebellious always at being dragged down of the free air and sunshine of to-day.

But this poet, this 'athlete, full of rich words, full of joy,' takes you by the hand, and turns you with your face straight forwards. The present is great enough for him, because he is great enough for it. It flows through him as a 'vast oceanic tide,' lifting up a mighty voice. Earth, 'the eloquent, dumb, great mother,' is not old, has lost none of her fresh charms, none of her divine meanings, still bears great sons and daughters, if only they would possess themselves and accept their birthright,—a richer, not a poorer, heritage than was ever provided before,—richer by all the toil and suffering of the generations that have preceded, and by the further unfolding of the eternal purposes. Here is one come at last who can show them how; whose songs are the breath of a glad, strong, beautiful life, nourished sufficingly, kindled to unsurpassed intensity and greatness by the gifts of the present.

Each moment and whatever happens thrills me with joy.

O the joy of my soul leaning poised on itself,—receiving identity through materials, and loving them,—observing characters, and absorbing them!
O my soul vibrated back to me from them!

O the gleesome saunter over fields and hillsides!
The leaves and flowers of the commonest weeds, the moist, fresh stillness of the woods,
The exquisite smell of the earth at daybreak, and all through the forenoon.

O to realize space!
The plenteousness of all—that there are no bounds;
To emerge, and be of the sky—of the sun and moon and the flying clouds, as one with them.

O the joy of suffering,—
To struggle against great odds, to meet enemies undaunted,
To be entirely alone with them—to find how much one can stand!

I used to think it was great to disregard happiness, to press on to a high goal, careless, disdainful of it. But now I see that there is nothing so great as to be capable of happiness; to pluck it out of 'each moment and whatever happens;' to find that one can ride as gay and buoyant on the angry, menacing, tumultuous waves of life as on those that glide and glitter under a clear sky; that it is not defeat and wretchedness which come out of the storm of adversity, but strength and calmness.

34. Edward Dowden on Whitman

1871

Extracts from 'The Poetry of Democracy: Walt Whitman', *Westminster Review* (July 1871). Reprinted, with some changes, in Dowden's *Studies in Literature* (1882). The following extracts are from the latter version, pp. 468–83, 519–23.

Concerning this article Professor Harold Blodgett has written:

Among early utterances on Whitman's claims it is conspicuous for its sobriety. . . . Although Dowden's article was by no means the first important European comment upon *Leaves of Grass*, it was signally effective in strengthening Whitman's position. . . . In Dublin Dowden played much the same role that William Michael Rossetti played in London [*American Literature*, May 1929].

Edward Dowden (1843–1913), Irish critic and poet, became professor of English literature at Trinity College in Dublin in 1867. His first book, *Shakespeare, his Mind and Art* (1875) was translated into German and Russian. His own volume of *Poems* (1876) went into a second edition. He wrote extensively on Shakespeare and is the author of the introductory studies to each of Shakespeare's plays in the Oxford University Press edition. He was best known to the public at large for his *Life of Shelley* (1886). He became the first Taylorian lecturer at Oxford in 1889 and served from 1892 to 1896 as Clark lecturer at Trinity College, Cambridge.

That school of criticism which has attempted in recent years to connect the history of literature and art with the larger history of society and the general movement of civilizations, creeds, forms of national life and feeling, and which may be called emphatically the critical school of the present century, or the naturalist as contradistinguished from the dogmatic school, has not yet essayed the application of its method and principles to the literature and art of America. For a moment one wonderingly inquires after the cause of this seeming neglect. The New

World, with its new presentations to the senses, its new ideas and passions, its new social tendencies and habits, must surely, one thinks, have given birth to literary and artistic forms corresponding to itself in strange novelty, unlike in a remarkable degree those sprung from our old-world, and old-world hearts. A moral soil and a moral climate so different from those of Europe must surely have produced a fauna and flora other than the European, a fauna and flora which the writers of literary natural history cannot but be curious to classify, and the peculiarities of which they must endeavour to account for by the special conditions of existence and of the development of species in the new country. It is as much to be expected that poems and pictures requiring new names should be found there as that new living things of any other kind, the hickory and the hemlock, the mocking-bird and the katydid, should be found. So one reasons for a moment, and wonders. The fact is, that while the physical conditions, fostering certain forms of life, and repressing others, operated without let or hindrance, and disclosed themselves in their proper results with the simplicity and sureness of nature, the permanent moral powers were met by others of transitory or local, but for the time, superior authority, which put a hedge around the literature and art of America, enclosing a little paradise of European culture, refinement, and aristocratic delicatesse from the howling wilderness of Yankee democracy, and insulating it from the vital touch and breath of the land, the winds of free, untrodden places, the splendour and vastness of rivers and seas, the strength and tumult of the people.

Until of late indigenous growths of the New World showed in American literature like exotics, shy or insolent. We were aware of this, and expected in an American poet some one to sing for us gently, in a minor key, the pleasant airs we know. Longfellow's was a sweet and characteristic note, but, except in a heightened enjoyment of the antique—a ruined Rhine castle, a goblet from which dead knights had drunk, a suit of armour, or anything frankly mediaeval—except in this, Longfellow is one of ourselves—an European. 'Evangeline' is an European idyl of American life, Hermann and Dorothea having emigrated to Acadie. 'Hiawatha' might have been dreamed in Kensington by a London man of letters who possessed a graceful idealizing turn of imagination, and who had studied with clear-minded and gracious sympathy the better side of Indian character and manners. Longfellow could amiably quiz, from a point of view of superior and contented refinement, his countrymen who went about blatant and blustering for a national art and literature which should correspond with the large proportions and freedom of the Republic.

> We want [cries Mr Hathaway in 'Kavanagh'] a national drama, in which scope enough shall be given to our gigantic ideas, and to the unparalleled activity and progress of our people. . . . We want a national literature, altogether shaggy and unshorn, that shall shake the earth, like a herd of buffaloes, thundering over the prairies!

And Mr Churchill explains that what is best in literature is not national but universal, and is the fruit of refinement and culture. Longfellow's fellow-countryman, Irving, might have walked arm-in-arm with Addison, and Addison would have run no risk of being discomposed by a trans-Atlantic twang in his companion's accent. Irving, if he betrays his origin at all, betrays it somewhat in the same way as Longfellow by his tender, satisfied repose in the venerable, chiefly the venerable in English society and manners, by his quiet delight in the implicit tradition of English civility, the scarcely-felt yet everywhere influential presence of a beautiful and grave Past, and the company of unseen beneficent associations. In Bryant, Europe is more in the background; prairie and immemorial forest occupy the broad spaces of his canvas, but he feels pleasure in these mainly because he is not native to their influences. The mountains are not his sponsors; there are not the unconscious ties between him and them which indicate kinship, nor the silences which prove entire communion. Moreover, the life of American men and women is almost unrepresented in the poetry of Bryant. The idealized Red man is made use of as picturesque, an interesting and romantic person; but the Yankee is prosaic as his ledger. The American people had evidently not become an object of imaginative interest to itself in the mind of Bryant.

That the historical school of criticism should not have occupied itself with American literature is then hardly to be wondered at. A chapter upon that literature until recently must have been not a criticism but a prophecy. It was this very fact, the absence of a national literature, which the historical school was called on to explain. And to explain it evident and sufficient causes were producible, and were produced. The strictly Puritan origin of the Americans, the effort imposed upon them of subduing the physical forces of the country, and of yoking them to the service of man, the occupation of the entire community with an absorbing industry, the proximity of Europe, which made it possible for America to neglect the pursuit of the sciences, literature, and the fine arts without relapsing into barbarism—these causes were enumerated by De Tocqueville as having concurred to fix the minds of the Americans upon purely practical objects.

I consider the people of the United States as that portion of the English people which is commissioned to explore the wilds of the New World; whilst the rest of the nation, enjoying more leisure, and less harassed by the drudgery of life, may devote its energies to thought, and enlarge in all directions the empire of the mind.

Beside which, before a nation can become poetical to itself, consciously or unconsciously, it must possess a distinctive character, and the growth of national as of individual character is a process of long duration in every case, of longer duration than ordinary when a larger than ordinary variety of the elements of character wait to be assimilated and brought into harmony.

In Emerson a genuine product of the soil was perhaps for the first time apparent to us. We tasted in him the flavour of strange sap, and knew the ripening of another sun and other winds. He spoke of what is old and universal, but he spoke in the fashion of a modern man, and of his own nation. His Greek head pivoted restlessly on true Yankee shoulders, and when he talked Plato he did so in a dialectical variety of Attic peculiar to Boston.* Lowell, at times altogether feudal and European, has also at times a trans-Atlantic air, in the earnest but somewhat vague spiritualism of his earlier poems, his enthusiasm about certain dear and dim general ideas, and more happily in a conception of the democratic type of manhood which appears in some of the poems of later years, especially in that very noble 'Ode recited at the Harvard Commemoration, July 21, 1865.' But taken as a whole, the works of Lowell do not mirror the life, the thoughts, and passions of the nation. They are works, as it were, of an English poet who has become a naturalized citizen of the United States, who admires the institutions, and has faith in the ideas of America, but who cannot throw off his allegiance to the old country, and its authorities.

At last steps forward a man unlike any of his predecessors, and announces himself, and is announced with a flourish of critical trumpets, as Bard of America, and Bard of democracy. What cannot be questioned after an hour's acquaintance with Walt Whitman and his *Leaves of Grass* is that in him we meet a man not shaped out of old-world clay, not cast in any old-world mould, and hard to name by any

* 'A Greek head on right Yankee shoulders.'—LOWELL.

old-world name. *In his self-assertion there is a manner of powerful nonchalantness which is not assumed;* he does not peep timidly from behind his works to glean our suffrages, but seems to say, 'Take me or leave me, here I am, a solid and not an inconsiderable fact of the universe.' He disturbs our classifications. He attracts us; he repels us; he excites our curiosity, wonder, admiration, love; or, our extreme repugnance. He does anything except leave us indifferent. However we feel towards him we cannot despise him. He is 'a summons and a challenge.' He must be understood and so accepted, or must be got rid of. Passed by he cannot be. His critics have, for the most part, confined their attention to the personality of the man; they have studied him, for the most part, as a phenomenon isolated from the surrounding society, the environment, the *milieu*, which has made such a phenomenon possible. In a general way it has been said that Whitman is the representative in art of American democracy, but the meaning of this has not been investigated in detail. It is purposed here to consider some of the characteristics of democratic art, and to inquire in what manner they manifest themselves in Whitman's work.

A word of explanation is necessary. The representative man of a nation is not always the nation's favourite. Hebrew spiritualism, the deepest instincts, the highest reaches of the moral attainment of the Jewish race, appear in the cryings and communings of its prophets; yet the prophets sometimes cried in the wilderness, and the people went after strange gods. *American democracy is as yet but half-formed. The framework of its institutions exists, but the will, the conscience, the mature desires of the democratic society are still in process of formation. If Whitman's writings are spoken of as the poetry of American democracy, it is not implied that his are the volumes most inquired after in the libraries of New York or Boston. What we mean is that these are the poems which naturally arise when a man of imaginative genius stands face to face with a great democratic world, as yet but half-fashioned, such as society is in the United States of the present day.* Successive editions of his works prove that Whitman has many readers. But whether he had them now, or waited for them in years to come, it would remain true that *he is the first representative democrat in art of the American continent.* Not that he is to be regarded as a model or a guide; great principles and great passions which must play their part in the future, are to be found in his writings; but these have not yet cleared themselves from their amorphous surroundings. At the same time he is before all else a living man, and must not be compelled to appear as mere official representative of anything. He will not be comprehended in a formula. No *view* of him can image the substance, the life and movement of his manhood, which contracts and dilates, and is all over sensitive and vital. Such views are, however, valuable in the study of literature, as hypotheses are in the natural sciences, at least for the colligation of facts. They have a tendency to render criticism rigid and doctrinaire; the critic must therefore ever be ready to escape from his own theory of a man, and come in contact with the man himself. Every one doubtless moves in some regular orbit, and all aberrations are only apparent, but what the precise orbit is we must be slow to pronounce. Meanwhile we may legitimately conjecture, as Kepler conjectured, if only we remain ready, as Kepler was, to vary our conjectures as the exigencies of the observed phenomena require.

The art of a democratic age exhibits characteristics precisely opposite to those of the art of an aristocracy. *Form and style modelled on traditional examples are little valued.* No canons of composition are agreed upon or observed without formal agreement. No critical dictator enacts laws which are accepted without dispute, and acquire additional authority during many years. Each new generation, with its new heave of life, its multitudinous energies, ideas, passions, is a law to itself. Except public opinion, there is no authority on earth above the authority of a man's own soul, and public opinion being strongly in favour of individualism, a writer is tempted to depreciate unduly the worth of order, propriety, regularity of the academic kind; he is encouraged to make new literary experiments as others make new experiments in religion; he is permitted to be true to his own instincts, whether they are beautiful instincts or the reverse. The appeal which a work of art makes is to the nation, not to a class and diversities of style are consequently admissible. Every style can be tolerated except the vapid, everything can be accepted but that which fails to stimulate the intellect or the passions.

Turning to Whitman, we perceive at once that his work corresponds with this state of things. If he had written in England in the period of Queen Anne, if he had written in France in the period of the *grand monarque*, he must have either acknowledged the supremacy of authority in literature and submitted to it, or on the other hand revolted against it. *As it is, he is remote from authority, and neither submits nor revolts.* Whether we call what he has written verse or prose, we have no hesitation in saying that it is no copy, that it is something uncontrolled by any model or canon, something which takes whatever shape it possesses directly from the soul of its maker. With the Bible, Homer, and Shakespeare familiar to him, Whitman writes in the presence of great models, and some influences from each have doubtless entered into his nature; but that they should possess authority over him any more than that he should possess authority over them, does not occur to him as possible. The relation of democracy to the Past comes out very notably here. Entirely assured of its own right to the Present, it is prepared to acknowledge fully the right of past generations to the Past. It is not hostile to that Past, rather claims kinship with it, but also claims equality, as a full-grown son with a father:—

I conn'd old times;
I sat studying at the feet of the great masters:
Now, if eligible, O that the great masters might return and study me!
In the name of These States, shall I scorn the antique?
Why These are the children of the antique, to justify it.

Dead poets, philosophs, priests,
Martyrs, artists, inventors, governments long since,
Language-shapers on other shores,
Nations once powerful, now reduced, withdrawn or desolate,
I dare not proceed till I respectfully credit what you have left, wafted hither:
I have perused it, own it is admirable (moving awhile among it);
Think nothing can ever be greater,—nothing can ever deserve more than it deserves;
Regarding it all intently a long while,—then dismissing it,
I stand in my place, with my own day, here.

35. 'Whitman's style . . . is his greatest contribution'

1872

Robert Buchanan, 'Walt Whitman', an appendix to *The Fleshly School of Poetry* (1872).

Robert Williams Buchanan (1841–1901), British poet, novelist, dramatist and critic, was the son of Robert Buchanan (1813–66), an Owenite lecturer and journalist. He wrote many successful plays and is the author of a long series of novels. The article on 'The Fleshly School of Poetry' was contributed under the pseudonym of Thomas Maitland to the *Contemporary Review* of October 1871. It evoked replies from Dante Gabriel Rossetti and from Swinburne (in *Under The Microscope*) to whom the Appendix reprinted here is, in its turn, an answer. Swinburne had objected that it was inconsistent for Buchanan to object to the sensuality of English poets like himself while accepting the same quality in Whitman.

There is at the present moment living in America a great ideal prophet, who is imagined by many men on both sides of the Atlantic to be one of the sanest and grandest figures to be found in literature, and whose books, it is believed, though now despised, may one day be esteemed as an especial glory of this generation. It is no part of my present business to eulogize Walt Whitman, or to protest against the popular misconceptions concerning him; but it just happens that I have been asked, honestly enough, how it is that I despise so much the Fleshly School of Poetry in England and admire so much the poetry which is widely considered unclean and animal in America? It is urged, moreover, that Mr. Rossetti and Mr. Swinburne merely repeat the immodesties of the author of *Leaves of Grass*, and that to be quite consistent I must condemn all alike. Very true, if Whitman be a poet of *this* complexion, if his poetry be shot through and through with animalism as certain stuffs are shot through and through with silk. But it requires no great subtlety of sight to perceive the difference between these men. To begin with, there are Singers, imitative and shallow; while that other is a Bard, outrageously original and creative in the form and substance of his so-called verse. In the next place, Whitman is in the highest sense a spiritual person; every word he utters is symbolic: he is a colossal mystic; but in all his great work, the theme of which is spiritual purity and health, there are not more than fifty lines of a thoroughly indecent kind, and these fifty lines are embedded in passages in the noblest sense antagonistic to mere lust and indulgence. No one regrets the writing and printing of these fifty lines more than I do. They are totally unnecessary, and silly in the highest degree—silly as some of Shakspere's dirt is silly—silly in the way of Aristophanes, Rabelais, Victor Hugo—from sheer excess of aggressive life. Fifty lines, observe, out of a book nearly as big as the Bible; lines utterly stupid, and unpardonable in themselves; but to be forgiven, doubtless, for the sake of the spotless love and chastity surrounding them. It is Whitman's business to chronicle *all* human sensations in the person of the 'Cosmical Man,' or typical Ego; and when he comes to the sexual instincts, he tries to blend emotion and physiology together, to the utter destruction of all natural effect. Judging from the internal evidence of these passages, I should say that Whitman was by no means a man of strong animal passions. There is a frightful violence in his expressions, which an epicure in lust would have avoided. This part of his book, I guess, cost him a good deal of trouble; it is not written *con amore;* and, apart from its double or mystic meaning, is just what an old philosopher might write if he were trying to represent passion by the dim light of memory. At all events, here Whitman is talking nonsense, as is the way of all wise men at some unfortunate moment or other. Elsewhere, he is perhaps the most mystic and least fleshly person that ever wrote.

It is in a thousand ways unfortunate for Walt Whitman that he has been introduced to the English public by Mr. William Rossetti, and been loudly praised by Mr. Swinburne. Doubtless these gentlemen admire the American poet for all that is best in him; but the British public, having heard that Whitman is immoral, and having already a dim guess that Messrs. Swinburne and Rossetti are not over-refined, has come to the conclusion that his nastiness alone has been his recommendation. All this despite the fact that Mr. William Rossetti has expurgated the fifty lines or so in his edition.

I should like to disclaim, in this place, all sympathy with Whitman's pantheistic ideas. My admiration for this writer is based on the wealth of his knowledge, the vast roll of his conceptions (however monstrous), the nobility of his *practical* teaching, and (most of all perhaps) on his close approach to a solution of the true relationship between prose cadence and metrical verse.[1] Whitman's style, extraordinary as it is, is his greatest contribution to knowledge. It is not impossible to forsee a day when Coleridge's feeling of the 'wonderfulness of prose' may become universal, and our poetry (still swathe-bound in the form of early infant speech, or rhyme) may expand into a literature blending together all that is musical in verse, and all that is facile and powerful in ordinary language. I do not think Whitman has *solved* the difficulty, but he sometimes comes tremendously close upon the arcana of perfect speech.

36. A belated appreciation

1873

Extracts from pseudonymous ('Matador') review, *New York Graphic* (25 November 1873). Reprinted in Bucke, pp. 209–10.

The interest of this brief essay lies in the candour with which it speaks of the author's change of heart about Whitman. Taste, unlike the love described by Marlowe in *Hero and Leander*, is not created by overpowering first impressions necessarily. It may develop rather slowly. This reader's avowal seems to be a perfect illustration of the truth of William Blake's Proverb:

> We are led to believe a lie
> When we see *with* not *through* the eye.

The progress of his experience is from seeing Whitman's work *with* his eye merely (at which time it appeared completely ridiculous) to seeing it *through* his eye with entire identification and sympathy. It then became something sublime. The lines that he chooses to illustrate Whitman's genius to those who are still sceptical (from the middle of section 21 of 'Song of Myself': 'I am he that walks with the tender and growing night') have been appreciated even by those critics and scholars, like Esther Shephard, who have been least charitable in their assessments of Whitman's character and poetic originality.

It takes seven years to learn to appreciate Walt Whitman's poetry. At least it took me precisely that time, and I divided it as follows: For four years I ridiculed *Leaves of Grass* as the most intricate idiocy that a preposterous pen had ever written. During the next two years I found myself occasionally wondering if, after all, there might not be some glimmer of poetic beauty in Whitman's ragged lines. And then during the last year of my Walt Whitman novitiate the grandeur and beauty and melody of his verse, its vast and measureless expression of all human thoughts and emotions, were suddenly revealed to me. I understand it now, I have learned its purpose and caught the subtle melody of its lines.

Carelessly looked at, *Leaves of Grass* is a formless aggregation of lines without definite purpose and without the slightest pretence of prosody. Closer search shows the thread that guides one through the maze, and demonstrates its artistic plan. Whitman professes to express all the thoughts and feelings common to humanity,—whatever you or I may have felt, whether in moments of joy or sorrow; whatever you or I may have thought, whether it was true or false, honorable or shameful, our feelings and thoughts are expressed in this cosmical poem. It is this vastness of design that forbids the easy comprehension of the poem; that, permitting to the careless observer only a view of a rough stone here or a misshapen gargoyle there, reveals its true proportions only to the slow and careful survey that sees it from all sides, and, passing over details, grasps the final meaning of the whole.

There is much that seems trivial and ugly and meaningless and repulsive in *Leaves of Grass* when viewed only in detail. These things, however, have their place. Without them the poem would not be complete. Without them it would lack the universality hinted at in the name, *Leaves of Grass*. . . .

There is another sort of descriptive poetry in which the poet, instead of setting definite objects before your sight, works by creating in you the feelings that naturally accompany certain situations. It is a method that is nowhere mentioned in books of rhetoric, but it is precisely analogous to the method of Beethoven and the grand masters of symphonic music. Their music is not descriptive in the sense of cataloguing scenes and events, but produces upon the mind of the listener directly the impression which such scenes and events would necessarily produce.

Of this sort of subjective and descriptive poetry *Leaves of Grass* contains frequent examples. Here is one:

Of the turbid pool that lies in the autumn forest,
Of the moon that descends the steeps of the soughing twilight,
Toss, sparkles of day and dusk—toss on the black stems that decay in the muck,
Toss to the moaning gibberish of the dry limbs.

There are few definite points given in these lines which attract the eye. There is really no feature given us, but only a vague mystery of hinted color, and yet you at once recognize the feeling it calls into being as that which belongs to a moonlight night spent in the depth of a lonely forest.

And again, take these lines that hint of a midsummer's night. They describe nothing, but they perfectly express the physical pleasure that we feel when kissed by the warm and wandering night winds:

I am he that walks with the tender and growing night,
I call to the earth and sea half-held by the night.

Press close bare-bosomed night—press close magnetic nourishing night!
Night of south winds—night of the large few stars!
Still nodding night—mad naked summer night.

Smile O voluptuous cool-breath'd earth!
Earth of the slumbering and liquid trees!
Earth of departed sunset—earth of the mountains misty topt!
Earth of the vitreous pour of the full moon just tinged with blue!

Do you say that this is meaningless when each phrase is taken as a distinct statement? So is the Seventh Symphony meaningless if you try to translate it bar by bar. I claim, however, that in these verses Walt Whitman follows the method of the tone poets, and that what you call vagueness and obscurity is simply the art of the musician, the only art that transcends the art of the poet.

37. Saintsbury on Whitman

1874

Extracts from review, *The Academy* (10 October 1874). Quoted in Dowden, pp. 248–9.

George Edward Bateman Saintsbury (1845–1933), English man of letters, was educated at Merton College, Oxford, from which he took his B.A. in 1868. He began his journalistic career as a critic for the *Academy* and later became an important member of the staff of the *Saturday Review*. From 1895 to 1915 he was professor of rhetoric and English literature at Edinburgh University. His work gives the impression of an immense range of reading. Among his many works are *A History of Criticism* (1900–4) in three volumes, *A History of English Prosody* (1906–21) in three volumes, *The History of English Criticism* (1911) and *A History of the French Novel* (1917–19).

There are few poets who require to be studied as a whole so much as Walt Whitman . . . It is impossible not to notice his exquisite descriptive faculty, and his singular felicity in its use. Forced as he is, both by natural inclination, and in the carrying out of his main idea, to take note of 'the actual earth's equalities,' he has literally filled his pages with the songs of birds, the hushed murmur of waves, the quiet and multiform life of the forest and the meadow. And in these descriptions he succeeds in doing what is most difficult, in giving us the actual scene or circumstance as it impressed him, and not merely the impression itself. This is what none but the greatest poets have ever, save by accident done, and what Whitman does constantly, and with a sure hand . . . No Englishman, no one indeed, whether American or Englishman, need be deterred from reading this book, a book the most unquestionable in originality, if not the most unquestioned in excellence, that the United States have yet sent us.

38. Peter Bayne on Whitman

1875

'Walt Whitman's Poems', *Contemporary Review*, XXVII (1875), 49–69.

The author of this very vigorous assault upon the claims made for Whitman as a poet, Peter Bayne (1830–96), was a Scottish journalist and author who was educated at Edinburgh University. His works include *The Christian Life, Social and Individual* (1855); *Essays, Bibliographical and Critical* (1859); *Martin Luther, His Life and Work* (1887); and *The Free Church oj Scotland.* Bayne notes affinities between Whitman and Rousseau and regards him as an evil portent for the future of the United States and perhaps of the democratic experiment in general. He notes that Whitman's advice: 'Resist much; obey little!' is an invitation to anarchy and licence rather than to a stable and ordered form of liberty, but he failed to notice (as an American perhaps should) the significance of the fact that this bit of advice is proffered by the poet not to the random individual but to *the states* in their relation presumably to the federal union which they compose. It is ironic, then, but hardly anarchic that Whitman, who was as strong a Unionist as Lincoln during the Civil War, should thus have indicated his sympathetic attitude towards states-rights (when not pushed to an extreme by 'a conspiracy of slaveholders') against a national bureaucracy whose increasing weight threatened to crush them.

Concerning this essay, Professor Harold Blodgett (*Walt Whitman In England*) makes the following interesting observation (p. 199): 'Edward Dowden, greatly dismayed at this article, called it "very vicious", but it should not be allowed to die. A very plausible Tory attack, it states with adequacy and vigor the formidable case that all respectable persons have against *Leaves of Grass.*'

The critic who calls our attention to true poetry does us one of the best possible services; for no imagery derived from the beauty or the bounteousness of nature—from golden islands of the sunset or pearly dews of dawn, from corn, or wine, or glowing fruit—can express too strongly the goodliness of poetry that is really such; but in proportion to the gracious beneficence of this service is the maleficence of critics who, by their wit or their authority, beguile us into reading atrociously bad verse. If I ever saw anything in print that deserved to be characterized as atrociously bad, it is the poetry of Walt Whitman; and the three critics of repute, Dr. Dowden, Mr. W. Rossetti, and Mr. Buchanan, who have praised his performances, appear to me to be playing off on the public a well-intentioned, probably good-humoured, but really cruel hoax. I shall state briefly what I found the so-called poetry to be, presenting a few examples of Whitman's work: if these are such as the English public will regard with any other feelings but scorn and disgust, I for one have mistaken the character of my countrymen.

The *Leaves of Grass*, under which designation Whitman includes all his poems, are unlike anything else that has passed among men as poetry. They are neither in rhyme not in any measure known as blank verse; and they are emitted in spurts or gushes of unequal length, which can only by courtesy be called lines. Neither in form nor in substance are they poetry; they are inflated, wordy, foolish prose; and it is only because he and his eulogists call them poems, and because I do not care to dispute about words, that I give them the name. Whitman's admirers maintain that their originality is their superlative merit. I undertake to show that it is a mere knack, a 'trick of singularity,' which sound critics ought to expose and denounce, not to commend.

The secret of Whitman's surprising newness—the principle of his conjuring trick—is on the surface. It can be indicated by the single word, extravagance. In all cases he virtually, or consciously, puts the question, What is the most extravagant thing which it is here in my power to say? What is there so paradoxical, so hyperbolical, so nonsensical, so indecent, so insane, that no man ever said it before, that no other man would say it now, and that therefore it may be reckoned on to create a sensation? He announced himself as poet with a contemptuous allusion—we shall see its terms farther on—to those poets whose fame has shed lustre on America, and he expressly declares war against all regulated and reasonable things.

I confront peace, security, and all the settled laws, to unsettle them,
I am more resolute because all have denied me than I could ever have been had all accepted me;
I heed not, and have never heeded, either experience, cautions, majorities, nor ridicule.
And the threat of what is called hell is little or nothing to me;
And the lure of what is called heaven is little or nothing to me.

Goethe said that the assent of even one man confirmed him infinitely in his opinion; Whitman is only the more peremptory in his egotism when he finds that people of sense disagree with him. In spite, however, of his Fakir-like gesticulations, his extravagance generally continues dull.

Divine am I inside and out, and I make holy whatever I touch or am touch'd from;
The scent of these armpits, aroma finer than prayer;
This head more than churches, Bibles, and all the creeds.
If I worship one thing more than another it shall be the spread of my own body or any part of it.

Mr. Ruskin insists that there are errors and blemishes of such exceeding and immedicable vileness that, if you find a single instance of their occurrence in the work of an artist, you may, with assured heart, turn once and for ever from his pictures, confident that, since the tree is corrupt, its fruit will always be noxious. Whether Mr. Ruskin is absolutely right as to the fact I shall not undertake to decide; but I challenge Professor Dowden, Mr. W. Rossetti, and Mr. Buchanan, to produce, from any poet of acknowledged excellence, a single passage so offensively silly as the preceding. I beg readers to force themselves to look well at the lines. It is a man who talks of himself as divine inside and out, and drivels nauseously about the scent of his armpits, whom we are called to welcome as a great poet. Whitman, as Professor Dowden will by-and-by attest for us, prints incomparably more indecent things than this, but the words are thoroughly characteristic. They have exactly the originality of Whitman, and we cannot refuse to admit that they are unique.

One of the most favourite extravagances of Whitman is extravagant conceit, and he occasionally indulges it in forms which in England would simply be regarded as evidence of idiocy.

> I conned old times;
> I sat studying at the feet of the great masters:
> Now, if eligible, O that the great masters might return and study me!

Much good would it do them. Equally silly, but more pompous in its silliness, is what follows:—

> The moth and the fish-eggs are in their place;
> The suns I see, and the suns I cannot see, are in their place;
> The palpable is in its place, and the impalpable is in its place.

Do men of talent mumble truisms like this? And is there any excuse for such pretentious twaddle after the doctrine that everything is right in its own time and place had been stated, with a pith and quaint humour not likely to be surpassed, by the author of the Proverbs of Solomon?

Whitman's writings abound with reproductions of the thoughts of other men, spoiled by obtuseness or exaggeration. He can in no case give the finely correct application of a principle, or indicate the reserves and expectations whose appreciation distinguishes the thinker from the dogmatist: intense black and glaring are his only colours. The mysterious shadings of good into evil and evil into good, the strange minglings of pain with pleasure and of pleasure with pain, in the web of human affairs, have furnished a theme for musing to the deepest minds of our species. But problems that were felt to be insoluble by Shakespeare and Goethe have no difficulty for this bard of the West. Extravagant optimism and extravagant pessimism, both wrong and shallow, conduct him to 'the entire denial of evil' (the words are Professor Dowden's), to the assertion that 'there is no imperfection in the present and can be none in the future,' and to the vociferous announcement that success and failure are pretty much the same.

> Have you heard that it was good to gain the day?
> I say also it is good to fall—battles are lost in the same spirit in which they are won.
> I beat and pound for the dead;
> I blow through my embouchures my loudest and gayest for them.
> Vivas to those who have fail'd!
> And to those whose war-vessels sank in the sea!
> And to those themselves who sank in the sea!
> And to all generals that lost engagements! and all overcome heroes!
> And the numberless unknown heroes, equal to the greatest heroes known.

Mr. Carlyle's lifelong effort to show that the success of the hero is, on the whole, a proof that he deserved to succeed, has, it seems, been a waste of power. 'Vivas to those who have failed!' 'Hurrah for the gallows!' I do not know that a better illustration could be found of the evil effect of Whitman's obliterating extravagance than these lines. They contain the blurred and distorted lineaments of a mysterious and melancholy truth. Noble innocence and courage have been indeed laid low; beauty and virtue have in every age been seen 'walking hand in hand the downward slope to death;' and all hearts thrill at the thought of murdered Naboth and his sons, and of Lear hanging over the white lips of Cordelia. But the soul of the pathos in all these instances lies in their exceptional nature. It is because we feel that they violate the law of justice, the fundamental ordinances of human society, that they move us. It is because whether from a veracious instinct, or from a blissful illusion, we believe success to be the natural reward of merit, and happiness the natural guerdon of virtue, that we are agonized by the death-shrieks of Desdemona or the slow torture of Joan of Arc. If human affairs were a mad welter of causeless failure and unmerited success, as they are represented in this passage of Whitman's, there could be no such thing as pathos either in life or in art.

Whitman is never more audaciously extravagant than when he takes some well-known poetical idea, and inflates it into bombast.

> Dazzling and tremendous, how quick the sunrise would kill me,
> If I could not now and always send sunrise out of me.

It is a beautiful and touching thought that our joy brightens the summer flowers, and that our sorrow lends mournfulness to winter's snow; but it is mere extravagant nonsense to say that sunrise would kill a man unless he sent sunrise out of him. The sun has been the prey of poetical charlatans time out of mind and Whitman cruelly bedrivels the long-suffering luminary:—

> I depart in air—I shake my white locks at the runaway sun;
> I effuse my flesh in eddies, and drift it in lacy jags.

It would be interesting to know what meaning Whitman's admirers attach to the second of these lines: to my thinking it is not one whit more rational, and infinitely less amusing, than the talk of the walrus and the carpenter in *Alice through the Looking-Glass*.

> Oxen that rattle the yoke and chain, or halt in the leafy shade! What is that you express in your eyes?
> It seems to me more than all the print I have read in my life.

Whitman's eulogists tell us that he reads Shakespeare, Homer, and the Bible. Can they pretend to believe it to be anything but fantastic affectation to say that there is more in the eyes of oxen than in these? Whitman must have been consciously affected when he wrote the words: they are stupid as affectation, incredible as anything else. But the brutes are rather a favourite theme with our poet.

I think I could turn and live with animals, they are so placid and self-contained;
I stand and look at them long and long.
They do not sweat and whine about their condition;
They do not lie awake in the dark and weep for their sins;
They do not make me sick discussing their duty to God;
Not one is dissatisfied—not one is demented with the mania of owning things;
Not one kneels to another, nor to his kind that lived thousands of years ago;
Not one is respectable or industrious over the whole earth.

Wise men have long been, and are likely to be, content to learn from the bee and the ant; but neither the sage of the past not the scientific man of the present can have anything to say for such teaching as this of Whitman's. His statements are neither accurate nor sagacious; they are a confused echo, extravagantly absurd, of teachings which he has not understood. Patiently and closely observant of the animals, Mr. Darwin and his followers have shown that they are much more like men than used to be thought; that they have, in germ, almost all human passions, as well as the institutions of marriage and property; that they exhibit in a pronounced form the human failings of jealousy, hatred, revenge, and cunning, and some faint adumbration of the human virtues of tenderness, faithfulness, and self-sacrifice. But it is a wild caricature of Darwin's teaching to panegyrize the animals for those qualities in which they are markedly below humanity; and there is curious infelicity in combining with this vague panegyric the particular libel of charging them with lack of industry, a virtue which, on pain of death, they are bound to exhibit. 'In beetledom are no poor laws,' and the beast that will not seek its livelihood perishes out of hand. 'Loafing and making poems,' which Whitman describes as his favourite modes of existence, are privileges or perversities peculiar to human nature. Nor would Whitman have learned from Darwin the pitiful extravagance of despising, or affecting to despise, human qualities for no reason, suggested or implied, but because they are human. There is no apparent reason why it should be more contemptible for men to build temples than for crows to build nests; and since it has been in all ages and generations a habit with mankind to discuss their duty to God, it would have been less inhumanly insolent in Whitman to evince some respect for the practice than to say that it turns him sick. The sneer about weeping in the dark for sins might have been expressly directed against one of the best known verses of Goethe, a man not given to sentimental brooding or self-questioning, but who knew that tears shed at midnight on solitary beds are not unpleasing to 'the heavenly powers.'

Let it not be thought, however, that because Whitman speaks scornfully of duty to God and of sin, he never praises religion, Self-contradiction is one of the commonest freaks of affectation, and Whitman never hesitates to contradict himself. He oscillates, in fact, from extreme to extreme, and parades now this extravagance, now that, consistent only in avoidance of the golden mean. We have seen that it makes him sick to hear men discussing their duty to God. His extravagance in its pious tune is almost equally offensive.

I say that the real and permanent grandeur of these States must be their religion;
Otherwise there is no real and permanent grandeur;
(Nor character, nor life worthy the name, without religion;
Nor land, nor man, nor woman, without religion.)

This is just as silly as to praise pigs and foxes for not worshipping God. Here is another illustration of Whitman's habit of exaggerating truth or half-truth into falsehood.

I believe a leaf of grass is no less than the journey-work of the stars,
And the pismire is equally perfect, and a grain of sand, and the egg of the wren,
And the tree-toad is a chef-d'œuvre for the highest,
And the running blackberry would adorn the parlours of heaven,
And the narrowest hinge in my hand puts to scorn all machinery,
And the cow, crunching with depress'd head, surpasses any statue,
And a mouse is miracle enough to stagger sextillions of infidels.

This is exceptionally good for Whitman. Several of the lines have a picturesque felicity. So recently as a quarter of a century ago they might have passed for true science and sound theology; but progress in understanding the constitution of nature has within the specified period been unprecedentedly rapid; truths which, five-and-twenty years ago, were but as streaks of pale crimson on the horizon, have flashed into general recognition; and the natural theology which revelled in talk like this, about the miracles of nature and the impotence of man, is irrevocably superseded. Those who have read with any carefulness in modern science know that throughout nature there is no perfection discoverable by man; everything is in perpetual change, perpetual movement; and the 'type of perfect,' of which Plato dreamed and Tennyson has sung, can be found neither in mouse nor in mountain. It has been recognized that man invents, and that nature, with her task set her at every point by mechanical necessity, does not invent. The hinge in the hand does not put machinery to scorn; and Helmholtz, without incurring the charge of arrogance from any scientific man, pronounces the eye an instrument 'full of defects.' The line about the mouse convincing sextillions of infidels is a mere platitude of the kind for which Paley used to stand sponsor; and we have to recollect that if the sextillions of infidels, when convinced by the miraculous mouse, began to discuss their duty to God, they would immediately make Mr. Whitman sick.

It must be confessed that this last would be a frame of mind or of body much more customary with him than that in which he points out the unreasonableness of infidels in declining to be 'staggered' by mice. Fierce disdain for faith in God, except as a phase of human fancying, is one of his recurrent moods, and though he may not express it in words, there is no maxim which he more energetically enforces than this—'Reverence nothing.'

Magnifying and applying come I,
Outbidding at the start the old cautious hucksters;
Taking myself the exact dimensions of Jehovah;
Lithographing Kronos, Zeus his son, and Hercules his grandson;
Buying drafts of Osiris, Isis, Belus, Brahma, Buddha;
In my portfolio placing Manito loose, Allah on a leaf, the crucifix engraved,
With Odin and the hideous Mexitli, and every idol and image;
Taking them all for what they are worth and not a cent more.

With a flourish of his pen, he accounts for and effaces all gods.

What do you suppose I would intimate to you in a hundred ways, but that man or woman is as good as God,
And that there is no God any more divine than yourself?

It is possible to hold with candid intelligence, and to teach without irreverence, the doctrine of man's divinity. The higher self of Mr. Matthew Arnold, the heroic in man of Carlyle, the rightly and perfectly developed humanity of Goethe, may, without much practical mischief, be an object of admiration to the pitch of worship. But theoretically the insanest, and practically the most pernicious, of all faiths or no-faiths, is the crude self-worship, the deification of the *profanum vulgus*, which, in so far as it admits of definition, is the creed of Whitman. Until I examined his book, I did not know that the most venomously malignant of all political and social fallacies—that 'one man is as good as another'—had been deliberately taught in print.

The messages of great poets [says Whitman, in his preface] to each man and woman, are, Come to us on equal terms—only then can you understand us. We are no better than you; what we enclose you enclose, what we enjoy you may enjoy. Did you suppose there could be only one Supreme? We affirm there can be unnumbered supremes, and that one does not countervail another, any more than one eyesight countervails another; and that men can be good or grand only of the consciousness of their supremacy within them.

Neither in Goethe nor Carlyle will Whitman find anything but detestation for the sentiment of these words. Those men might teach hero-worship; he teaches self-worship and fool-worship. Goethe said that poets raised men to the gods, and brought down the gods to men; but that every man was himself as good as either god or poet, Goethe would have denied with keenest brilliancy of scorn. Carlyle bade men reverence the hero, discern the heroic in man as constituting his true majesty, detect and honour it under all disguises, refuse to accept any sham heroism, however dignified, in its place; but so disgusted was he to find that his unmasking of sham kings and nobles was being mistaken for a doctrine of anarchic levelling and the kingship of blockheads and scamps, that, in too violent recoil, he has latterly insisted that the rule of one despot is better than that of multitudinous fools, each fool proclaiming his own 'supremacy.' It is because of their subtle and pervasive flattery of the mob that Whitman's writings are not harmless as they are worthless, but poisonously immoral and pestilent.

Whitman is an intrepid destroyer of other people's thoughts, but he sometimes speaks a language wholly his own. No other human being would have said this about 'touch:'—

Blind, loving, wrestling touch! sheath'd, hooded, sharp-tooth'd touch!
Did it make you ache so, leaving me?
Parting, track'd by arriving—perpetual payment of perpetual loan;
Rich, showering rain, and recompense richer afterward:
Sprouts take and accumulate—stand by the curb prolific and vital:
Landscapes, projected, masculine, full-sized, and golden.

Thoughts quite his own being rare with him, he hugs them accordingly. No one, I suppose, will dispute his paternity of the thought, or rather the conceit, that grass is 'the beautiful uncut hair of graves.' In my opinion it is a far-fetched and stupid conceit, but it might have passed without blame in half a line, if the reader's imagination had been left to make the best of it. Whitman wire-draws it thus:—

Tenderly will I use you, curling grass
It may be you transpire from the breasts of young men;
It may be if I had known them I would have loved them;
It may be you are from old people, and from women, and from offspring taken
  out of their mothers' laps.
This grass is very dark to be from the white heads of old mothers;
Darker than the colourless beards of old men;
Dark to come from under the faint-red roofs of mouths.
O, I perceive after all so many uttering tongues!
And I perceive they do not come from the roofs of mouths for nothing.

If this is not mawkish there is no passage known to me in literature deserving to be so characterized.

Whitman's 'poetry' contains a vast deal about himself. 'I celebrate myself,' he frankly remarks. He professes to 'inaugurate' a religion, of which the one duty, the sole worship, is to be the 'dear love of comrades,' and he speaks with the authority of a founder of a new church.

> No dainty dolce affettuoso I;
> Bearded, sunburnt, gray-necked, forbidding, I have arrived,
> To be wrestled with as I pass, for the solid prizes of the universe;
> For such I afford whoever can persevere to win them.

The two last lines either mean nothing at all, or announce that Whitman is a god. Whichever alternative is chosen, the man is a demonstrated quack.

Take another piece of self-portraiture.

Sure as the most certain sure, plumb in the uprights, well entretied, braced in the
  beams,
Stout as a horse, affectionate, haughty, electrical,
I and this mystery, here we stand.

Are these the words of a sane man? Is there common sense in saying that you stand plumb in the uprights, well entretied, strong as a horse, electrical, and side by side with a mystery?

If there is anything in Whitman decidely better than mere extravagant affectation, anything that may claim the dignity of legitimate mannerism, it is a certain feeling for magnitude, an amplitude of mental vision and descriptive grasp. America he discerns to be a very large place, the United States a republic of federated nations, the Mississippi an immense river; and he is impressed with the idea that a specially redundant and sonorous style is appropriate to these conditions. This feeling for magnitude might be of value if associated with consummate power, if dominated by a fine sense of proportion, grace, and order. But an itch of hugeness has much more frequently aped than evidenced the strength of genius. Every one familiar with the history of art is aware that a multitude of bad painters have betrayed their badness by spasmodic aspiration after bigness, vapouring about their capacity to rival Angelo and Tintoret, if they had only walls large enough to display their conceptions. When they were permitted to work on their chosen scale, they did nothing but smear acres of canvas. It would be an insult to the memory of Barry or Haydon to compare them with Walt Whitman; but the long lists of names, the auctioneer catalogues, the accumulation of words out of all proportion to ideas, which make up the body of Whitman's poems, recall their vain attempt to prove themselves great painters by using very large brushes and filling very large frames. Whitman, however, must speak for himself. Here is part of a bird's-eye view with which he favours us of sailors and their doings throughout the world:—

I behold the mariners of the world;
Some are in storms—some in the night, with the watch on the look-out;
Some drifting helplessly—some with contagious diseases.
I behold the sail and steamships of the world, some in clusters in port, some on their voyages;
Some double the Cape of Storms—some Cape Verde, others Cape Guardafui, Bon, or Bajadore;
Others Dondra Head—others pass the Straits of Sunda—others Cape Lopatka—others Behring's Straits;
Others Cape Horn—others sail the Gulf of Mexico, or along Cuba, or Hayti—others Hudson's Bay, or Baffin's Bay;
Others pass the Straits of Dover—others enter the Wash—others the Frith of Solway—others round Cape Clear—others the Land's End;
Others traverse the Zuyder Zee, or the Scheldt;
Others add to the exits and entrances at Sandy Hook;
Others to the comers and goers at Gibraltar, or the Dardanelles;
Others sternly push their way through the northern winter-packs;
Others descend or ascend the Obi or the Lena;
Others the Niger, or the Congo—others the Indus, the Burampooter and Cambodia;
Others wait at the wharves of Manhattan, steam'd up, ready to start;
Wait, swift and swarthy, in the ports of Australia;

Wait at Liverpool, Glasgow, Dublin, Marseilles, Lisbon, Naples,
Hamburg, Bremen, Bordeaux, the Hague, Copenhagen;
Wait at Valparaiso, Rio Janeiro, Panama;
Wait at their moorings at Boston, Philadelphia, Baltimore,
Charleston, New Orleans, Galveston, San Francisco.

In ages when the science of geography was in its earliest dawn—when not one man in ten thousand had heard of towns or rivers beyond the frontiers of his own province—a catalogue of names and countries might be what only a pre-eminently well-informed poet could give, and what every intelligent listener would appreciate and admire. Many interests, besides those of geographical curiosity, interests of a patriotic and clannish nature, enhanced the eager fascination with which the old Greeks heard the names of the nations that sent ships to Troy, or of the ports at which Jason or Ulysses touched. But any boy or girl of twelve, who can spell names of places on a map and write them down on a page, could fill a volume with such descriptive lines as these of Whitman's. Observe, there is no concatenation, no ordered sequence, no quickening or illuminating thought, in the list. The conception of a coherent and reasoned account of the water-ways of the world, on the principle of their historical development or their commercial or political importance, is beyond him. Nothing could be more void of significance than his throwing together the Wash and the Frith of Solway instead of the Thames, the Severn, the Mersey, or the Clyde, by way of indicating the marine activity of Britain. There is no cause why Bristol and London should not be named as well as Glasgow and Liverpool. The thing, in fact, could not be done more brainlessly. A poor piece of mannerism at best, it is here wretchedly worked, and though Whitman sometimes executes it with less dulness, this is a fair average sample of his success. When we consider that nine-tenths of Whitman's poetry consists of these catalogues—that they, in fact, constitute, in respect both of manner and of matter, one of the differentiating elements in his work—it will be seen that no small importance attaches to the facility of the artifice. It is, in fact, the most childishly easy of all artifices. Think of the materials afforded for such compilation in these days. Every town contains a library in which there are dictionaries of classical antiquity, translations from foreign languages, travellers' volumes on every country under the sun. Every daily newspaper contains correspondence filled with the most picturesque and exciting details the correspondent can rake together. There is absolutely nothing in Whitman's lists that you could not match after a few hours' turning over of the leaves of Lemprierre, Livingstone, Du Chaillu, Figuier, or a few volumes of any one of fifty encyclopædias. The world could, on these terms, be filled with poetry, if it were not an absurdity to apply the name to rant and rubbish. Having got at his secret, you soon learn to take stock of the American bard. Almost anything will do to start him off in his jingle, as all roads will suit if you don't want to go anywhere in particular, but merely to raise a dust. Take, for example, the glorious burst of noise which breaks from the minstrel when he mentions the broad-axe.

The axe leaps!
The solid forest gives fluid utterances;
They tumble forth, they rise and form,
Hut, tent, landing, survey,
Flail, plough, pick, crowbar, spade,
Shingle, rail, prop, wainscot, jamb, lath, panel, gable,
Citadel, ceiling, saloon, academy, organ, exhibition house, library,
Cornice, trellis, pilaster, balcony, window, shutter, turret, porch,
Hoe, rake, pitch-fork, pencil, wagon, staff, saw, jack-plane, mallet, wedge, rounce,
Chair, tub, hoop, table, wicket, vane, sash, floor,
Work-box, chest, string'd instrument, boat, frame, and what not.

What not, indeed? There is no assignable reason why everything else that ever was made of wood night not be added. But why, it is relevant to ask, give these? Ought expression to have no relation to sense? Ought words to have no proportion to ideas? Is there any definition of linguistic silliness, of verbiage, of hopelessly bad writing, more just than that which turns upon extension of sound without corresponding extension of meaning? And this is what Mr. W. Rossetti publishes in England with eulogistic preface! This is the kind of thing which we are commanded to receive as the rhythmic utterance of Western democracy, the voice of America! It is pleasing to reflect that, if people like such poetry, they may have plenty of it. Every auctioneer's clerk will be a poet of the new era. Suppose the subject to be 'Occupations'—a poetical subject enough. Who does not see how the bard of democracy would begin setting it to music? Here goes:—

Oil-works, silk-works, white-lead works, the sugar-house, steam-saws, the grist-mills, and factories;
Stone-cutting, shapely trimmings for façades or window or door-lintels, the mallet, the tooth-chisel, the jib to protect the thumb.

Is this not up to Whitman's mark? Is it not the genuine gurgle of the democratic Castalia? Listen:—

> Leather-dressing, coach-making, boiler-making, rope-twisting,
> Distilling, sign-painting, lime-burning, cotton-picking,
> Electro-plating, electro-typing, stereotyping.

The enlightened reader doubtless asks for more; and it is easy to oblige him:—

> The pens of live pork, the killing-hammer, the hog-hook,
> The scalder's tub, gutting, the cutter's cleaver, the packer's maul,
> And the plenteous winter-work of pork-packing.

Am I outrageously caricaturing the favourite of Dr. Dowden, Mr. Rossetti, and Mr. Buchanan? Every line, or rather every amorphous agglomeration of broken clauses, is Whitman's own. Page after page of the like will be found flung together in what he calls a 'Carol of Occupations.' Mr. Rossetti expresses majestical pity for us if we have no ear for such music. Time was when Englishmen knew quackery when they saw it.

It must be evident that, on the terms and by the methods of which we are now able to form some idea, there would be no difficulty in multiplying the number, or expanding the dimensions of Whitman's works. They are the most flagrant and offensive example ever met with by me of big badness trying to palm itself off as great excellence. Quantity of production is without question one index of power; and it is true not only that the poet who produces a hundred immortal poems is greater than the poet who produces one, but that the hand of the great artist has a sweep and freedom, corresponding to the largeness of scale on which he likes to work. No artist whose characteristic pictures cannot be appreciated without a lens—though he paint, fold for fold, on the limbs of Titania, the woven air of Cashmere—is a great artist. But it is equally true, and it is much more apt to be forgotten, that, throughout nature as known to man, the transition from inorganic to organic, and from ruder forms to finer forms, is from largeness to smallness. A bird is a more exquisite piece of nature's workmanship than a megalosaurus. And if amount of work is one measure of greatness, there is perhaps no test of the quality of genius so sure as capacity to excel within narrow limits. A weak artist may mask his weakness by showing us enormous limbs a-sprawl on ceilings, but only a consummate artist will conceive and execute a faultless vignette. You might suspect sham work, random smudging and brush-flinging, in Turner's great storms, or billowy plains, or crowding hills, or scarlet and golden sunsets; but you learn to trust them when the same hand traces for you the shadows, and touches for you the rose-buds, in that garden arbour which forms one of the minor illustrations to Rogers's poems, or when it works into a few square inches, with tiny flower-pots in fairy-like rows, and gem-like burnishing of flower-petals, a perfect picture of the conservatory at Farnley. All art which is great in quality as well as in quantity presupposes such work as we have in Turner's drawing of Farnley conservatory. Turner could not have given the misty curve of his horizons, the perspective of his rivers winding in the distance, unless he had gone through such work as is attested in the minute drawing; and if you take any ten pages in Carlyle's greatest books, in his *French Revolution*, or his *Cromwell*, and examine them by reference to the sources you will find that, broad and bold as is his touch, magnificently free as is his sweep of hand, he has been as strenuously careful in the preliminary mastery of details as was Turner in conning the grammar of his art. Magnitude without worth, breadth of scale without fineness of execution, is the refuge of aspiring and immodest incompetence both in painting and in literature.

But we must devote more particular attention to what Whitman's admirers have to say in his favour. We are met at the outset by the circumstance that they make admissions of a disparaging nature, such as no advocates ever made on behalf of their client. They enable me, to my extreme satisfaction, to refer judge and jury to them on certain points which it would otherwise have been impossible for me to make an English audience understand. Quotation of much that is most characteristic in Whitman's writings is out of the question, and I am not equal to the task of making description do the work of sample.

If there be any class of subjects [says Professor Dowden] which it is more truly natural, more truly human *not* to speak of, than to speak of (such speech producing self-consciousness, whereas part of our nature, it may be maintained, is healthy only while it lives and moves in holy blindness and unconsciousness of self), if there be any sphere of silence, then Whitman has been guilty of invading that sphere of silence.

This is a felicitously correct account of what Whitman has done; and most readers will, I think, agree with me that it is a grave offence, an abominable blunder. The man who does not know what to speak of, and what not to speak of, is unfit for society; and if he puts into his books what even he would not dare to say in society, his books cannot be fit for circulation. As Dr. Dowden has defined for us the nature, he will also kindly tell us the extent, of Whitman's offence against civilized manners. 'Whitman,' says Dr. Dowden, 'in a few passages falls below humanity—falls even below the modesty of brutes.' This is strictly true; and would, I submit, be enough to sink a ship-load of poems with ten times the merits of Whitman's; and although I shall not say that he often falls below the modesty of brutes, I do say that, not in a few but in many passages, he is senselessly foul. But 'it ought not,' pleads Professor Dowden, 'to be forgotten that no one asserts more strenuously than does Whitman the beauty, not indeed of asceticism, but of holiness and healthiness, and the shameful ugliness of unclean thought, desire, and deed.' If such were his theory, the less pardonable would be his practice; but the truth—to which the critic's generosity seems to blind him—is that Whitman has no fixed theory or settled practice in this or in any other case, but confounds good and bad, delightful and disgusting, decent and indecent, in his chaotic extravaganza. He may be foul on one page and condemn himself for being so on another, just as he may say on one page that there can be no man or woman without religion, and on another that it makes him sick to hear people discussing their duty to God. Mr. Rossetti puts in the plea that eminent writers of all ages have sinned in this matter as well as Whitman. He cites no passages, names no authors, and I content myself with affirming generally that his plea cannot be sustained. There is no author of reputation of whom Dr. Dowden could say that he sinks in immodesty below the brutes. And there is no author whatever who, like Whitman, is indecent from mere extravagance and affectation. They all give us something to redeem what, nevertheless, are blots on their work. Chaucer is gross, but he has humour; Fielding, but he has wit; Whitman has no fun in him. Homer is never gross: he has a vehement sympathy with all natural joys, and there is no monastic coldness in his description of the embraces of Jupiter and Juno, or of the ivory bed of Ulysses; but he is the gentleman always, less than the gentleman never; and his heroes, though they may kill mutton, never infringe that first law of good manners which we have heard Dr. Dowden define. Had Whitman ventured upon the hundredth part of his grossness in the camp of the Greeks, he would have been cudgelled more cordially than Thersites.

On the intellectual side, Whitman's critics make admissions which are almost as strange as that which certifies his occasional descent, in moral respects, below the level of the brutes. Dr. Dowden speaks of 'the recurring tendency of his poems to become catalogues of persons and things.' It is curious, by the way, that our bard's panegyrists cannot speak of him without using language that sounds like irony. 'Selection,' says Professor Dowden, 'seems forbidden to him; if he names one race of mankind, the names of all the other races press into his page; if he mentions one trade or occupation, all other trades or occupations follow.' Exactly; but it used to be understood that the poet was bound not only to apply the process of selection, but of selection so searching and so keen that, like dross and slag from metal placed in a furnace heated sevenfold, every imperfection was purged away by it, and only the fine stream of liquid gold flowed out. 'Writing down the headings of a trades directory,' says Dr. Dowden again, 'is not poetry.' No. 'But this,' he adds, 'is what Whitman never does.' I respectfully insist that it is a literal description of what Whitman, on Dr. Dowden's own showing, frequently does; but Professor Dowden must admit, at least, that there are no other compositions passing current as poetry of which he would have thought it necessary to make the remark. He states that 'the logical faculty is almost an offence to Whitman,' and owns to suspecting that his matter belongs at times rather to chaos than to cosmos, and that his form corresponds to his matter. But of all the concessions made by Whitman's eulogists, one tendered by Mr. Rossetti pleases me most. 'Each of Whitman's poems is,' he says, 'a menstruum saturated with form in solution.' To this I explicitly subscribe; when the solution crystallizes it will be time to inquire whether the crystals are poetry. A marble statue in a state of solution is mud.

We find, then, that the gentlemen who propose to assign Whitman's writings a place of honour in the literature of the world admit that logic is an offence to him, that his matter is occasionally chaotic, that the form of his poems is 'form in solution,' and that his immodesty passes the immodesty of brutes. Having reached this point, might we not expect to be told that the right thing to do with his productions is to cast them away, accepting with philosophical resignation, the implied suggestion as to their treatment made by the poet himself, in the most reasonable of all his prophecies?—

> I bequeath myself to the dirt. . . .
> If you want me again, look for me under your boot-soles.

But Whitman's admirers, of course, refuse to take the hint, and we are bound to give them audience when they attempt to prove that the unparalleled concessions they have made as to his defects are more than balanced by his merits. The main ground on which they commend Whitman is, that he has at last founded a distinctively American school of poetry. The new world, argues Dr. Dowden, may be expected to give birth to 'literary and artistic forms corresponding to itself in strange novelty,' to 'a fauna and flora other than the European,' requiring a new nomenclature, like other American things—'hickory,' for example, and 'mocking-bird.' American democracy being a great, new, unexampled thing, with faults enough, but yet deserving recognition and respect, the poet of American democracy may, in like manner, though his works are surprising and questionable deserve applause. Whitman himself set out, as was mentioned, with a determination to write differently from his contemporaries and predecessors. The American poetry which he found existing was, he intimated,

either the poetry of an elegantly weak sentimentalism—at bottom nothing but maudlin puerilities, or more or less musical verbiage, arising out of a life of depression and enervation as their result—or else that class of poetry, plays, &c., of which the foundation is feudalism, with its ideas of lords and ladies, its imported standard of gentility, and the manners of European high-life-below-stairs in every line and verse.

'*I* am the poet of America,' virtually says the modest Whitman; and our English critics bow assent.

When we reflect that, among the American poets thus slightly waived aside, were, to mention no others, Longfellow, Bryant, Emerson, Lowell, and Edgar Poe, the justice of the remark that Whitman shows effrontery will be apparent. But his feelings, as affected by the abundance, apart from all question as to the excellence, of existing poetry, when he first thought of becoming himself a poet, was not unreasonable. It arose from a more or less vague but substantially just perception of the fact that literature is old, that the libraries of the world are well stocked, that subjects, motives, images, incidents, plots, which were novel some thousands of years ago, have become stale. The first broad aspects, the salient facts and features, of that nature which man seeks to present again—represent—in his art, have long since been seized. The interest of dart-throwing and of heroic skull-cleaving was pretty well exhausted by Homer. Goethe says that if Shakespeare had written in German, he (Goethe) would, at the outset of his literary career, have been oppressed with something like despair; and the years which have passed since Goethe experienced this feeling, with their Scott poetry, their Byron poetry, their Wordsworth, Coleridge, Shelley, Campbell, Tennyson poetry, not to mention half a dozen American poets whose names are known throughout Europe, have incalculably enhanced the difficulty and hazard that face one who, using the English language, aspires to the fame of a poet. Under such circumstances, the temptation to false originality, to one or other form of affectation, is almost irresistible. I am deliberately of opinion that no young poet or painter,—for what has been said applies *mutatis mutandis*, to pictorial as well as to literary art,—be his powers what they may, wholly escapes its influence. It causes men of undoubted genius to say things with a queerness, a quaintness, which I, at least cannot conceive to be natural to them. Mr. Morris, for example, thus describes an occurrence which, though interesting and delightful, has for many ages been a poetical commonplace:—

In that garden fair
Came Lancelot walking; this is true, the kiss
Wherewith we kissed in meeting that spring day,
I scarce dare talk of the remembered bliss,
When both our mouths went wandering in one way;
And, aching sorely, met among the leaves,
Our hands being left behind strained far away.

To say that Lancelot and Guinevere kissed each other would certainly have been ordinary, and Mr. Morris's way of stating the fact is original; but since it is not possible that the kiss could have been performed as he describes it—for although the lovers might have restrained their natural impulse to embrace as well as kiss, and might have kept their hands before them or at their sides, it is inconceivable that they should have poked their hands out behind them while craning their necks forward to bring their lips together—we must conclude that Mr. Morris considered it a less evil to be fantastic than to be commonplace. Mr. D. G. Rossetti has written several poems which seem to me imperishably great; but he also has suffered from the tyrannical necessity of being original, after nature has been laid under contribution by poets for thousands of years. It would have been as commonplace for Mr. Rossetti to say that he sat musing on the grass, as for Mr. Morris to say that Lancelot took Guinevere into his arms and kissed her. Accordingly Mr. Rossetti writes thus:—

The wind flapped loose, the wind was still,
Shaken out dead from tree and hill:

I had walked on at the wind's will,—
I sat now, for the wind was still.

Between my knees my forehead was,—
My lips, drawn in, said not, Alas!
My hair was over in the grass,
My naked ears heard the day pass.

Original, no doubt, but is it not somewhat odd? The posture described is grotesque, and in a room, when attempted by persons making no claim to the character of poet, cannot be achieved; but even on a peculiarly formed bank in the country, it would be uncomfortable. The feat performed by Mr. Rossetti might be recommended to professors of gymnastics, and, perhaps, if one sat with his head between his knees and his hair in the grass for an hour, the acoustic nerve would become so sensitive through torture that he could 'hear the day pass;' but it is not easy to believe that the lines would have been as they are, if Mr. Rossetti had felt it admissible to say so commonplace a thing as that he sat on a green bank and meditated. From the works of Mr. Browning, and even from those of Mr. Tennyson, illustration might be derived of the shuddering horror with which modern poets avoid commonplace; and the oddities and eccentricities of painters during the present century have been equally conspicuous. I recollect seeing a picture of St. George and the Dragon, by an artist admired by many eloquent young ladies, in which the dragon looked like a large green lizard, and St. George like a medical gentleman administering to it, by means of a long glass bottle which he poked into its mouth, a dose of castor-oil. I was given to understand that the piece had a profound spiritual significance, but I had not soul enough to comprehend it.

If the necessity of being original lies hard upon poets in these days, is it not all the more, on that account, the duty of critics to press upon them the equally inexorable necessity of resisting the fascinations of false and affected originality? Novelty is essential to art; every genuine art-product, in sculpture, in painting, in poetry, is unique; but it is intensely untrue that everything that is novel and unparalleled is art; and so easy is it to ape or to travesty right newness, that Whitman's conscious and trumpeted purpose to produce something original ought to have been, in the eyes of critics so acute as Dr. Dowden and so accomplished as Mr. W. Rossetti, a presumption that the originality forthcoming would be spurious. Every art-product is new, but every art-product is also old; and the operation of producing a true poem or picture—an operation too subtle to be described in words or executed by rule—consists essentially in combining newness of form and colour and musical harmony with oldness of principle and law. An illustration of this union, applicable, to my thinking, with scientific accuracy to the case in hand, is afforded by nature every spring. When the brown hill-side breaks, as Goethe finely says, into a wave of green, every hollow of blue shade, every curve of tuft, and plume, and tendril, every broken sun-gleam on spray of young leaves, is new. No spring is a repetition of any former spring. And yet the laws of chemistry and of vegetable life are unchanging. The novelty that the poet must give us is the novelty of spring; and the transcendent but inevitable difficulty of poetical originality lies in this, that the limits of variation within which he is permitted to work are narrow. His poetry must be as different from that of any other poet as one spring is different from another; *but it must not be more so*. It is a fundamental principle, laid down by that ancient nation which was inspired to write the bible of art, that all gigantesque, eccentric, distorted, extravagant art is barbarous. By working in the spirit of the lesson taught it once and for ever by Greece, Europe has gone beyond Greece; but as far as Europe, in Shakespeare, has transcended Greece, so far will America fall behind and below not Europe only, but Egypt, Babylon, and Assyria, if she cast the lesson of Greece to the winds and consent to the identification of democracy with lawless extravagance. It would, I believe, be unfair to the Americans to speak of them as pledged to admiration of Whitman. They are not afraid to give every one a hearing, and in this they are bravely right; but they have a way, also, of getting, sooner or later, at the true value of a man, and I rather think they have found Whitman out. I have produced abundant evidence to prove that he exceeds all the bounds fixed to sound poetical originality, and is merely grotesque, and surprising.

It is instructive to note that, whenever Whitman is, comparatively speaking, rational and felicitous, his writing becomes proportionally like that of other people. Of really good poetical work there is, indeed, in those of his poems known to me—and I have read, with desperate resolution, a great deal both of his prose and his verse, including productions which his eulogists specifically extol—very little. Even his best passages have this characteristic of inferior writing, that they deal with sensational subjects and fierce excitements. His lack of delicate and deep sensibility is proved by his producing horror when he aims at pathos. The true masters of pathos obtain their greatest effects by means that seem slight. A Shakespeare, a Goethe, will make all generations mourn over the sorrows of an Italian girl, of a German grisette; a daisy, a mouse, a wounded hare, evoke touches of immortal pathos from Burns. Whitman must have his scores massacred, his butcherly apparatus of blood and mangled flesh, his extremity of peril in storm, his melodramatic exaggeration of courage in battle. But it is in the few sketches of such scenes, occurring in the poem called 'Walt Whitman,' that he is most successful; and then his affectations fall, to a refreshing extent, from his loins, and he makes some approach to the perspicuity, compression, vividness, and force of good writing in general. If his English critics had contented themselves with discriminating between what is passably good and what is insufferably bad in his work, commending the former and condemning the latter, not a word would have been written by me upon the subject. Dr. Dowden, Mr. Rossetti, Mr. Buchanan, and, most vociferously of all, Mr. Swinburne, accept him at his own valuations as 'the greatest of American voices,'* and the poet of democracy. To do so is to wrong the true poets whom America has produced, and to strike a pang as of despair into the hearts of those who, amid all short-comings and delinquencies, amid Fiske tragedies and Tammany Rings, refuse to believe that democracy means dissolution, and that the consummation of freedom must be an exchange of the genial bonds and decent amenities of civilization for infra-bestial license. Originality, true and clear, characterizes the real poets of America. There is in them a fragrance and flavour native to the American soil, a something that gives them a character as distinctive as marks off the Elizabethans from Milton, or distinguishes Pope and his school from recent English poets. More than this was not to be looked for or desired; the strong presumption was that more than this would indicate monstrosity, debility, or affectation; and this presumption has been verified by Whitman. Nature in America is different from nature in Europe, but we do not, in crossing the Atlantic, pass from cosmos into chaos; and Mr. Carlyle's expression, 'winnowings of chaos,' would be a candidly scientific description of Whitman's poetry if only it were possible to associate with it the idea of any winnowing process whatever. Street-sweepings of lumberland—disjointed fragments of truth, tossed in wild whirl with disjointed fragments of

* These words are Mr. Swinburne's, and perhaps would not be endorsed by the others. I take this opportunity of protesting against certain comments made by Mr. Swinburne (in a republished essay on the text of Shelley) on an article written by me for this REVIEW in the year 1867. I did *not* say what Mr. Swinburne represents me as saying, and what I *did* say can be proved to be grammatically correct.

falsehood—gleams of beauty that have lost their way in a waste of ugliness—such are the contents of what he calls his poems. If here and there we have tints of healthful beauty, and tones of right and manly feeling, they but suffice to prove that he can write sanely and sufferably when he pleases, that his monstrosities and solecisms are sheer affectation, that he is not mad, but only counterfeits madness. He is in no sense a superlatively able man, and it was beyond his powers to make for himself a legitimate poetical reputation. No man of high capacity could be so tumid and tautological as he—could talk, for instance, of the 'fluid wet' of the sea; or speak of the aroma of his armpits, or make the crass and vile mistake of bringing into light what nature veils, and confounding liberty with dissolute anarchy. The poet of democracy he is not; but his books may serve to buoy, for the democracy of America, those shallows and sunken rocks on which, if it is cast, it must inevitably, amid the hootings of mankind, be wrecked. Always, unless he chooses to contradict himself for the sake of paradox, his political doctrine is the consecration of mutinous independence and rabid egotism and impudent conceit. In his ideal city 'the men and women think lightly of the laws.' His advice is to resist much and to obey little. This is the political philosophy of Bedlam, unchained in these ages chiefly through the influence of Rousseau, which has blasted the hopes of freedom wherever it has had the chance, and which must be chained up again with ineffable contempt if the self-government of nations is to mean anything else than the death and putrescence of civilization. Incapable of true poetical originality, Whitman had the cleverness to invent a literary trick, and the shrewdness to stick to it. As a Yankee phenomenon, to be good-humouredly laughed at, and to receive that moderate pecuniary remuneration which nature allows to vivacious quacks, he would have been in his place; but when influential critics introduce him to the English public as a great poet, the thing becomes too serious for a joke. While reading Whitman, in the recollection of what had been said of him by those gentlemen, I realized with bitter painfulness how deadly is the peril that our literature may pass into conditions of horrible disease, the raging flame of fever taking the place of natural heat, the ravings of delirium superseding the enthusiasm of poetical imagination, the distortions of tetanic spasm caricaturing the movements, dance-like and music-measured, of harmonious strength. Therefore I suspended more congenial work to pen this little counterblast to literary extravagance and affectation.

39. Lanier on Whitman

1878

Extract from a letter from Sidney Lanier to Bayard Taylor, 3 February 1878. Published in *Letters of Sidney Lanier*, 1866–81, (1899), ed., H. W. Lanier and Mrs Sidney Lanier, p. 208.

Sidney Lanier (1842–81), American poet, was born in Macon, Georgia and served in the Civil War from 1861 to 1865, returning home in broken health. In 1879 he became lecturer on English literature at the Johns Hopkins University, and his lectures there served as the basis of his *Science of English Verse* published in 1880. That a southern soldier and a traditional prosodist should find the verse of Whitman to his taste is as unexpected a tribute as he himself evidently felt it to be.

I read through the three volumes on Sunday: and upon a sober comparison I think Walt Whitman's *Leaves of Grass* worth at least a million of *Among My Books* and *Atalanta in Calydon*. In the two latter I could not find anything which has not been much better said before; but *Leaves of Grass* was a real refreshment to me—like rude salt spray in your face—in spite of its enormous fundamental error that a thing is good because it is natural, and in spite of the world-wide difference between my own conception of art, and its author's.

40. Some views of the 1880s

(*a*) The American poet and critic Edmund Clarence Stedman (1833–1908). Extract from *Scribner's Monthly* (1880), XXI. Stedman edited a volume of *Cameos* from Landor (1873). *A Library of American Literature* in eleven volumes (1887–90), *The Works of Edgar Allan Poe* (1894–95), *A Victorian Anthology* (1895) and *An American Anthology* (1900). He wrote a number of volumes of poetry and an elaborate commemorative ode on Hawthorne, which he read before the Harvard Phi Beta Kappa Society in 1877: No one more conspicuously shines by difference. Others are more widely read, but who else has been so widely talked about, or who has held even a few readers with so absolute a sway? . . . In two things he [Whitman] fairly did take the initiative, and might, like a wise advocate, rest his case upon them. He essays, without reserves or sophistry, the full presentment of the natural man. He devoted his song to the future of his own country, accepting and outvying the loudest peak-and-prairie brag, and pledging These States to work out a perfect democracy and the salvation of the world.

(*b*) The English academician and critic, John Todhunter (1839–1916). Extract from *A Study of Shelley* (1880), pp. 1–2; quoted in Dowden, p. 252. John Todhunter was the occupant of the Chair of English Literature at Alexandra College in Dublin, He is described by Professor Harold Blodgett (in his *Walt Whitman in England*) as an 'enthusiastic Shelleyite': The present age has produced three great poets of Democracy—three men whose utterances are full of prophetic fervour, and who seem to gaze forward into the future with eyes that lighten with the vision of some boundless hope for mankind—Shelley, Victor Hugo, and Walt Whitman . . . Walt Whitman is neither, like Shelley, a dreamer aloof from every-day life, in pursuit of ethereal abstractions, of a 'something removed from the sphere of our sorrow,' nor is he like Hugo, led into extravagance by love of theatrical effect. He is rather the idealist of real life, in every common event of which his full-blooded imagination discerns an underworking spiritual force—'a hope beyond the shadow of a dream.'

(*c*) The Irish historian and editor, Fitzgerald Molloy (1858–1908). Extract from 'Leaders of Modern Thought, No. xxvii, Walt Whitman,' *Modern Thought* (September 1882); quoted in Dowden, p. 253. Mr. Molloy was a prolific author. Among his works are: *Royalty Restored*, or *London under Charles II*, in two volumes, *The Russian Court in the Eighteenth Century* in two volumes (1906), *Court Life Below Stairs*, or *London under the first Georges* (1882–3), *Famous Plays, their histories and their authors* (1888), *The Life and Adventures of Edmund Kean* (1888), *The Life and Adventures of Peg Woffington* (1887): Walt Whitman was the outcome of a great era and a great country—they worthy of him in all things, he worthy of them; and as a poet and a prophet he sings of all that he sees in the present, and of the future, peering beyond the surface of things, and crying aloud of the changes to come in the fulness of time.

(*d*) The English professor and lecturer on literature G. C. Macaulay. Extract from 'Walt Whitman', *Nineteenth Century* (December 1882); quoted in Dowden, p. 254. Professor George C. Macaulay edited *The Chronicles of Froissart* and *The Complete Works of John Gower*. He wrote a critical study of Francis Beaumont, a translation of Herodotus, and is the author of the volume on James Thomson in the English Men of Letters series (Macmillan). He is described by Professor Blodgett (in *Walt Whitman in England*) as being generally like the other English and Irish academicians who admired Whitman and spoke up for him in public 'distinguished among their colleagues for their independence and nonconformist spirit': If we were asked for justification of the high estimate of this poet, which has been implied, if not expressed, in what has been hitherto said, the answer would be perhaps first, that he has a power of passionate expression, of strong and simple utterance of the deepest tones of grief, which is almost or altogether without its counterpart in the world.

(*e*) The Scottish novelist and essayist Robert Louis Stevenson (1850–94). Extract from 'Books Which Have Influenced Me' (1887), p. 7: I come next to Whitman's *Leaves of Grass*, a book of singular service which tumbled the world upside down for me, blew into space a thousand cobwebs of genteel and ethical illusions, and, having thus shaken up my tabernacle of lies, set me back again upon a strong foundation of all the original and manly virtues. But it is, once more, only a book for those who have the gift of reading.

41. 'caviare to the multitude'

1881

Unsigned review of the seventh edition of *Leaves of Grass*, the *Critic*, No. 22 (5 November 1881), pp. 302–3.

The anonymous reviewer's remarks on the Osgood edition of 1881 are interesting in the light of the fact that some very careful and knowledgeable readers of Whitman like Professor Crawley, who have compared all the editions of *Leaves of Grass* that appeared during his lifetime, have given the preference to that of 1881. The reviewer also makes an imaginative and interesting point in comparing Whitman's assimilatory attitude towards foreign languages with that of America itself towards the immigrant masses who were crowding into the country during this time.

Practically, but not actually, this is the first time that Mr. Whitman has issued his poems through a publishing house instead of at his private cost. The two volumes called *Leaves of Grass* and *The Two Rivulets*, which he had printed and himself sold at Camden, N. J., are now issued in one, under the former title, without special accretions of new work, but not without a good deal of re-arrangement in the sequence of the poems. Pieces that were evidently written later, and intended to be eventually put under *Leaves of Grass* now find their place; some that apparently did well enough where they were have been shifted to other departments. On the whole, however, the changes have been in the direction of greater clearness as regards their relation to the sub-titles. It is not apparent, however, that the new book is greatly superior to the old in typography, although undeniably the fault of the privately printed volumes, a variation in types used, is no longer met with. The margins are narrower, and the look of the page more commonplace. The famous poem called 'Walt Whitman' is now the 'Song of Myself.' It still maintains:

> I too am not a bit tamed, I too am untranslatable;
> I sound my barbaric yawp over the roofs of the world.

It still has the portrait of Whitman when younger, standing in a loose flannel shirt and slouched hat, with one hand on his hip, the other in his pocket. 'Eidolons' has been taken from the second volume and placed, for good reasons that the reader may not be ready to understand, among the first pieces gathered under the sub-title 'Inscriptions.' It ends with the 'Songs of Parting,' under which the last is 'So Long,' a title that a foreigner and perhaps many an American might easily consider quite as untranslatable as Mr. Whitman proclaims himself to be. The motive for the publication seems to be to take advantage of that wider popularity which is coming somewhat late in life to him whom his admirers like to call 'the good gray poet.'

One great anomaly of Whitman's case has been that while he is an aggressive champion of democracy and of the working-man, in a broad sense of the term working-man, his admirers have been almost exclusively of a class the farthest possibly removed from that which labors for daily bread by manual work. Whitman has always been truly caviare to the multitude. It was only those that knew much of poetry and loved it greatly who penetrated the singular shell of his verses and rejoiced in the rich, pulpy kernel. Even with connoisseurs, Whitman has been somewhat of an acquired taste, and it has always been amusing to note the readiness with which persons who would not or could not read him, raised a cry of affectation against those who did. This phenomenon is too well known in other departments of taste to need further remark; but it may be added that Mr. Whitman has both gained by it and lost. He has gained a vigorousness of support on the part of his admirers that probably more than outbalances the acrid attacks of those who consider his work synonymous with all that is vicious in poetical technique, and wicked from the point of morals. As to the latter, it must be confessed that, according to present standards of social relations, the doctrines taught by Whitman might readily be construed, by the overhasty or unscrupulous, into excuses for foul living: for such persons do not look below the surface, nor can they grasp the whole idea of Whitman's treatment of love. However fervid his expressions may be, and however scornful he is of the miserable hypocrisies that fetter but also protect the evilly disposed, it is plain that the idea he has at heart is that universal love which leaves no room for wickedness because it leaves no room for doing or saying unkind, uncharitable, unjust things to his fellow-man. With an exuberance of thought that would supply the mental outfit of ten ordinary poets, and with a rush of words that is by no means reckless, but intensely and grandly labored. Whitman hurls his view of the world at the heads of his readers with a vigor and boldness that takes away one's breath. This century is getting noted among centuries for singular departures in art and literature. Among them all, there is none bolder or more original than that of Whitman. Perhaps Poe in his own line might be cited as an equal. It is strange, and yet it is not strange, that he should have waited so long for recognition, and that by many thousands of people of no little culture his claims to being a poet at all are either frankly scouted or else held in abeyance. Literature here has remarkably held aloof from the vital thoughts and hopes of the country. It seems as if the very crudity of the struggle here drove people into a petty dilettante atmosphere of prettiness in art and literature as an escape from the dust and cinders of daily life. Hence our national love for 'slicked up' pictures, for instance, by which it is often claimed in Europe that promising geniuses in painting, there, have been ruined for higher work. Hence our patronage of poets that have all the polish of a cymbal, but all a cymbal's dry note and hollowness. Hence, at one time, our admiration for orators that were ornate to the verge of inanity. Into this hot-house air of literature Walt Whitman bounded, with the vigor and suppleness of a clown at a funeral. Dire were the grimaces of the mourners in high places, and dire are their grimaces still. There were plenty of criticisms to make, even after one had finished crying Oh! at the frank sensuality, the unbelievable nakedness of Walt. Everything that decent folk covered up, Walt exhibited, and boasted of exhibiting! He was proud of his nakedness and sensuality. He cried, Look here, you pampered rogues of literature, what are you squirming about, when you know, and everybody knows, that things are just like this, always have been, always will be? But it must be remembered that this was what he wrote, and that he did with a plan, and by order from his genius. It has never been heard of him that he was disgusting in talk or vile in private life, while it has been known that poets celebrated for the lofty tone of their morality, for the strictness of their Christianity, the purity of their cabinet hymns, can condescend in private life to wallow in all that is base. That is the other great anomaly of Whitman. He rhapsodizes of things seldom seen in print with the enthusiasm of a surgeon enamoured of the wonderful mechanism of the body. But he does not soil his conversation with lewdness. If evil is in him, it is in his book.

Whitman's strength and Whitman's weakness lie in his lack of taste. As a mere external sign, look at his privately printed volumes.

For a printer and typesetter, reporter and editor, they do not show taste in the selection and arrangement of the type. A cardinal sin in the eyes of most critics is the use of French, Spanish, and American-Spanish words which are scattered here and there, as if Whitman had picked them up, sometimes slightly incorrectly, from wandering minstrels, Cubans, or fugitives from one of Walker's raids. He shows crudely the American way of incorporating into the language a handy or a high-sounding word without elaborate examination of its original meaning, just as we absorb the different nationalities that crowd over from Europe. His thought and his mode of expression is immense, often flat, very often monotonous, like our great sprawling cities with their endless scattering of suburbs. Yet when one gets the 'hang' of it, there is a colossal grandeur in conception and execution that must finally convince whoever will be patient enough to look for it. His rhythm, so much burlesqued, is all of a part with the man and his ideas. It is apparently confused; really most carefully schemed; certainly to a high degree original. It has what to the present writer is the finest thing in the music of Wagner—a great booming movement or undertone, like the noise of heavy surf. His crowded adjectives are like the mediæval writers of Irish, those extraordinary poets who sang the old Irish heroes and their own contemporaries, the chiefs of their clans. No Irishman of to-day has written a nobler lament for Ireland, or a more hopeful, or a more truthful, than has Walt Whitman. Yet it is not said that he has Irish blood. Nor is there to be found in our literature another original piece of prose so valuable to future historians as his notes on the war. Nor is there a poet of the war-time extant who has so struck the note of that day of conflict as Whitman has in 'Drum Taps.' He makes the flesh creep. His verses are like the march of the long lines of volunteers, and then again like the bugles of distant cavalry. But these are parts of him. As he stands complete in *Leaves of Grass*, in spite of all the things that regard for the decencies of drawing-rooms and families may wish away, he certainly represents, as no other writer in the world, the struggling, blundering, sound-hearted, somewhat coarse, but still magnificent vanguard of Western civilization that is encamped in the United States of America. He avoids the cultured few. He wants to represent, and does in his own strange way represent, the lower middle stratum of humanity. But, so far, it is not evident that his chosen constituency cares for, or has even recognized him. Wide readers are beginning to guess his proportions.

42. 'taken in hand by a reputable publisher'

1882

Unsigned review of the seventh edition of *Leaves of Grass*, the *Dial* (January 1882), pp. 218–19.

Though the Osgood edition was praised in most of the reviews and enjoyed, according to its publisher, 'a fair success' commercially as well, reviews like this one may have encouraged the District Attorney of Boston on 1 March 1882 to classify *Leaves of Grass* as obscene literature and to notify Osgood that legal proceedings would be started against him if certain poems in it were not taken out. After negotiations with Whitman in which the poet offered some concessions but not enough to satisfy the District Attorney, Osgood withdrew as the publisher of the book. William Douglas O'Connor again came to Whitman's defence with letters to the newspapers, and the press as a whole condemned the Boston District Attorney. For a time the latter had succeeded in having the Boston postmaster ban *Leaves of Grass* from the post, but this order did not last long, possibly, according to Gay Wilson Allen, as a result of the representations made by O'Connor to the Attorney General.

After a quarter of a century's probation in the obscurity of author's editions and desultory proof sheets, Walt Whitman's *Leaves of Grass* have at last been taken in hand by a reputable publisher. To Mr. Whitman, this success, after so long a period of suppression and literary outlawry, is no doubt particularly grateful; and in the enjoyment of his triumph he may not unnaturally reject all hints afforded by its long postponement as to the value of his literary wares. Though the period during which he has been known as a writer has been one of great activity and enterprise in the publishing trade, and one in which publishers have keenly sought for what was new and fresh in literature, none of them have been willing to risk either money or reputation on him in an unedited state, and his refusal to abridge or modify his work is understood to have been imperative. He is doubtless glad now that it was so, and will be very likely to find his personal independence and self-sufficiency reinforced by the event: though we could not easily call to mind a case in which reinforcements of this sort are less needed. The self-poise of one whose motto is 'I blab myself' is not to be suspected lightly. Not wishing to repress sympathy rightly due to perseverance in the face of obstacles, we would yet suggest that congratulations in the present case may not imprudently be restricted as regards both promptness and effusiveness. A literary revolt, like a political one, must not be lauded too hastily. Having found a publisher, it remains to be seen if Mr. Whitman shall find a public. Before declaring him to be the new messiah of poetry, it may be well to take time at least to note the magnitude of the task to which he has set himself—which, practically, is not to found a new poetic school, but to work a poetic revolution. We do not purpose to undertake now any extended analysis of Mr. Whitman's characteristics. The most obvious and distinguishing of them—that which relates to poetic form—is, in our judgment, one which it is a waste of time to consider seriously. If his method of writing poetry be correct or even admissible, we might as well drop distinctions between poetry and prose, at least so far as expression is concerned,—a merchant's inventory or lawyer's brief being as good poetry as a ballad or sonnet, and the average political 'leader' being as truly poetical (we will not say imaginative) as Shelley's 'Ode to the West Wind'. The untutored citizen who avowed his inability to see anything in Whitman's poetry beyond 'a lot of —— cataloging' is an entirely competent witness in the case; and we would be quite willing to rest it upon his evidence, without recourse to the concurrent testimony of all poets who ever wrote—from the Hebrew melodists and the 'impudent Highlander' Macpherson to the Sweet Singer of Michigan. Mr. Whitman, indeed, appears not to be content with the abrogation of all conventional notions of poetry and artificial contrivances for constructing and testing it. Not only are rhymes avoided by him and even measures shunned—spondees, dactyls, trochees, iambics, anapests, odes, ballads, and sonnets, kicked into chaos together, as frippery suited only to poets who lull their readers with 'piano tunes,'—but he overrides and crushes out with remorseless effort even those innocently recurring cadences and natural rhythms which are so often the involuntary accompaniment of the expression of impassioned thought. He thus succeeds not only in avoiding all semblance of piano tunes or any other musical thing, but in producing singularly harsh and disagreeable prose. Whatever may be Mr. Whitman's powers of imagination and description, his lack of a sense of poetic fitness, his failure to understand the business of a poet, is certainly astounding. His disqualifications in these respects are scarcely less phenomenal than those of a painter who should be insensible to shades of color, or of a draughtsman without perception of form. As the particular apostle and expounder of Nature, there is something inexplicable in his obtuseness to the existence of rhythm and cadence as elements in both Nature and the human soul. In view of his savage contempt for anything musical in poetry, it will be a fine stroke of the irony of fate if he shall be destined to be remembered only by the few pieces which are marked by the 'piano-tune' quality that he derides—the true and tender lyric of 'My Captain' and the fine poem on 'Ethiopia's Saluting the Colors.' These pieces, with the magnificent threnody on Lincoln—'When Lilacs Last in the Dooryard Bloomed'—and a few others in which there is an approach to metrical form, with fine lines and passages scattered here and there, are likely to be preserved in memory when his more characteristic pieces—those which are without form and void—shall exist only as curiosities of literature or are performing for their author the very proper function of sounding his 'barbaric yawp over the roofs of the world.' Of the more purely intellectual quality of these writings we have but little to say. It is not to our taste, even in prose, to dissociate the thing said from the manner of saying it; and such separation is quite impossible in poetry. We are aware how strongly Mr. Whitman is praised for his virility and freedom; but his virility, as applied to the purposes of poetry, seems to us not unlike what the virility of a buffalo bull might be as applied to carriage purposes, and his freedom such as might more properly be expected of an irresponsible and rampant savage. His democracy, so loudly proclaimed and oft reiterated, is of a sentimental and dramatic kind which addresses everyone with stage cries of '*Camerado*,' salutes as equal the 'Caffre, Patagonian, Hottentot, Feejeeman, Greenlander, Lapp, Austral Negro, naked, red, sooty, with protrusive lip,' and causes surprise only at his moderation in not including in his good-fellowship apes and baboons also. The grossness of Mr. Whitman's poetry is also a matter on which we do not care to dwell. In fact, some of his pieces are so very gross that it is almost indelicate to call attention to them even for purposes of condemnation. Grossness in literature is bad enough when introduced incidentally and apologetically; but when it is paraded without veil or foil, and not only toleration for it but admiration for its author's candor is demanded, it is difficult to avoid a feeling of injury and resentment. We have no wish to make this matter in any way a question of personal moral quality. We are inclined to the opinion that if Mr. Whitman had been possessed of but a little humor, his poetry would have been less immoral; and we prefer to think that it is but a part of his general lack of the sense of poetic fitness and propriety that he fails to distinguish between what is erotic in poetry and what is simply bestial. The pieces of this class are not numerous in his volume, but it would be both difficult and undesirable to express their rankness of quality. The real gems which he offers us are furnished with a most unclean and offensive setting—in disregard of the fact that selection and decoration are precisely the business of the poet. It is doubtful if there was ever before a writer, much less a poet, who showed such utter lack of taste in the selection of material. Under the plea—repeated so often as almost to discredit its sincerity—that he despises affectations and hypocrisies, and wishes to be as open and as free as Nature is, he invites us to clinical studies of men's lusts and to æsthetic considerations of carrion. The really good and beautiful things in his pages are blotched and fouled by their associations. The literary delicacies which he offers are garnished with garbage; he requires his readers to extract scattering grains of nourishment after the fashion of barnyard fowls. Perhaps his most serious error is in estimating the strength of the common poetic stomach by his own. Nature's impulses are usually unmistakable; and it is a triumph of that original Adam in man which Mr. Whitman celebrates that most unvitiated stomachs reject with involuntary but decided symptoms of disapproval the mixture of wine and bilge-water, nectar and guano, which he has compounded and for which Messrs. Osgood & Co. have consented (let us hope not without some furtive qualms and indignation of the nostrils) to become the cup-bearers.

43. A writer of almost insane violence

1882

Extract from John Nichol, *American Literature: An Historical Sketch, 1620–1880* (Edinburgh, 1882), pp. 207–11.

Mr Nichol takes up the argument against Whitman where Peter Bayne had left it seven years earlier, yet he seems to be striving towards a more balanced view of his subject, particularly in the comparison between Whitman and Blake which he adopts from Swinburne's suggestion. The 'great English poet' whose view of Whitman is criticized at the end is Swinburne (see No. 32).

John Nichol (1833–94) was a friend of Swinburne and professor of English literature at the University of Glasgow for a quarter of a century. He first wrote of Whitman in his article on American Literature in the ninth edition of the *Encyclopaedia Britannica* in 1875.

With one exception the best work of the other Western poets of note is vigorous, fresh, and rude: they think and feel better than they speak: they are eager, impatient, loud, apt to confound poetry with rhetoric, impetuosity with power; but they have contributed something distinctly new to the literature of the world. This most applies to the writer who, in the estimate of several claiming to direct modern criticisms, is the grandest single product of America.

The 'Saturday Club' of Boston is one of the choicest of social circles. There were wont to meet the leading metaphysicians, humorists, poets, and lecturers of Harvard and its neighbourhood—Dr. Howe, the recreator of Laura Bridgman; Mr. Fields, the New England Murray; Ticknor, the critic of *The Cid*; Hillard, the editor of Landor's *Hellenics*; Lowell, fresh from his *Commemoration Ode;* Bowen, dreaming over Kant; Holmes, brightest of talkers and kindliest of wits; Emerson, giving serene utterance to some careful paradox; and, at the head of the table, diffusing over it a mellow sunshine, the author of *Hiawatha*. We can imagine the door flung open wide, and bursting on this august and polished company a strange figure, tall, stalwart, and disorderly, a 'specimen of native raw material,' a cross between John the Baptist and a Cherokee Indian. We fancy him striding to the front, throwing down a bundle of manuscripts, and shouting—'The kingdom of heaven is here: I am America: I am Europe: I am Asia: I am Africa and the Polynesian Islands: I am the North Pole, and the South Pole, and the Equator: I am the Mississippi: I am Manhattan: I am the past and the future, there is no difference: I am female and male and gymnastical: I am Humanity: I am a Libertad: I sound my barbaric yawp over the roofs of the world,—

Did you ask dulcet rhymes from me,
Did you find what I sang erewhile so hard to follow, to understand?
Why, I was not singing, erewhile, for you to follow, nor am I now.
What to such as you anyhow such a poet as I, therefore leave my work
And go lull yourself with what you can understand;
For I lull nobody, and you will never understand me:—

but the daintiest of Oxford have written odes to me, and the most cynical of Cambridge. My English Editor, with all his purification of my pages—where there is nothing pure or impure, but all is immense —my Editor admits that I am "oceanic and colossal," "beyond compare the greatest of American poets . . . one of the greatest now living in any part of the world." You, what are you? Your verse is "either the poetry of an elegantly weak-sentimentalism, or at bottom nothing but maudlin puerilities, or more or less musical verbiage, arising out of a life of enervation, or else that class of plays, etc. of which the foundation is feudalism, with its ideas of lords and ladies, its imported gentility, and the manners of European high life below stairs in every line and verse."

'But listen to one of my *Drum Taps*—

Beat! beat! drums!—Blow! bugles! blow!
Through the windows—through doors—burst like a ruthless force,
Into the solemn church, and scatter the congregation;
Into the school where the scholar is studying;
Leave not the bridegroom quiet—no happiness must he have now with his bride;
Nor the peaceful farmer any peace, ploughing his field or gathering his grain;
So fierce you whirr and pound, you drums—so shrill you bugles blow.

Beat! beat! drums!—Blow! bugles! blow!
Make no parley—stop for no expostulation;
Mind not the timid—mind not the weeper or prayer;
Mind not the old man beseeching the young man;
Let not the child's voice be heard, nor the mother's entreaties;
Make even the trestles to shake the dead, where they lie awaiting the hearses,
So strong you thump, O terrible drums—so loud you bugles blow!

'Now, like Nebuchadnezzar, you shall digest a *Leaf of Grass*—

What do you see, Walt Whitman?
Who are they you salute, and that one after another salute you?
I see a great round wonder rolling through the air;
I see diminute farms, hamlets, ruins, grave-yards, jails, factories, palaces, hovels, huts of barbarians, tents of nomads, upon the surface;
I see the shaded part on one side, where the sleepers are sleeping—and the sunlit part on the other side,
I see the curious silent change of the light and shade,
I see distant lands, as real and near to the inhabitants of them as my land is to me.

I see plenteous waters;
I see mountain-peaks—I see the sierras of Andes and Alleghanies, where they range;
I see plainly the Himalayas, Chian Shahs, Altays, Ghauts;
I see the giant pinnacles of Elburz, Kazbec, Bazardjusi;
I see the Rocky Mountains, and the Peak of Winds;
I see the Styrian Alps, and the Karnac Alps;

I see the superior oceans and the inferior ones—the Atlantic and Pacific, the sea of Mexico, the Brazilian sea, and the sea of Peru,
The Japan waters, those of Hindostan, the China Sea, and the Gulf of Guinea,
The spread of the Baltic, Caspian, Bothnia, the British shores, and the Bay of Biscay,
The clear-sunned Mediterranean, and from one to another of its islands,
The inland fresh-tasted seas of North America,
The White Sea, and the sea around Greenland.

I behold the mariners of the world;
Some are in storms—some in the night, with the watch on the lookout;
Some drifting helplessly—some with contagious diseases.'

These passages, far from being perversely selected, are among the gems chosen by the poet's most enthusiastic admirer; nor do I deny that the first has merit. The second is a short section from a long diorama of names, accumulated in the same fashion.

I saw the vision of the world and all the wonder that should be

is the text and pith of the whole, amplified, by a simple process, from Lord Salisbury's large maps and a copious gazetteer, into two pages of hearing and thirteen pages of seeing: smelling, tasting, and touching are in this instance fortunately omitted; but it is by no means always so. Walt Whitman is undoubtedly a writer of great force, but he is ruined as an artist by his contempt for art—an impeachment nowise weakened by the fact that, in edition after edition, he has added and altered many times, without bettering the original scrawl. He has a teeming brain on a big body, and he tosses everything that the one or the other engenders into his powerful or monstrous book. The result is a chaos of impressions, thoughts, or feelings thrown together without rhyme, which matters little; without metre, which matters more; and often without reason, which matters much. There is no principle of prosody on which he can be harmoniously read; for, when we are merely rejoicing in the run of some discernible rhythm, a block laid across the line throws us off the rails. His words sometimes belong to no language, or they are used in a contorted sense, which is the *ne plus ultra*—of a pedantry never before found in conjunction with so much barbarism. A fervid admirer admits that he is a Democratic formalist; and, protesting against the objections taken to his views of life, confesses that

never before was high poetry so puddled and adulterated with mere doctrine in its crudest form. Never was there less assimilation of the lower dogmatic with the higher prophetic element . . . it is one thing to sing the song of all trades, and quite another to tumble down together the names of all possible crafts and implements in one unsorted heap; to sing the song of all countries is not simply to fling out on the page at random, in one howling mass, the titles of all divisions of the earth, and so leave them.

We go further than this writer—'*οὐ γὰρ πρό γε τῆς ἀληθείας τιμητέος ἀνήρ*[1]'—in reprobating this reckless manner. If Shakespeare, Keats, and Goethe are poets, Whitman is not. He *is*, in this respect, 'Athanasius contra mundum.' Nor, despite a wholesome dread of merely conventional morals, can we wholly pardon the taste of his presentation of *Nature naturans* in her most unabashed forms, or acquiesce in his audacious denial of all that civilisation has done to raise man above the savage or the chimpanzee. No considerable writer has been more devoid of the remotest sense of humour; by

[1] 'A man should not be honoured before the truth!'

consequence, no one else who has written even tolerably has perpetrated such utter absurdities. On the other hand, Whitman exhibits some genius in his perception of natural beauty, the charm of which in the *Leaves of Grass* underlies a cartload of crude Pantheism and naked Animalism, and is especially conspicuous in his descriptions of the sea. The battle-piece of sections 35–36, 'Would you hear of an old-time sea-fight', has the vigour of Tennyson's 'Revenge'; but how inferior the form! His normal excellences are his absolutely unaffected democratic philanthropy; a confidence, like Shelley's, in the world's great age beginning anew—like that of Burns, in all the dwellers on its surface being brothers at last; and his intense pathetic sympathy with his fellow-workers under every form of struggle, sickness, or sorrow. Rough, even insolent, as the man at times appears, it should not be forgotten that, during the terrible war, he went about the most dangerous fields, ministering with gentle hands to the wounded and the dying. Half the *Drum Taps* are clarions; the rest dirges or idylls, which only fall short of masterpieces because their passionate regrets are expressed in stammering speech. Few nobler laments have been written in America than *Lincoln's Burial Hymn*, the closing strophe of which gathers up the preceding images in a burst of irregular melody.

I cease for my song from thee;
From my gaze on thee in the west, fronting the west, communing with thee,
O comrade lustrous, with silver face in the night,
Yet each I keep, and all, retrievements out of the night . . .

44. Gerard Manley Hopkins on Whitman

1882

Gerard Manley Hopkins (1844–89) was born in the same year as his friend, Robert Bridges, who became the English Poet Laureate. It was owing to this friendship that Hopkins's book of poems was published many years after the author's death. He came of middle-class stock we are told. The most significant events in his life, apart from the writing of his poems, were his conversion to the Catholic Church in 1866 and his ordination to the priesthood in 1877. His poetry was highly experimental and could hardly be appreciated before the twentieth century. His reflections in this letter to Robert Bridges are those of one radical experimentalist upon another and are therefore of the highest interest and significance. We should note that Whitman, with all of his strenuous efforts at publicizing himself and his work (which may be what Hopkins is alluding to in calling him a scoundrel), did not succeed in achieving general recognition sooner than his more retiring contemporaries, Hopkins and Emily Dickinson. Real fame came to all three around the time of the First World War, the traumatic shock of which may have impelled humanity to take stock of itself and the worth of its intellectual productions during the preceding century. Concerning Hopkins's own technical explorations, Herbert Read has written:

> His originality . . . is both verbal and metrical, and perhaps the innovations he introduced into metre prevent more than anything else the appreciation of his poetry. Except for a few early poems, which need not be taken into account, practically every poem written by Hopkins presents rhythmical irregularities. The poet himself attempted a theoretical justification of these, and it is an extremely ingenious piece of work. . .

The sophistication of Hopkins's prosodic theory, whether or not it is a rationalization of the intuitive practice prompted by his own genius (as Read surmises) deserves the close attention and reflection of every student of poetry in general and of Whitman in particular.

Dearest Bridges,—I have read of Whitman's (1) 'Pete' in the library at Bedford Square (and perhaps something else; if so I forget), which you pointed out; (2) two pieces in the *Athenaeum* or *Academy*, one on the Man-of-War Bird, the other beginning 'Spirit that formed this scene'; (3) short extracts in a review by Saintsbury in the *Academy*: this is all I remember. I cannot have read more than a half a dozen pieces at most.

This, though very little, is quite enough to give a strong impression of his marked and original manner and way of thought and in particular of his rhythm. It might be even enough, I shall not deny, to originate or, much more, influence another's style: they say the French trace their whole modern school of landscape to a single piece of Constable's exhibited at the Salon early this century.

The question then is only about the fact. But first I may as well say what I should not otherwise have said, that I always knew in my heart Walt Whitman's mind to be more like my own than any other man's living. As he is a very great scoundrel that is not a pleasant confession. And this also makes me the more desirous to read him and the more determined that I will not.

Nevertheless I believe that you are quite mistaken about this piece, and that on second thoughts you will find the fancied resemblance diminish and the imitation disappear.

And first of the rhythm. Of course I saw that there was to the eye something in my long lines like this, that the one would remind people of the other. And both are in irregular rhythms. There the likeness ends. The pieces of his I read were mostly in an irregular rhythmic prose: that is what they are thought to be meant for and what they seemed to me to be. Here is a fragment of a line I remember: 'or a handkerchief designedly dropped'. This is in a dactylic rhythm—or let us say anapaestic; for it is a great convenience in English to assume that the stress is always at the end of the foot; the consequence of which assumption is that in ordinary verse there are only two English feet possible, the iamb and the anapaest, and even in my regular sprung rhythm only one additional, the fourth paeon: for convenience' sake assuming this, then the above fragment is anapaestic—'or[1] a[2] hánd[3] | ker[1]-chief[2] . . .[3] | .[1] de[2]sígn[3] | ed[1]ly[2] drópped[3]'—and there is a break down, a designed break of rhythm, after 'handkerchief', done no doubt that the line may not become downright verse, as it would be if he had said 'or a handkerchief purposely dropped'. Now you can of course say that he meant pure verse and that the foot is a paeon—'or a hánd | kerchief desígn | edly drópped'; or that he means, without fuss, what I should achieve by looping the syllable *de* and calling that foot an outriding foot—for the result might be attained either way. Here then I must make the answer which will apply here and to all like cases and to the examples which may be found up and down the poets of the use of sprung rhythm—*if they could have done it they would:* sprung rhythm, once you hear it, is so eminently natural a thing and so effective a thing that if they had known of it they would have used it. Many people, as we say, have been 'burning', but they all missed it; they took it up and mislaid it again. So far as I know—I am enquiring and presently I shall be able to speak more decidedly—it existed in full force in Anglo saxon verse and in great beauty; in a degraded and doggerel shape in *Piers Ploughman* (I am reading that famous poem and am coming to the conclusion that it is not worth reading); Greene was the last who employed it at all consciously and he never continuously; then it disappeared—for one cadence in it here and there is not sprung rhythm and one swallow does not make a spring. (I put aside Milton's case, for it is altogether singular.) In a matter like this a thing does not exist, is not *done* unless it is wittingly and willingly done; to recognise the form you are employing and to mean it is everything. To apply this: there is (I suppose, but you will know) no sign that Whitman means to use paeons or outriding feet where these breaks in rhythm occur; it seems to me a mere extravagance to think he means people to understand of themselves what they are slow to understand even when marked or pointed out. If he does not mean it then he does not do it; or in short what he means to write—and writes—is rhythmic prose and that only. And after all, you probably grant this.

Good. Now prose rhythm in English is always one of two things (allowing my convention about scanning upwards or from slack to stress and not from stress to slack)—either iambic or anapaestic. You may make a third measure (let us call it) by intermixing them. One of these three simple measures then, all iambic or all anapaestic or mingled iambic and anapaestic, is what he in every case means to write. He dreams of no other and he *means* a rugged or, as he calls it in that very piece 'Spirit that formed this scene' (which is very instructive and should be read on this very subject), a 'savage' art and rhythm.

Extremes meet, and (I must for truth's sake say what sounds pride) this savagery of his art, this rhythm in its last ruggedness and decomposition into common prose, comes near the last elaboration of mine. For that piece of mine is very highly wrought. The long lines are not rhythm run to seed: everything is weighed and timed in them. Wait till they have taken hold of your ear and you will find it so. No, but what it *is* like is the rhythm of Greek tragic choruses or of Pindar: which is pure sprung rhythm. And that has the same changes of cadence from point to point as this piece. If you want to try it, read one till you have settled the true places of the stress, mark these, then read it aloud, and you will see. Without this these choruses are prose bewitched; with it they are sprung rhythm like that piece of mine.

Besides, why did you not say *Binsey Poplars* was like Whitman? The present piece is in the same kind and vein, but developed, an advance. The lines and the stanzas (of which there are two in each poem and having much the same relation to one another) are both longer, but the two pieces are greatly alike: just look. If so how is this a being untrue to myself? I am sure it is no such thing.

The above remarks are not meant to run down Whitman. His 'savage' style has advantages, and he has chosen it; he says so. But you cannot eat your cake and keep it: he eats his offhand, I keep mine. It makes a very great difference. Neither do I deny all resemblance. In particular I noticed in 'Spirit that formed this scene' a preference for the alexandrine. I have the same preference: I came to it by degrees, I did not take it from him.

About diction the matter does not allow me so clearly to point out my independence as about rhythm. I cannot think that the present piece owes anything to him. I hope not, here especially, for it is not even spoken in my own person but in that of St. Winefred's maidens. It ought to sound like the thoughts of a good but lively girl and not at all like—not at all like Walt Whitman. But perhaps your mind may have changed by this.

I wish I had not spent so much time in defending the piece.

Believe me your affectionate friend

GERARD.

45. Swinburne on Whitmania

1887

Algernon Charles Swinburne, 'Whitmania', *Fortnightly Review* (1887). Reprinted in *The Complete Works of Algernon Charles Swinburne*, (1926), ed. Sir Edmund Gosse and Thomas James Wise, V, 307–18.

For an earlier statement by Swinburne, see No. 32.

The little-known Jephson with whom Swinburne in his last sentence chooses to compare Whitman is Robert Jephson (1736–1803), an Irish dramatist who, after serving with the British army, retired in England where he was a friend of Johnson, Goldsmith, Burke, Reynolds and other distinguished men. His plays include a tragedy *Braganza* (1775), *Conspiracy* (1796) and *The Law of Lombardy* (1779). He was also the author of *The Confessions of Jacques Baptiste Couteau*, a satire on the French revolutionaries.

The remarkable American rhapsodist who has inoculated a certain number of English readers and writers with the singular form of ethical and aesthetic rabies for which his name supplies the proper medical term of definition is usually regarded by others than Whitmaniacs as simply a blatant quack—a vehement and emphatic dunce, of incomparable vanity and volubility, inconceivable pretension and incompetence. That such is by no means altogether my own view I need scarcely take the trouble to protest. Walt Whitman has written some pages to which I have before now given praise enough to exonerate me, I should presume, from any charge of prejudice or prepossession against a writer whose claims to occasional notice and occasional respect no man can be less desirous to dispute than I am. Nor should I have thought it necessary to comment on the symptoms of a disorder which happily is not likely to become epidemic in an island or on a continent not utterly barren of poetry, had the sufferers not given such painfully singular signs of inability to realise a condition only too obvious to the compassionate bystander. While the preachers or the proselytes of the gospel according to Whitman were content to admit that he was either no poet at all, or the only poet who had ever been born into this world—that those who accepted him were bound to reject all others as nullities—they had at least the merit of irrefragable logic; they could claim at least the credit of indisputable consistency. But when other gods or godlings are accepted as participants in the divine nature; when his temple is transformed into a pantheon, and a place assigned his godhead a little beneath Shakespeare, a little above Dante, or cheek by jowl with Homer; when Isaiah and Æschylus, for anything we know, may be admitted to a greater or lesser share in his incommunicable and indivisible supremacy—then, indeed, it is high time to enter a strenuous and (if it be possible) a serious protest. The first apostles alone were the depositaries of the pure and perfect evangel: these later and comparatively heterodox disciples have adulterated and debased the genuine metal of absolute, coherent, unalloyed and unqualified nonsense.

To the better qualities discernible in the voluminous and incoherent effusions of Walt Whitman it should not be difficult for any reader not unduly exasperated by the rabid idiocy of the Whitmaniacs to do full and ample justice: for these qualities are no less simple and obvious than laudable and valuable. A just enthusiasm, a genuine passion of patriotic and imaginative sympathy, a sincere though limited and distorted love of nature, an eager and earnest faith in freedom and in loyalty—in the loyalty that can only be born of liberty; a really manful and a nobly rational tone of mind with regard to the crowning questions of duty and of death; these excellent qualities of emotion and reflection find here and there a not inadequate expression in a style of rhetoric not always flatulent or inharmonious. Originality of matter or of manner, of structure or of thought, it would be equally difficult for any reader not endowed with a quite exceptional gift of ignorance or of hebetude to discover in any part of Mr. Whitman's political or ethical or physical or proverbial philosophy. But he has said wise and noble things upon such simple and eternal subjects as life and death, pity and enmity, friendship and fighting; and even the intensely conventional nature of its elaborate and artificial simplicity should not be allowed, by a magnanimous and candid reader, too absolutely to eclipse the genuine energy and the occasional beauty of his feverish and convulsive style of writing.

All this may be cordially conceded by the lovers of good work in any kind, however imperfect, incomposite, and infirm; and more than this the present writer at any rate most decidedly never intended to convey by any tribute of sympathy or admiration which may have earned for him the wholly unmerited honour of an imaginary enlistment in the noble army of Whitmaniacs. He has therefore no palinode to chant, no recantation to intone; for if it seems and is unreasonable to attribute a capacity of thought to one who has never given any sign of thinking, a faculty of song to one who has never shown ability to sing, it must be remembered, on the other hand, that such qualities of energetic emotion and sonorous expression as distinguish the happier moments and the more sincere inspirations of such writers as Whitman or as Byron have always, in common parlance, been allowed to pass muster and do duty for the faculty of thinking or the capacity of singing. Such an use of common terms is doubtless inaccurate and inexact, if judged by the 'just but severe law' of logical definition or of mathematical precision: but such abuse or misuse of plain words is generally understood as conveying no more than a conventional import such as may be expressed by the terms with which we subscribe an ordinary letter, or by the formula through which we decline an untimely visit. Assuredly I never have meant to imply what most assuredly I never have said—that I regarded Mr. Whitman as a poet or a thinker in the proper sense; the sense in which the one term is applicable to Coleridge or to Shelley, the other to Bacon or to Mill. Whoever may have abdicated his natural right, as a being not born without a sense of music or a sense of reason, to protest against the judgment which discerns in 'Childe Harold' or in 'Drum-Taps' a masterpiece of imagination and expression, of intelligence or of song, I never have abdicated mine. The highest literary quality discoverable in either book is rhetoric: and very excellent rhetoric in either case it sometimes is; what it is at other times I see no present necessity to say. But Whitmaniacs and Byronites have yet to learn that if rhetoric were poetry John Bright would be a poet at least equal to John Milton, Demosthenes to Sophocles, and Cicero to Catullus. Poetry may be something more—I certainly am not concerned to deny it—than an art or a science; but not because it is not, strictly speaking, a science or an art. There is a science of verse as surely as there is a science of mathematics: there is an art of expression by metre as certainly as there is an art of representation by painting. To some poets the understanding of this science, the mastery of this art, would seem to come by a natural instinct which needs nothing but practice for its development, its application, and its perfection: others by patient and conscientious study of their own abilities attain a no less unmistakable and a scarcely less admirable success. But the man of genius and the dullard who cannot write good verse are equally out of the running. 'Did you ask dulcet rhymes from me?' inquires Mr. Whitman of some extraordinary if not imaginary interlocutor; and proceeds, with some not ineffective energy of expression, to explain that 'I lull nobody—and you will never understand me.' No, my dear good sir—or camerado, if that be the more courteous and conventional address (a modest reader might deferentially reply): not in the wildest visions of a distempered slumber could I ever have dreamed of doing anything of the kind. Nor do we ask them even from such other and inferior scribes or bards as the humble Homer, the modest Milton, or the obsolete and narrow-minded Shakespeare —poets of sickly feudality, of hidebound classicism, of effete and barbarous incompetence. But metre, rhythm, cadence not merely appreciable but definable and reducible to rule and measurement, though we do not expect from you, we demand from all who claim, we discern in the works of all who have achieved, any place among poets of any class whatsoever. The question whether your work is in any sense poetry has no more to do with dulcet rhymes than with the differential calculus. The question is whether you have any more right to call yourself a poet, or to be called a poet by any man who knows verse from prose, or black from white, or speech from silence, or his right hand from his left, than to call yourself or to be called, on the strength of your published writings, a mathematician, a logician, a painter, a political economist, a sculptor, a dynamiter, an old parliamentary hand, a civil engineer, a dealer in marine stores, an amphimacer, a triptych, a rhomboid, or a rectangular parallelogram. 'Vois-tu bien, tu es baron comme ma pantoufle!'[1] said old Gillenormand—the creature of one who was indeed a creator or a poet:[2] and the humblest of critics who knows any one thing from any one other thing has a right to say to the man who offers as poetry what the exuberant incontinence of a Whitman presents for our acceptance, 'Tu es poète comme mon—soulier.'

But the student has other and better evidence than any merely negative indication of impotence in the case of the American as in the case of the British despiser and disclaimer of so pitiful a profession or

[1] 'See here, you're about as much of a baron as my shoe is!'

[2] The poet is Victor Hugo; Gillenormand is a character in *Les Misérables*.

ambition as that of a versifier. Mr. Carlyle and Mr. Whitman have both been good enough to try their hands at lyric verse: and the ear which has once absorbed their dulcet rhymes will never need to be reminded of the reason for their contemptuous abhorrence of a diversion so contemptible as the art of Coleridge and Shelley.

> Out of eternity
>   This new day is born:
> Into eternity
>   This day shall return.

Such were the flute notes of Diogenes Devilsdung: comparable by those who would verify the value of his estimate with any stanza of Shelley's 'To a Skylark.' And here is a sample of the dulcet rhymes which a most tragic occasion succeeded in evoking from the orotund oratist of Manhattan:—

> The port is near, the bells I hear, the people all exulting,
> *While follow eyes the steady keel*, the vessel grim and daring;
>
> For you bouquets and ribbon'd wreaths—for you the shores a-crowding; (*sic*)
> For you they call, the surging mass, their eager faces turning.

Ἰοὺ ἰού, ὤ ὤ κακά.[1] Upon the whole, I prefer Burns—or Hogg—to Carlyle, and Dibdin—or Catnach—to Whitman.

A pedantic writer of poems distilled from other poems (which, as the immortal author of the imperishable *Leaves of Grass* is well aware, must 'pass away')—a Wordsworth, for example, or a Tennyson—would hardly have made 'eyes' follow the verb they must be supposed to govern. Nor would a poor creature whose ear was yet unattuned to the cadence of 'chants democratic' have permitted his Pegasus so remarkable a capriole as to result in the rhythmic reverberation of such rhymes as these. When a boy who remains unable after many efforts to cross the Asses' Bridge expresses his opinion that Euclid was a beastly old fool, his obviously impartial verdict is generally received by his elders with exactly the same amount of respectful attention as is accorded by any competent reader to the equally valuable and judicial deliverances of Messrs. Whitman, Emerson, and Carlyle on the subject of poetry—that is, of lyrical or creative literature. The first critic of our time—perhaps the largest-minded and surest-sighted of any age—has pointed out, in an essay on poetry which should not be too long left buried in the columns of the *Encyclopædia Britannica*, the

1 'Alas, Alas, ah ah troubles!'

exhaustive accuracy of the Greek terms which define every claimant to the laurel as either a singer or a maker. There is no third term, as there is no third class. If then it appears that Mr. Walt Whitman has about as much gift of song as his precursors and apparent models in rhythmic structure and style, Mr. James Macpherson and Mr. Martin Tupper, his capacity for creation is the only thing that remains for us to consider. And on that score we find him, beyond all question, rather like the later than like the earlier of his masters. Macpherson could at least evoke shadows: Mr. Tupper and Mr. Whitman can only accumulate words. As to his originality in the matter of free speaking, it need only be observed that no remarkable mental gift is requisite to qualify man or woman for membership of a sect mentioned by Dr. Johnson—the Adamites, who believed in the virtue of public nudity. If those worthies claimed the right to bid their children run about the streets stark naked, the magistrate, observed Johnson, 'would have a right to flog them into their doublets'; a right no plainer than the right of common sense and sound criticism to flog the Whitmaniacs into their strait-waistcoats; or, were there any female members of such a sect, into their straight-petticoats. If nothing that concerns the physical organism of men or of women is common or unclean or improper for literary manipulation, it may be maintained, by others than the disciples of a contemporary French novelist who has amply proved the sincerity of his own opinion to that effect, that it is not beyond the province of literature to describe with realistic exuberance of detail the functions of digestion or indigestion in all its processes—the objects and the results of an aperient or an emetic medicine. Into 'the troughs of Zolaism,' as Lord Tennyson calls them (a phrase which bears rather unduly hard on the quadrupedal pig), I am happy to believe that Mr. Whitman has never dipped a passing nose: he is a writer of something occasionally like English, and a man of something occasionally like genius. But in his treatment of topics usually regarded as no less unfit for public exposition and literary illustration than those which have obtained notoriety for the would-be bastard of Balzac—the Davenant of the (French) prose Shakespeare—he has contrived to make 'the way of a man with a maid' (Proverbs xxx. 19) almost as loathsomely ludicrous and almost as ludicrously loathsome—I speak merely of the æsthetic or literary aspect of his effusions—as the Swiftian or Zolaesque enthusiasm of bestiality which insists on handling what 'goeth into the belly, and is cast out into the draught' (St. Matthew xv. 17). The Zolas and the Whitmen, to whom nothing, absolutely and literally nothing, is unclean or common, have an obvious and incalculable advantage over the unconverted who have never enjoyed the privilege of a vision like St. Peter's, and received the benefit of a supernatural prohibition to call anything common or unclean. They cannot possibly be exposed, and they cannot possibly be put to shame: for that best of all imaginable reasons which makes it proverbially difficult to 'take the breeks off a Highlander.'

It would really seem as though, in literary and other matters, the very plainness and certitude of a principle made it doubly necessary for those who maintain it to enforce and reinforce it over and over again; as though, the more obvious it were, the more it needed indication and demonstration, assertion and reassertion. There is no more important, no more radical and fundamental truth of criticism than this: that, in poetry perhaps above all other arts, the method of treatment, the manner of touch, the tone of expression, is the first and last thing to be considered. There is no subject which may not be treated with success (I do not say there are no subjects which on other than artistic grounds it may not be as well to avoid, it may not be better to pass by) if the poet, by instinct or by training, knows exactly how to handle it aright, to present it without danger of just or rational offence. For evidence of this truth we need look no further than the pastorals of Virgil and Theocritus. But under the dirty clumsy paws of a harper whose plectrum is a muck-rake any tune will become a chaos of discords, though the motive of the tune should be the first principle of nature—the passion of man for woman or the passion of woman for man. And the unhealthily demonstrative and obtrusive animalism of the Whitmaniad is as unnatural, as incompatible with the wholesome instincts of human passion, as even the filthy and inhuman asceticism of SS. Macarius and Simeon Stylites. If anything can justify the serious and deliberate display of merely physical emotion in literature or in art, it must be one of two things: intense depth of feeling expressed with inspired perfection of simplicity, with divine sublimity of fascination, as by Sappho; or transcendent supremacy of actual and irresistible beauty in such revelation of naked nature as was possible to Titian. But Mr. Whitman's Eve is a drunken apple-woman, indecently sprawling in the slush and garbage of the gutter amid the rotten refuse of her overturned fruit-stall: but Mr. Whitman's Venus is a Hottentot wench under the influence of cantharides and adulterated rum. Cotytto herself would repudiate the ministration of such priestesses as these.

But what then, if anything, is it that a rational creature who has studied and understood the work of any poet, great or small, from Homer down to Moschus, from Lucretius down to Martial, from Dante down to Metastasio, from Villon down to Voltaire, from Shakespeare down to Byron, can find to applaud, to approve, or to condone in the work of Mr. Whitman? To this very reasonable and inevitable question the answer is not far to seek. I have myself repeatedly pointed out—it may be (I have often been told so) with too unqualified sympathy and too uncritical enthusiasm—the qualities which give a certain touch of greatness to his work, the sources of inspiration which infuse into its chaotic jargon some passing or seeming notes of cosmic beauty, and diversify with something of occasional harmony the strident and barren discord of its jarring and erring atoms. His sympathies, I repeat, are usually generous, his views of life are occasionally just, and his views of death are invariably noble. In other words, he generally means well, having a good stock on hand of honest emotion; he sometimes sees well, having a natural sensibility to such aspects of nature as appeal to an eye rather quick than penetrating; he seldom writes well, being cabined, cribbed, confined, bound in, to the limits of a thoroughly unnatural, imitative, histrionic and affected style. But there is a thrilling and fiery force in his finest bursts of gusty rhetoric which makes us wonder whether with a little more sense and a good deal more cultivation he might not have made a noticeable orator. As a poet, no amount of improvement that self-knowledge and self-culture might have brought to bear upon such exceptionally raw material could ever have raised him higher than a station to which his homely and manly patriotism would be the best claim that could be preferred for him; a seat beside such writers as Ebenezer Elliot—or possibly a little higher, on such an elevation as might be occupied by a poet whom careful training had reared and matured into a rather inferior kind of Southey. But to fit himself for such promotion he would have in the first place to resign all claim to the laurels of Gotham, with which the critical sages of that famous borough have bedecked his unbashful brows; he would have to recognise that he is no more, in the proper sense of the word, a poet, than Communalists or Dissolutionists are, in any sense of the word, Republicans; that he has exactly as much claim to a place beside Dante as any Vermersch or Vermorel or other verminous and murderous muck-worm of the Parisian Commune to a place beside Mazzini; in other words, that the informing principle of his work is not so much the negation as the contradiction of the creative principle of poetry. And this it is not to be expected that such a man should bring himself to believe, as long as he hears himself proclaimed the inheritor of a seat assigned a hundred years ago by the fantastic adulation of more or less distinguished literary eccentricities to a person of the name of Jephson—whose triumphs as a tragic poet made his admirers tremble for Shakespeare.

46. Knut Hamsun on Whitman

1889

'The Primitive Poet, Walt Whitman', translated by Evie Allison Allen, in *Walt Whitman Abroad* (1955), ed. Gay Wilson Allen, pp. 112–23 (reprinted by permission of the translator and the editor).

Allen states: 'Title supplied by the editor. This essay was an expansion of an address Hamsun gave in the Copenhagen Student Union during the winter of 1889, and published in *Fra det moderne Amerikas Aandsliv*, Copenhagen, 1889, pp. 63–85.'

Knut Hamsun (1859–1952), Norwegian novelist, was born the son of poor parents. He started to write when he was nineteen at a time when he was a shoemaker's apprentice. Later he earned his livelihood as coal trimmer and country schoolmaster. He eventually went to America where he became a streetcar conductor in the city of Chicago. His bad impressions of America may be, at least in part, responsible for the vehemence of his attack upon Whitman. In 1888, he published, in a Danish magazine, the fragment of a novel, which was later translated into English and became well-known under the title *Hunger*. The work immediately attracted attention because of the beauty of its style and originality of treatment. In his attraction to the analysis of psychologically morbid types of character, he is said to resemble the Russians. His best known work perhaps is *Growth of the Soil*. In 1920, he received the Nobel Prize for Literature. His collaboration with the German occupation forces in Norway during the Second World War helped to embitter the last years of his life. It is only quite recently that a revival of interest in his works has become noticeable in America. Among the unfavourable responses evoked by Whitman, Hamsun's seems to me the wittiest and, in some respects, the weightiest. I like to imagine Whitman himself who, though he is sometimes denied the quality of humour by his critics (like

Wordsworth and Milton in this respect), once hazarded the guess to a friend that he might go down to posterity wearing 'the cap and bells of a jester', enjoying some of the keenly humorous and satiric thrusts of Hamsun.

In 1855 a book was published in Boston which evoked a letter from Emerson, a reprint in London and an essay by Rudolf Schmidt. The book was called *Leaves of Grass* and the author, Walt Whitman. When this book appeared Whitman was thirty-six years old.

The author called the work poetry; Rudolf Schmidt also called it poetry; Emerson, on the contrary, had plainly not been able to hit on any designation for this work with its extremely weak system of thought. In reality it is not poetry at all; no more than the multiplication tables are poetry. It is composed in pure prose, without meter or rhyme. The only way in which it resembles verse is that one line may have one, two, or three words, the next twenty-eight, thirty-five, or literally up to forty-three words.

The author called himself a 'cosmos'; Rudolf Schmidt called him a 'cosmos'. I, on the other hand, can only with difficulty find any connection with a term so extremely comprehensive, so that for my part he could equally well be a cosmos, a pigeon-hole, or anything else. I will modestly and simply call Walt Whitman a savage. He is a voice of nature in an uncultivated, primitive land.

He is somewhat of an Indian both in his language and emotions; and, accordingly, he celebrates the sea, the air, the earth, the grass, the mountains, the rivers, in brief, the natural elements. He always calls Long Island, his birthplace, by its Indian name, Paumanok; he constantly uses the Indian term *maize* instead of the English *corn*. Again and again he refers to American places—even whole states—by Indian names; in his poetry there are entire stanzas of American aboriginal names. He feels so moved by the primitive music of these places that he crams long series of them into passages where they have no connection whatever with the text; often he mentions a score of state names in a row without saying a word about the states. It is a pretentious game with savage words. One of his poems goes thus:

From Paumanok starting I fly like a bird,
Around and around to soar to sing the idea of all,
To the north betaking myself to sing there arctic songs,

To Kanada till I absorb Kanada in myself, to Michigan then,
To Wisconsin, Iowa, Minnesota, to sing their songs,
(they are inimitable;)
Then to Ohio and Indiana to sing theirs, to Missouri and Kansas and Arkansas to sing theirs,
To Tennessee and Kentucky, to the Carolinas and Georgia to sing theirs,
To Texas and so along up toward California, to roam accepted everywhere;
To sing first (to the tap of the war-drum if need be).
The idea of all, of the Western world one and inseparable,
And then the song of each member of these States.

The innate primitiveness of his nature, the barbaric Indian feeling of kinship with the elements about him, is expressed everywhere in his book and often bursts into brilliant flame. When the wind whispers or an animal howls, it seems to him that he hears a group of Indian names. He says:

... sounds of rain and winds, calls as of birds and animals in the woods, syllabled to us for names,

Okonee, Koosa, Ottawa, Monongahela, Sauk, Natchez, Chattahoochee, Kaqueta, Oronoco,
Wabash, Miami, Saginaw, Chippewa, Oshkosh, Walla-Walla,
Leaving such to the States they melt, they depart, charging the water and the land with names.

It requires at least twice as much inspiration to read such verse as it does to write it.

His style is not English: his style belongs to no culture. His style is the difficult Indian picture-writing, without the pictures, influenced by the ponderous and hard to comprehend Old Testament. His language rolls heavily and confusedly over the pages of his book, roaring along with columns of words, regiments of words, each one of which makes the poem more unintelligible than the other. He has poems which are completely grandiose in their unreadableness. In one of them, an unusually profound poem in three lines, over half of which is in parentheses, he 'sings' as follows:

Still though the one I sing
(One, yet of contradictions made,) I dedicate to Nationality,
I leave in him revolt, (O latent right of insurrection!
O quenchless, indispensable fire!)

That could just as well be a birthday greeting as an Easter hymn. It could as easily be a poem as a rule of three. However, we refuse to believe that in this primitive poem the author means to sing that he is a patriot and at the same time a complete rebel.

O'Connor said that one must have seen Whitman to understand his book; Bucke, Conway, and Rhys also say that one must have seen him first to be able to understand his book. But it seems to me that the impression of dream-like barbarianism one gets from reading *Leaves of Grass* would be strengthened rather than weakened by seeing the author. He is certainly the last specimen of a modern man who was born a savage.

Thirty or forty years ago people in New York, Boston, New Orleans, and later Washington met on the streets a man of unusually powerful physique, a large, serene man of somewhat crude appearance, always dressed in careless fashion, reminding one of a mechanic, or a sailor, or some other workman. He almost always went without a coat, often without a hat; in warm weather he kept to the sunny side of the street and let the sun beat down on his great head. His features were large but handsome; he had at once a proud and benign expression; his blue eyes were gentle. He frequently spoke to passersby whether he knew them or not; sometimes tapped strange men on the shoulder. He never laughed; usually he wore gray clothes, which were always clean but often lacked buttons; he wore colored shirts and a white paper collar about his neck. Such was the appearance of Whitman at that time.

Now he is a sick old man of seventy years. I have seen a picture of him taken a few years ago. As usual he is in shirt-sleeves; as usual he inappropriately has on his hat. His face is large and handsome, his thick hair and beard, which he never cut, cascade over his shoulders and chest. On the forefinger of his extended hand he holds an artificial butterfly with wings outstretched; he sits and observes it.

These portraits of Whitman do not civilize his book; as a literary production it is a poetic desecration. Some people have wanted to regard him as the American folk-poet. This can only be considered ironical. He lacks all the unity and simplicity of a folk-poet. His primitive emotions ante-date those of the people. And his language is not calm but raucous power; it mounts now and then to high orchestral outbursts, frightful shouts of victory which remind the stunned reader of Indian war dances. And everywhere, on closer inspection, we find it is only a wild carnival of words. The author made a great effort to express something in his poems but he could not get it said for the words. He has poems which consist of almost nothing except names, poems of which single lines could be used as titles for poems:

Americanos! conquerors! etc.

> Chants of the prairies,
> Chants of the long-running Mississippi, and down to the Mexican sea,
> Chants of Ohio, Indiana, Illinois, Iowa, Wisconsin and Minnesota,
> Chants going forth from the centre of Kansas, and thence equidistant,
> Shooting in pulses of fire ceaseless to vivify all.

End! In the next poem [section of the poem] he talks of something entirely different; in the next poem [*sic*] he records how he 'in old times' sat 'studying at the feet of the great masters', but now the old masters 'might return and study me'. When we consider that he puts first among the old masters, Christ, Socrates, and Plato, it is understandable that a civilized reader of the poem feels a little incredulous.

It was obviously the long series and groups of repeated names and terms in Whitman's poetry which aroused the interest of Emerson and the English authors. These repetitions, catalogic columns, are absolutely the most unique and original quality of his poetry. They are literary phenomena. They are without parallel. His whole book is stuffed full of these lists. In a poem of twelve sections, 'Song of the Broad-Axe,' there is scarcely a stanza that does not have a catalogue. One section reads thus:

> Welcome are all earth's lands, each for its kind,
> Welcome are lands of pine and oak,
> Welcome are lands of the lemon and fig,
> Welcome are lands of gold,
> Welcome are lands of wheat and maize, welcome those of the grape,
> Welcome are lands of sugar and rice,
> Welcome are the cotton-lands, welcome those of the white potato and sweet potato,
> Welcome are mountains, flats, sands, forests, prairies,
> Welcome are the rich borders of rivers, table-lands, openings,
> Welcome the measureless grazing lands, welcome the teeming soil of orchards, flax, honey, hemp;
> Welcome just as much the other more hard-faced lands,
> Lands rich as lands of gold or wheat and fruit lands,
> Lands of mines, lands of the manly and rugged ores,
> Lands of coal, copper, lead, tin, zinc,
> Lands of iron—lands of the make of the axe.

The ninth section of the same catalogic poem begins with one of the author's usual incomprehensible parentheses and continues:

(America! I do not vaunt my love for you,
I have what I have.)

The axe leaps!
The solid forest gives fluid utterances,
They tumble forth, they rise and form,
Hut, tent, landing, survey,
Flail, plough, pick, crowbar, spade,
Shingle, rail, prop, wainscot, jamb, lath, panel, gable,
Citadel, ceiling, saloon, academy, organ, exhibition-house, library,
Cornice, trellis, pilaster, balcony, window, turret, porch,
Hoe, rake, pitchfork, pencil, wagon, staff, saw, jack-plane, mallet, wedge, rounce,
Chair, tub, hoop, table, wicket, vane, sash, floor,
Work-box, chest, string'd instrument, boat, frame, and what not,
Capitols of States, and capitol of the nation of States,
Long stately rows in avenues, hospitals for orphans or for the poor or sick,
Manhattan steamboats and clippers taking the measure of all the seas.

It is heresy to say it, perhaps almost blasphemy, but I confess that in the darkness of night when I could not sleep and yielded to the impulse to think of writing poetry, it has happened that I had to grit my teeth in order not to say frankly: I could write poetry like that too!

What did Whitman want? Did he want to abolish the slave trade in Africa or forbid the use of walking sticks? Did he want to build a new school house in Wyoming or introduce woolen hunting jackets? No one knows! In the art of talking much and saying absolutely nothing I have never met his equal. His words are warm; they glow; there is passion, power, enthusiasm in his verse. One hears this desperate word music and feels his breast heave. But one does not know why he is enthusiastic. Thunder rolls through the whole book and lightning flashes; but the spark never comes. One reads page after page and is not able to find the meaning of anything. One is confused or intoxicated by these enthusiastic word-tables; one is paralyzed; crushed to earth in stupid hopelessness; their eternal unending monotony finally affects the reader's understanding. By the time one has read the last poem one cannot count to four. One really stands before an author who strains an ordinary person's mentality. The poet merely went along the road ('Song of the Open Road') and felt himself overcome by ecstasy—'the road shall be more to me than my poems'—and afterwards as he wandered on this often-mentioned road, he found 'divine things well envelop'd.' He was like the man of the desert who waked one morning at an oasis and fell into a revery as he looked at the grass. 'I swear to you there are divine things more beautiful than words can tell,' he exclaims constantly in regard to this road which he mentions over and over again. But he never expresses the divine things, so does not make the reader any wiser.

Even with the author's own picture vividly before the eyes, *Leaves of Grass* is still like 'unspeakable' darkness for the poor reader, like a book without pictures. It is perhaps highly doubtful whether one could understand the poems better if one actually knew the poet. At most he personally might explain what he meant by his various catalogues; however, they were not expressed in understandable words but remain in writing which supposedly contains 'songs'. Moreover, according to his own and his biographer's account, Whitman meant to celebrate Democracy in his book. He is 'the poet of Democracy.' Furthermore, he is also, according to Rhys, the 'Poet of the Universe'; so one must presume the singer is a highly gifted man. One does not fail to observe that at times he must have had difficult problems with his catalogues.

How is he 'the poet of Democracy'? In 'I Hear America Singing,' which is a program-poem, he is the poet of democracy in the following manner and fashion:

I hear America singing, the varied carols I hear,
Those of mechanics, each one singing his as it should be blithe and strong.
The carpenter singing his as he measures his plank or beam,
The mason singing his as he makes ready for work, or leaves off work,
The boatman singing what belongs to him in his boat, the deckhand singing on the steamboat deck,
The shoemaker singing as he sits on his bench, and hatter singing as he stands,
The wood-cutter's song, the ploughboy's on his way in the morning, or at the noon intermission or at sundown,
The delicious singing of the mother, or of the young wife at work, or of the girl sewing or washing,
Each singing what belongs to him or her and to none else,
The day what belongs to the day—at night the party of young fellows, robust, friendly,
Singing with open mouths their strong melodious songs.

In this poem he forgot, if meter means anything, to count at all; and if verse is all-inclusive, he forgot to hear saddlers or streetcar conductors, or general managers sing! If a poet of democracy here at home wrote such a poem—whether it was about a shoemaker who sings as he sits on his bench or a hatter who sings as he stands—and brought it to a newspaper or the Danish editor of an almanac, I venture to believe that they would want to feel the singer's pulse and maybe offer him a glass of water. If he refused to admit that he was ill, one would at least feel that he jested very crudely.

Walt Whitman is a gifted American lyricist; as such he is a rare phenomenon. He has read little or nothing and had less experience with life. Little has happened to him. He was born in 1819; at twenty he was cheated of his betrothed; during the war over slavery he was a nurse; in 1868 he was discharged from his position in the Department of the Interior but was later taken back again; in 1873 his mother died and at the same time, according to his own statement, something in him died. This is his life story in brief. Besides *Leaves of Grass* he has written and published a few other things, among them *Specimen Days and Collect* and *Democratic Vistas*, which, however, have in no way strengthened his position in literary history. When Whitman's name is mentioned it is in connection with *Leaves of Grass*; his essays are not read and are in part unreadable.

If he had been born in a land of culture and been intelligently educated, he might possibly have been a little Wagner; his spirit is sensitive and his disposition musical; but born in America, that remote corner of the world where he could always shout Hurrah and where the only recognized talent is salesmanship, he had to be a changeling, a mixture of primitive being and modern man. 'In our country,' says the American author, Nathaniel Hawthorne, 'there is no shadow, no antiquity, no mystery, no picturesque and gloomy wrong.' For an original primitive like Whitman his innate inclination is to do more or less primitive reading; thus for him reading the Bible is the highest poetic enjoyment; in this way he undoubtedly developed his savage tendencies more than he repressed them. Everywhere in his poetry the language and the imagery of the Bible reappear; in places the similarity to the Bible is so striking that we must almost marvel at the completeness with which he has been able to assimilate such a peculiar form. In 'Song of the Answerer' he says:

A young man comes to me bearing a message from his brother,
How shall the young man know the whether and when of his brother?
Tell him to send me the signs

And I stand before the young man face to face, and take his right hand in my left hand and his left hand in my right hand,
And I answer for his brother and for men, and I answer for him that answers for all, and send these signs . . .

Doesn't that read like an excerpt from one of the Old Testament writers? Whitman's constant study of biblical poetry has certainly increased his literary boldness, so that he frankly mentions things that are tabu. He is modern in so far as he always writes brutally with the intense literalness felt and thought by uncultivated minds. But it is scarcely because of any conscious feeling of artistic courage that he has poeticised Reality; it is much more the result of the naivete of a child of nature. The section of erotic poems in *Leaves of Grass* for which he has been censured and about which supercilious Bostonians shouted to heaven, in reality contains nothing more than can be said with impunity in any literature; it is another matter entirely that the audaciousness is rather crudely, illiterately spoken, as it certainly is. With somewhat less naivete and a little less biblical influence, one could say twice as much as he says and give it double the literary value merely by a superficial use of literary dexterity, such as shifting a word here, revising another there, deleting a vulgarity and replacing it with an acceptable term. The language in Whitman's poetry is by far the boldest and warmest in all literature, but in the main it is naive and lacking in taste.

Walt Whitman's naivete is so incongruously great that it can actually be captivating, and now and then the reader can put up with it. It is this strange naivete which has won him a few disciples among *men of letters.* His catalogues, those impossible reiterations of persons, states, household furniture, tools, articles of dress are certainly the most naive poetry with which a literature has yet been augmented, and had it not been sung from a naive heart, it would certainly never have been read, because it shows not a vestige of talent. When Whitman celebrates something he says so in the first line, then mentions another thing in the second line and a third in the next line, without celebrating any of them except by mentioning them. He knows no more of things than the names, but he knows many names—hence all the enthusiastic name-calling. His disposition is too impatient, his thought too uneducated to grasp the single idea long enough to celebrate it; he pictures life on parade, not the fine variety of individual things but all the noisy multiplicity of things; he always sees masses. One can open the book anywhere and search any page only to find everywhere that he says he will celebrate this or that thing, which he ultimately only mentions. In this connection his little three-line poem called 'Farm Picture' is interesting. Here, according to the nature of the theme, he needed to describe, to picture, and he did it thus:

Through the ample open door of the peaceful country barn,
A sunlit pasture field with cattle and horse feeding,
And haze and vista, and far horizon fading away.

The end! That is his farm picture. Barn, country, meadow, cattle, horses, haze, vista, horizon. That the door is wide and the barn admirably peaceful, that the country is sunny at the same time that it is hazy, and hazy at the same time there is a vista—and finally the horizon fading away—it is a 'description' which a reader can remember a year and a day! Whitman's incomprehensible naivete seduced him into putting his poetry into print; his naivete led him further to believe that he had produced a new and sorely needed type of poetry. In many of his poems he comes back to that. He exclaims in one place:

Shut not your doors to me proud libraries,
For that which was lacking on all your well-fill'd shelves, yet needed most, I bring.

There is no doubt in his mind as to his special mission as an author.

This good man's naivete is so fresh and amiable, so fundamentally the nature of primitive man that it never gives the impression of conceit. Even in places where it is most blatantly expressed and least motivated, one does not have the feeling of standing before a vain person. He is a good fellow, this man; one feels as if one were arm in arm with him as the poet sings his lists of household furniture. In 'By Blue Ontario Shore' [*sic*] he undertakes to 'chant a poem that comes from the soul of America,' which likewise would be 'a carol of victory,' also a song 'of the throes of Democracy.' After having struggled through fourteen heavy strophes with that complex task, after having for the ninety-ninth time ransacked 'Missouri, Nebraska and Kansas' as well as 'Chicago, Kanada and Arkansas,' he suddenly pulls up and stops short. He has finally come to a conclusion; he dips his pen and writes:

I swear I begin to see the meaning of these things,
It is not the earth, it is not America who is so great,
It is I who am great or to be great . . .

At last he says that America is himself:

America isolated yet embodying all, what is it finally except myself?
These States, what are they except myself?

And yet there is no impression of arrogant conceit; it is only naivete, a wild, boisterous naivete.

Among the poems which Whitman has collected under the title of *Calamus* are to be found the best in the book. Here he sings of the love for men which beats strongly in his good warm breast and occasionally finds an echo in others. Through 'love of Comrades' he will rejuvenate the corrupt American democracy; by it he will 'make the continent indissoluble'; 'make inseparable cities with their arms about each other's necks'; 'make the most splendid race the sun ever shone upon'; 'plant companionship thick as trees along all the rivers.' There occur isolated coherent passages in these poems; they stand out therefore as strange exceptions in his book. His primitively unrestrained emotional nature is here expressed in somewhat civilized English, which is thus intelligible even to his compatriots. In a poem entitled 'Sometimes With One I Love' he is so extraordinarily clear that, in surprise, one supposes these two or three lines must have been written by his mother or some other intelligent person:

Sometimes with one I love I fill myself with rage for fear I effuse unreturn'd love,
But now I think there is no unreturn'd love, the pay is certain one way or another,
(I loved a certain person ardently and my love was not return'd,
Yet out of that I have written these songs.)

Here—if we overlook the author's break in rhythm in the first and second lines—we can find a comprehensible thought expressed in intelligible language—actually in language which, remembering that it is lyrical, is used legitimately; but he cannot restrain himself long; a few lines further he is again the incomprehensible savage. In one poem he indicates in all seriousness that he is personally present with each individual reader of his book; 'Be not too certain but I am now with you,' he warns. In the next poem ['That Shadow My Likeness'] he lapsed into despair concerning Walt Whitman's shadow:

That shadow . . .
How often I find myself standing and looking at it where it flits,
How often I question and doubt whether it is really me; . . .

It seems to me that this doubt is not wholly unjustified; always one is endowed with a shadow which can fly while one stands and watches.

Whitman is a very genial person, a man of native capacity, born too late. In 'Song of the Open Road' he plainly reveals what a benevolent disposition he has, mingled with all the naivete of his ideas. If his verse were written in a little more regular style, much of it would be poetry;

on the other hand, it is novel for an author to continually hinder the understanding of his poetry because of the incomprehensible word-mechanism he uses. He cannot say a thing once emphatically; he is incapable of making a point. He says a thing five times and always in the same grand but meaningless way. He does not control his material, he lets it control him; that is evident in his colossal form which accumulates and overwhelms him. In all this song of the highway his heart is warmer than his brain is cool; therefore he can neither describe nor celebrate; he can only exult—exult in wild outbursts over everything and nothing. One feels a heart beating violently in the pages of his book, but one seeks in vain for a probable reason why that heart has been so strongly moved. One cannot conceive that a mere road could make a heart palpitate so. Whitman is intoxicated by it; his bosom heaving with emotion, he says frankly: 'I think I could stop here myself and do miracles.' How his great joyous heart leads him astray:

I think whatever I shall meet on the road I shall like, and whoever beholds me shall like me.

He says in his strange inaccurate language:

Whoever denies me it shall not trouble me,
Whoever accepts me he or she shall be blessed and shall bless me.

He is impressive, very impressive. At times his great goodness astonishes even himself, so that the naive and simple soul goes on to sing:

I am larger, better than I thought,
I did not know I held so much goodness.

He is rather an exuberant man than a talented poet. Walt Whitman certainly cannot write. But he can feel. He lives an emotional life. If he had not received that letter from Emerson his book would have failed, as it deserved to fail.

47. Harriet Monroe on Whitman

1892

'A Word About Walt Whitman', The *Critic* (16 April, 1892), p. 231.

Harriet Monroe, who was a poet herself, later became the editor and publisher of the influential *Poetry: A Magazine of Verse* in the city of Chicago. This magazine, which has entered literary history because it published some of the earliest work of T. S. Eliot, Ezra Pound, Carl Sandburg and other notable figures in the twentieth century, bore for a long time on its masthead a saying by Walt Whitman: 'To have great poets, one must have great audiences, too.'

The persistence of prejudice is illustrated by various phases of Walt Whitman's reputation at home and abroad. In spite of the appreciative sympathy of fellow-poets who feel the wide swing of his imagination and the force of its literary expression, in spite of the tardy acknowledgments of critics who have gradually learned to find power and melody in some of his rugged verse, it cannot be said that the venerable bard is widely honored in his own country. Songs which celebrate the toils and pleasures of the masses have thus far found small audience among the common people of the nation, being read chiefly by the cultivated few. Aristocratic rhymesters, weavers of triolets and madrigals, have reached a greater number of humble homes than this prophet of democracy, and the toilers of the land care more for jingles than for the barbaric majesty of his irregular measures. The poet of the people is neglected by the people, while the works of scholarly singers like Longfellow and Bryant find a place in every farmer's library.

Humanity does not enjoy the scientific method of reasoning from facts and theories, preferring unphilosophically to adjust the facts to its preconceived ideas. In this country we are proud of the swift conquests of civilization, and too willing to forget the free simplicity and uncouth heroism of pioneer times. We boast of our borrowed culture and keep our truly great achievements in the background. We look forward to a powerful future and too often obliterate the memory of a valiant past, allowing details to slip unrecorded into oblivion which might serve as the foundation of epics as majestic as Homer's. Reason about it as we will, Americans have an instinctive feeling that the formative period of the national character should be out of sight and out of mind as soon as possible, so that our virgin republic may at once take a place of assured wisdom among the gray and hardened dames of the old world, decked like them with the splendid trophies of twenty centuries of civilization.

Walt Whitman tries to arrest this ill-directed current of false vanity, to reveal to the nation her true glory of physical and moral prowess, to unveil a superb figure of strong and courageous youth playing a new part in the world with all of youth's tameless energy and daring. He finds her achievements beautiful and heroic, worthy to be celebrated and immortalized by art, and feels that the adornments of culture and civilization must be gradually wrought out from her own consciousness, not imitated from outworn models or adopted ready-made. Thus he strives to discard from his singing all the incidents of American life which are not indigenous to American soil, bringing himself closely in contact with the primeval elements of nature and of man.

Long I roamed the woods of the North—long I watched Niagara pouring;
I travelled the prairies over, and slept on their breast—I crossed the Nevadas,
I crossed the plateaus;
I ascended the towering rocks along the Pacific, I sailed out to sea;
I sailed through the storm, I was refreshed by the storm.

Then from the majesty of ocean and plain to the higher majesty of cities:—

What, to pavements and homesteads here—what were those storms of the mountains and sea?
What, to passions I witness around me to-day, was the sea risen?

The glory of cataracts and thunders, of crowds and wars, appeals to him for utterance, and with the scrupulous loyalty of a true poet he does his utmost to answer the call. Whether his answer is adequate or not, we must honor his fidelity. The spirit of modern criticism becomes too finical, too much a command that the aspirant should fling away ambition, should be content with pleasant little valleys, and avoid the unexplored heights where precipices and avalanches threaten to destroy.

This spirit is a blight upon all high endeavor, and he who resists it and travels upward, even though he fall exhausted by the wayside, achieves a nobler success than a thousand petty triumphs could have brought him.

It is too soon for the world to decide how far this barbaric poet has fulfilled his mission. At present the mass of his countrymen brush aside his writings with a gesture of contempt, finding there what they most wish to forget—a faithful reflection of the rudeness, the unsettled vastness, the formlessness of an epoch out of which much of our country has hardly yet emerged. But theirs is not the final verdict; their desire to be credited with all the decorative embellishments which older states enjoy may yield when ours shall have won these ornaments and learned to regret the old unadorned strength and simplicity. Races which have passed their youth appreciate these vigorous qualities, which put them once more in touch with primitive nature, with the morning, with the wisdom of children, which is, after all, the serenest wisdom. Thus in England Walt Whitman's singing has thus far been more effectual than at home. There his work humors the prepossessions of the people, who find in him the incarnation of young democracy. To minds puzzled by the formality of other American poets, by Longfellow's academic precision, Whittier's use of time-worn measures, and Poe's love of rich orchestral effects of rhythm, Whitman's scorn of prosodical rules and of the accepted limitations of artistic decorum brings the revelation of something new in the brown old world. They greet him as a poet fresh from the wilds of which, to their persistent ignorance, both Americas are still made up. To them his songs seem as free and trackless as his native prairies, revealing once more the austerity and joyousness of primeval nature, so different from their elaborate civilization. It is possible that the next century of our own national life may find the same relief in his open-air honesty and moral ruggedness. It may turn to him to gain ideal comprehension of the forces which peopled this continent and redeemed its wastes from barrenness. His poetry is unruly and formless, but so were the times it mirrors—no harmony of fulfilment, but a chaos of forces struggling and toiling together for the evolution of a great nation. He sweeps the continent and gathers up all he finds, good, bad and indifferent, serenely conscious that to omniscience all is good, that to omnipotence all is important. The result is not art, perhaps; for art chooses and combines, gives form and life and color to nature's elements of truth. Art realizes the limitations of our finite humanity, appreciates our poverty of time for the multitudinous objects of thought, and indulgently omits all that is trivial and inessential from her epitome of truth. What does not emphasize she discards; to her fine judgment an hundred details serve but to weaken the force of one. Thus Walt Whitman may never be called an artist. What he finds he gives us with all the exact faithfulness of an inventory. In the mass of his discoveries there is much that is precious, many a treasure of rare and noble beauty; but its beauty is that of rich quartz, of uncut jewels, rather than that of the coin and the cameo. He offers us a collection of specimens from the splendid laboratory of nature. It will scarcely be strange if the future guards them in cabinets instead of circulating them far and wide among the people.

1893–1914

48. John Addington Symonds on Whitman

1893

Extracts from John Addington Symonds, *Walt Whitman: A Study* (1893), pp. 1–11.

John Addington Symonds (1840–93), English critic, poet and historian, must undoubtedly be given one of the most important places in the circle of Whitman's earliest disciples. The authority with which he spoke because of his own accomplishments in letters undoubtedly played a role in sustaining the old poet's confidence in himself and in supporting his conviction that he was destined in the future to receive a more respectful and sympathetic hearing than was his portion in his own time.

The world has lost another good and great man. Walt Whitman died in March 1892 at Camden, New Jersey, U.S.A., after a lingering and painful illness, which terminated in distressing debility, borne by him with serenity and fortitude. A spiritual force has been resumed through his death into the occult stock of universal energy; and it is too early as yet to sum up any final account of his achievement as the teacher of a new way of regarding life, the prophet of a democratic religion, and the poet of a revolutionary school.

Whitman, indeed, is extremely baffling to criticism. I have already said in print that 'speaking about him is like speaking about the universe.' I meant this to be appreciative, in so far as the largeness and comprehensiveness of the man's nature are concerned. But the saying has, like the famous Delphian knife, a double handle. Not merely because he is large and comprehensive, but because he is intangible, elusive, at first sight self-contradictory, and in some sense formless, does Whitman resemble the universe and defy critical analysis.

The peculiar surroundings of the man during his lifetime rendered it difficult to be impartial with regard to him. Assuming from the first an attitude of indifference to public opinion, challenging conventionalities, and quietly ignoring customary prejudice, he was exposed at the beginning of his career to unmerited insults and a petty persecution. Not only did critics and cultivated persons fling stones at him; but even a Minister of State thought it his duty to deprive him of a modest office which he held. This opposition was far from abating his courage or altering the calm of his essentially masculine nature. But it excited the pugnacious instincts of those few devoted followers and disciples who had gathered round him. Whitman began to be enveloped in a dust of controversy—indecent abuse upon the one hand, extravagant laudation on the other—outrage and depreciation, retaliated by what the French call *réclame* and *claque*. Sane criticism found it necessary to stand aloof from the ignoble fray; feeling confident that Whitman's worth would obtain due and ultimate recognition; knowing, as Sam Johnson used to say, that 'no man is written up or down except by himself'; dreading lest the sterling qualities of such magnificent work should be brought into discredit by clamorous and undiscriminating advocacy.

Whitman's own personality augmented these difficulties. No one was ever more generous and frank of nature, more ready to accept differences of opinion, more tolerant of criticism. At the same time he displayed a desire to diffuse his doctrines, an eagerness to be acknowledged in his lifetime. He craved for responsive affection in the audience to whom he appealed, and regarded his literary teaching in the light of a cause. He acted like one who did not trust to the certainty of the eventual success of genius. He collected and distributed trifling panegyrics of himself, culled from the holes and corners of American journalism. He showed small sense of proportion in criticism, and seemed to value people by the amount of personal zeal they displayed in the propagation of his views. This spirit was somewhat grotesquely exhibited in his table-talk at a banquet held in honour of his seventy-second birthday.* The kindness of his words about his friends and followers must have touched all who were concerned, as much, I hope, as they touched me. When I read what he said of me, I recognised the acumen of his insight into several points of my character. I felt that probably my name would survive in those unpremeditated remarks long after my own writings shall have been forgotten. Yet I could not

* *See* Walt Whitman's Birthday, 31 May 1891, *Lippincott's Magazine.*

help being amused by one sentence, which gave a special flavour to his praise: 'The best thing about Symonds is his splendid aspiration. He was quite willing to leap into the gulf.' Whitman, as the context proves, did not mean that Symonds is a Quintus Curtius[1] open to undertake a job of self-devotion at a moment's notice. He was only testing me by the standard of discipleship, which he applied to each and all of his acquaintances in turn. Early in the history of *Leaves of Grass* I accepted the book, and staked my critical reputation upon an open avowal of its sterling merit—indifferent to what my brother-students thought about it. That is no topic for eulogy: certainly none which need have been dwelt upon by Whitman. It may be false delicacy, it may be the result of effete culture, it may be feudalism in my blood. But I confess that I have always found this note in Whitman and his circle difficult to keep in tune with.

As Ernest Renan said of Victor Hugo, writing on the day after his death:

> Who would now interrogate the general upon the subject of the manœuvres he employed, the sacrifices which were the conditions of his success? The general is forced to be egotistic. He is the army; and a glaring exhibition of personality, unpardonable in the rest of men, is imposed on him by circumstances. Hugo (*and in like manner Whitman*) had become a symbol, a principle, an affirmation, the affirmation of idealism and emancipated art. He owed the whole of himself to his own religion. He was like a god, who had to be his own high priest. His lofty and vigorous nature lent itself to the playing of this part, which would have been unbearable to one of different calibre. A mighty instinct came to manifestation through him. He was like the main-spring of a spiritual world. He could not find the time to have taste; good taste, moreover, would have been of little service to him.

There is irony in everything which Renan wrote; and these sentences (transferred by me from his panegyric of Hugo to Whitman) are steeped in irony. To dispense with taste, or the refinements of gentle feelings, is what no man, not even the greatest, can do with impunity. No general, not even Napoleon, no founder, not even Christ, was great enough for that. Whitman then appeared omnivorous of praise, indiscriminative as to its quality, lacking the repose which belongs to the highest type of greatness. Instead of leaving his fame and influence to the operation of natural laws, he encouraged the *claque* and the *réclame* which I have pointed out as prejudicial.

[1] Symonds has here confused the legendary Roman hero *Marcus* Curtius with the biographer of Alexander the Great, *Quintus* Curtius Rufus.

I sincerely regard him, and have long regarded him, as a man born to remind the world of many important and neglected truths, to flash the light of authentic inspiration upon many dark and puzzling questions, and to do so with the force of admirable courage, flawless candour. But the ways he chose for pushing his gospel and advertising his philosophy, put a severe strain on patience. Were Buddha, Socrates, Christ, so interested in the dust stirred up around them by second-rate persons, in third-rate cities, and in more than fifth-rate literature?

In addition to what I have been advancing upon the difficulty of dealing fairly with Whitman during his lifetime—passing now to higher and more serious planes of reflection—his very originality, his individuality, the unique qualities which made him so remarkable a master, render the task of seizing and formulating the essential truth about him, both as teacher and as poet, well-nigh impracticable at the present time. Those of us who feel his influence most deeply, believe that his work has secured attention, and hope ardently that its import will be gradually absorbed and assimilated, so that in course of time a living image of himself shall exist in thousands, and the exposition be rendered easy.

Like Nature, he seemed, at first sight, to be a mass of contradictions and insoluble problems, of potent stuffs irreducible by any known method of analysis. We could feel him, submit to his impact, be enamoured of his charm. But we knew that it was impossible to find a formula for all that is implied in the two letters W. W. Critics, saddened, and made shy by their thankless task, judged it better to leave him to his predestined working in the sphere of thought, feeling assured that, like Nature, he could take care of himself.

How ill it fared with even superior intelligences in their efforts to evaluate W. W. might be illustrated by two examples. When 'Songs before Sunrise' were re-issued in 1883, Mr. Swinburne suffered an eloquent ode 'To Walt Whitman in America' to be reprinted. It contains the following impassioned stanza:

O strong-winged soul with prophetic
  Lips hot with the bloodbeats of song,
With tremor of heartstrings magnetic,
  With thoughts as thunders in throng,
With consonant ardours of chords
That pierce men's souls as with swords
  And hale them hearing along.

On reading this ode, and especially the lines just quoted, I, for my part, felt that true things had here been said regarding Whitman, but with rather more of the *claque* and the *réclame* flavour than I judged desirable. Still, I welcomed and appreciated the poem as a noteworthy contribution to the tradition gradually forming in support of Whitman's credit. Sad then was my disappointment to discover, before the eighties were over (that is within seven years of this dithyrambic blessing), that Mr. Swinburne was cursing Whitman by all his gods in prose, and stigmatising the muse of *Leaves of Grass*, as a drunken apple-woman reeling in a gutter. I forget the exact verbiage of the scurrility; and I do not impute the change of attitude implied in it, so much to Mr. Swinburne's levity, as to the bewilderment created in his mind by Whitman's incongruities.

The next instance is that of a critic not so lavish of the hyperboles of praise and blame as Mr. Swinburne is. My friend Mr. R. L. Stevenson once published a constrained and measured study of Walt Whitman, which struck some of those who read it as frigidly appreciative. He subsequently told me that he had first opened upon the key-note of a glowing panegyric, but felt the pompous absurdity of its exaggeration. He began again, subduing the whole tone of the composition. When the essay was finished in this second style, he became conscious that it misrepresented his own enthusiasm for the teacher who at a critical moment of his youthful life had helped him to discover the right line of conduct.

I feel that I may not unfairly be accused by the school of Whitman of having been lukewarm toward him in his lifetime, and of having started this memorial notice in a somewhat carping strain. Here, as elsewhere, however, it is my single desire to live in the Whole, and to see things, so far as may be possible, in their relation to the Whole. I am sure, moreover, that Whitman's genial and manly spirit, so lately resumed into the sum of things, approves of any earnest attempt on his disciple's part to show what his relative value is. No one, not Buddha, not Socrates, not Christ, has an absolute value. True criticism dares not forget that 'the eternal things,' 'the abiding relations' of the universe, extend around, above us all, sustaining and environing individualities however potent.

In 1889 I allowed the following words of mine to be circulated in a collection of what may be called testimonials to the bard of Camden:

Leaves of Grass, which I first read at the age of twenty-five, influenced me more perhaps than any other book has done, except the Bible; more than Plato, more than Goethe. It is impossible for me to speak critically of what has so deeply entered into the fibre and marrow of my being.

The time has now come for attempting some explanation of what I meant. Whitman threw clear light upon truths which I had but dimly perceived, and gave me the courage of opinions previously held with some timidity and shyness.

49. T. W. Rolleston on Whitman

1893

Extracts from an article by T. W. Rolleston, translated from the German by Alfred Forman and Richard Maurice Bucke, in *In Re*, pp. 285–95.

Thomas W. Rolleston (1857–1920) was a critic, editor, translator and correspondent with Whitman. His exchange of letters with the poet appears in the volume *Whitman and Rolleston: A Correspondence* edited by Herst Frenz (Dublin, 1952). Professor Harold Blodgett (*Walt Whitman in England*) informs us that he was an associate of Standish O'Grady (also an admirer of Whitman) in the Irish literary revival. He

was a scholar who brought to Whitman the scholar's talent for studious exposition and translation. Rolleston discovered Whitman in 1877, when he contributed a youthful poem on Walt to *Kotabos*, a brilliant Trinity College publication founded by Tyrrell. Two years later Rolleston went to Germany, and at the end of a four years' absorption in German literature and philosophy he published at Dresden, jointly with H. B. Cotterill, a pamphlet entitled *Uber Wordsworth und Walt Whitman: Zwei Vortrage Gehalten vor dem Literarischen Verein zu Dresden* . . . Rolleston's part in this enterprise was a twenty-two page discussion of Whitman and a translation of the 'Song of the Answerer.'

. . . . And now a word upon Walt Whitman's writings. They consist of two volumes—one of poetry, *Leaves of Grass*; the other of prose, *Specimen Days and Collect*, containing a varied collection of autobiographical sketches, descriptions of nature, and all sorts of impressions, with, further, a philosophic essay upon the import and the future of American Democracy. His poetry, however, is the prime work of his life; the rest must be considered as supplement or commentary. It is, therefore, with the *Leaves* that we shall chiefly occupy ourselves. The best introduction would perhaps be to quote one of the small poems called 'Inscriptions,' which stand at the beginning of the book.

Here, then, are the first words of *Leaves of Grass*:

One's-Self I sing, a simple separate person,
Yet utter the word Democratic, the word En-Masse.

Of physiology from top to toe I sing,
Not physiognomy alone nor brain alone is worthy for the Muse, I say the Form
  complete is worthier far,
The Female equally with the Male I sing.

Of Life immense in passion, pulse, and power,
Cheerful, for freest action form'd under the laws divine,
The Modern Man I sing.

Here is announced, with the finest accuracy, the material of Whitman's verse. And what material! The poets of the present, while occupying themselves merely with the surface of life, have arrived at so fine a technical result that we seldom feel any want in this respect. And yet there is wanting that which gives to every phenomenon of our days its real worth and importance. Where is the poet who has taken complete possession of the mind conquests of this singular age, and who has taken into himself, and poetically presented, modern man with his terrible energy, his unexampled intellectual activity and his infinite boldness in word and deed? If this age is actually to be represented in literature, it must be done by one who is able to reconcile the all-denying spirit of analytics with the all-affirming spirit of democracy —who can embrace in himself the intricate spiritual strivings of the age, demonstrate their true direction, and, by the inexplicable powers of a magic personality, impart to that which is now impotent through dispersion the mightiest effectiveness. That is Walt Whitman's task, and that task he has fulfilled. But do not let us be in a hurry to imagine that in a way so easy and off-hand we shall be able to acknowledge in this Yankee the world-poet of the age. As I have already indicated, his recognition demands a self-examination such as we each hesitate to undertake. Moreover, the first impression of the book, considered as art, is not an attractive one, but rather one of surprise or even consternation. In it we have an entirely new literary form, a new method of treatment, and subjects strange to all preceding poetry. All rules, all deeply meditated definitions, are demolished; of antecedent poetry nothing remains—except the poetry.

It is now high time for me to give my hearers some idea of the actual contents of this work—of the doctrine which is its special mark. But the book does not easily lend itself to an interpreter, because, among other things, so much depends upon the personality of the author. And further, although I have been familiar with *Leaves of Grass* for some six years, I am certain that I have still only a superficial idea of its contents. But, superficial as it may be compared with the full meaning which still lies beyond me, even this seems worth reporting.

There are many things in Whitman's works which should assure him special consideration in Germany. He is the greatest poetic representative of that which is usually considered a prime focal point in German philosophy. In the philosophy of the modern world there are apparently only two principal currents—the one starting from England, the other from Germany. In England, as is well known, thinkers are chiefly occupied with the laws of phenomena—the manner of their origin, and how they condition each other; with all, in short, which may be called their visible activities. But in the philosophy especially characteristic of Germany the starting point is from the inner, the subjective, not from the outer, the objective; that is to say, it does not consider the material of speculation as so given in experience that we have nothing more to do than to observe certain relations and sequences.

German thought prefers to absorb itself in the content of the soul-life—it seeks to formulate continually deeper and clearer the various ideas and experiences which go to make up this content—it desires, in fact, to be certain of its premises before it proceeds to draw conclusions. And when the problem is thus presented it becomes clear that the true task of philosophy is not to draw conclusions on this and that, but really to lift the inner life more and more into the light of consciousness. German philosophy keeps thus firm hold of the center of the thinking soul, and does not lose itself in observation. Phenomena and their laws are not regarded as independent facts, setting bounds to the activity of the soul, but rather as expressions of its activity—as faces, rather than as fetters, of the soul. Now, in Walt Whitman this principle of procedure—the principle, namely, of continuously working in towards the center, towards the primitive actuality of things—receives the most manifold and interesting application. For example, religions, social theories, political institutions and the like become for him vapor and dust the moment that either in word or deed they claim or are given an independence which places them beyond or in contradistinction to the life of man. But they are deprived of their significance only in order to receive for the first time their real significance. For they are all utterances of the human spirit, and for every one who regards them from the proper point of view they emit some ray of the godhood that they contain.

Here I should be glad to insert an extended specimen which might be taken as typical of his first period style as well as of his views:

I heard what was said of the universe,
Heard it and heard it of several thousand years;
It is middling well as far as it goes—but is that all?

Magnifying and applying come I,
Outbidding at the start the old cautious hucksters,
Taking myself the exact dimensions of Jehovah,
Lithographing Kronos, Zeus his son, and Hercules his grandson,
Buying drafts of Osiris, Isis, Belus, Brahma, Buddha,
In my portfolio placing Manito loose, Allah on a leaf, the crucifix engraved,
With Odin and the hideous-faced Mexitli and every idol and image,
Taking them all for what they are worth and not a cent more,
Admitting they were alive and did the work of their days,
(They bore mites as for unfledg'd birds who have now to rise and fly and sing for themselves.)
Accepting the rough deific sketches to fill out better in myself, bestowing them freely on each man and woman I see,
Discovering as much or more in a framer framing a house,
Putting higher claims for him there with his roll'd-up sleeves driving the mallet and chisel,
Not objecting to special revelations, considering a curl of smoke or a hair on the back of my hand just as curious as any revelation,
Lads ahold of fire-engines and hook-and-ladder ropes no less to me than the gods of the antique wars,
Minding their voices peal through the crash of destruction,
Their brawny limbs passing safe over charr'd laths, their white foreheads whole and unhurt out of the flames;
By the mechanic's wife with her babe at her nipple interceding for every person born,
Three scythes at harvest whizzing in a row from three lusty angels with shirts bagg'd out at their waists,
The snag-tooth'd hostler with red hair redeeming sins past and to come,
Selling all he possesses, travelling on foot to fee lawyers for his brother and sit by him while he is tried for forgery;
What was strewn in the amplest strewing the square rod about me, and not filling the square rod then,
The bull and the bug never worshipp'd half enough,

Dung and dirt more admirable than was dream'd,
The supernatural of no account, myself waiting my time to be one of the supremes,
The day getting ready for me when I shall do as much good as the best, and be as prodigious;
By my life-lumps! becoming already a creator,
Putting myself here and now to the ambush'd womb of the shadows.

Monstrous and unpoetic as these expressions, these metaphors, may sound, I beg my hearers to believe that they sound the same in English as in German.

At Whitman's first appearance he was ridiculed as a lunatic—save where it was shocked by his audacity—by the whole literary world, the highest spirits, such as Tennyson and Emerson, alone excepted.

But along with his glorification of the begetting spirit we may set the following glorification of the begotten, which is composed in a milder key:

Not you alone proud truths of the world,
Nor you alone ye facts of modern science,
But myths and fables of eld, Asia's, Africa's fables,
The far-darting beams of the spirit, the unloos'd dreams,
The deep diving bibles and legends,
The daring plots of the poets, the elder religions;
O you temples fairer than lilies pour'd over by the rising sun!
O you fables spurning the known, eluding the hold of the known, mounting to heaven!
You lofty and dazzling towers, pinnacled, red as roses, burnish'd with gold!
Towers of fables immortal fashion'd from mortal dreams!
You too I welcome and fully the same as the rest!
You too with joy I sing.

Walt Whitman is essentially and in the first place a poet, not a philosopher; but that he has occupied himself with philosophic questions, and in a philosophic manner, will be clear to every reader. And in this respect he stands in a special relationship to his age, in which thought has achieved an unexampled influence over action. In these days a purely mechanical conception of the universe has found the most extraordinary dissemination. Is the origin of this mode of thinking to be sought in the spirit of freedom, which during this and the preceding century has arisen in Europe, and which not seldom in the extremity of its insolence degenerates into the Platonic ὕβρις? It is certain, in any case, that the philosophy of the present day is characterized by a strong disinclination to acknowledge any authority whatever. No one is willing to take up the position of a learner—of a non-knower—nor to believe that another can see light and symmetry where for himself nothing but darkness exists. The cuteness which discovers logical connections is plentifully at hand—but not so the wholesome and noble scepticism which not only questions the insight of others, but also, and chiefly, its own. For example, when a thinker like Herbert Spencer seeks to go to the foundation of the idea of duty, he begins with the first conception of it that comes to hand in his (in certain directions) very limited understanding, thus: that duty is merely an impulse which at times forces us to the voluntary endurance of avoidable unpleasantness—believing hereby that he has exhausted the meaning of the idea of duty, and proceeding calmly in his examination without any suspicion that duty can really be anything other than what he takes it for and what he has assumed it to be. Now, for those who reject such mechanical philosophy the great problem of the century is the upholding and strengthening of the idea that moral conceptions have (rooted in the nature of the mind itself and independently of objectivity) an aim and a determinate place in the general scheme.

Those holding these latter views will find a powerful friend in Whitman. It is doubtless true that Whitman does not furnish us with the facile, cut and dried, proof such as might, without giving us any trouble, dispel all our uncertainties. In matters of this sort, in the long run, logic is of no avail; and what Whitman does for us goes to the heart of the problem, for he helps us to see with our own eyes all objects of thought as they exist. He gradually strengthens in us the religious sense. We feel ourselves, at last, in relationship not with merely dead, mechanical objects, but with utterances of a living essence. We experience with respect to the whole objective world the same transformation as that which happens when our formal opinions become converted into vital convictions. We know that it is not only possible, but that it also frequently happens, that we can firmly believe in a thing without this belief having any actual influence upon our life or mode of thought.

For example: how many are there now in the world who are convinced of the truth of the Christian doctrine of the immortality of the soul—that is to say, that there is a future life in which the material victories and defeats of the present will count for nothing, but where the spirit in which we have acted will count for all! And yet it strikes us as an altogether abnormal exception when we meet with a man who goes through life with the peace of mind which is the logical outcome of this belief. According to Cardinal Newman, who, in an extremely interesting work, has examined the psychology of the subject, this state in which our views and feelings stand opposed to each other might rightly be called one of 'formal' belief—a state which he distinguishes from that of effective, 'actual' belief. Now, it happens not unfrequently that a formal belief of this description passes into an actual belief. How can such a change have been effected? Only, as it seems to me, by the fact that a new relation between us and the object of our belief has been in some manner brought about by means of which the object is no longer for us a mere name, a logical conclusion, a tradition, but a thing, an actuality, touching the deeps of our consciousness. No matter in what way we describe the thing, every one is acquainted with it, and I need only call attention to the fact that this process of actualization can take place equally where the result may be described not as an assent, or belief, 'formal' or 'actual', but as a vital, spiritual perception, *σύλληψις*, of the object in question. The bringing about of such a relationship between the human soul and the whole inner and outer world is a prime feature of Whitman's effect upon his readers. When he has accomplished this, he believes that he has accomplished everything, for the perception in their actuality of the things of ordinary experience is religion and begets ethics.

On this point Whitman stands in close relationship with another great poet, William Wordsworth. If Whitman has any predecessor, this predecessor is Wordsworth. For each equally primarily sets himself to the unlocking of the springs of reverence, joy and noble passion which lie contained in our relationships to the facts of daily life. Whence it is that they derive the faculty for the solving of this riddle, what it is that makes their words so effective, is precisely the inexplicable element in poetry. But it is the privilege of poets to be able to express their own perception of things in such a manner as to enable us also to perceive with their eyes, provided we are morally qualified—provided, that is, that knowledge, insight into the soul of things, is of more consequence to us than that empty acquaintanceship with names and appearances which usually passes for knowledge. . . .

I have said that Whitman claims to derive the conviction of the divine from every form of experience. From every form? Even from that which we call evil? Yes, most certainly—from evil also. . . .

Whitman knows nothing of exceptions. To him God is in evil as well as in good. Is such doctrine immoral? If it is, then are we in a truly lamentable condition, for the reverse doctrine is certainly highly immoral—the belief, namely, that evil, as such, has an independent existence as a primeval principle. Such a theory must degenerate either into a revolting devil-worship or into equally revolting cruelties practised upon those who stand presumably in the devil's service. Or, should I rather say, it would thus degenerate were we not, as already remarked, often so little aware of the real content of our belief? But is not the doctrine of pantheism also necessarily immoral in the fact that it seems indiscriminately to mix and accept evil with good? It might easily become so, but Whitman's conception of it escapes such danger. . . .

Walt Whitman contemplates the world, as presented to our consciousness, in the form of a continually ascending succession of struggles and acquisitions. The theory of the origin of moral evil (of which alone we, naturally, are speaking here), which seems to be involved in Whitman's teaching, stands in direct conjunction with this general theory of evolution. The first appearance of evil marks the beginning of a new step—the birth of a new ideal. The stage of self-consciousness has been reached—then inexplicably arise among men the ideas of faith, love, justice, etc., each man becoming more or less aware of the presence and claims of these—and in so far as he becomes so aware, in so far does any violation of them become sin. Sin, therefore, is the offspring of the gradually unfolding consciousness of an ideal. A sinful act is, in and for itself, an expression of life like everything else, and contains, for those who have been enlightened by the spirit of Whitman, that which stimulates to the most resolute battle.

Walt Whitman's poems resemble in many respects the productions of nature; among other things, in that they seem to have been created without any regard to the verdict of unthinking men. For were it otherwise he would certainly never have uttered such views as, for instance, the following:

Partaker of influx and efflux I, extoller of hate and conciliation,
Extoller of amies and those that sleep in each others' arms.

I am he attesting sympathy
(Shall I make my list of things in the house and skip the house that supports them?)

I am not the poet of goodness only, I do not decline to be the poet of wickedness also.

What blurt is this about virtue and about vice?
Evil propels me and reform of evil propels me, I stand indifferent,
My gait is no fault-finder's or rejecter's gait,
I moisten the roots of all that has grown.

In politics Whitman is a rigid democrat. His works are the first embodiment of the genuine democratic spirit in literature; for it is undeniable that no other has seen, as he has seen and presented in his writing, what infinite unsurmised meanings are contained in this word democracy. By him the struggle between republicanism and monarchism is regarded in an almost religious light. If it could be proved that disseminated well-being, peace and order, were only possible under a despotic government, Whitman would still adhere to republicanism, for in his view, as already said, the course of the development of mankind is primarily towards the widening and deepening of his consciousness—that is to say, that mankind may more and more enter into relationship with the existence and ethical experiences of others, and that it may grow more and more to feel and reverence the actuality of these experiences. This point of view being justified, the strivings of democracy are also justified, and at the same time aim and limit are given to them. Political and social institutions, though always with caution, must in the long run be directed to placing and leaving mankind in the most vivid possible contact with life. But under a despotism, be it however enlightened, the sharp impression of life is blurred; it may be embellished, but the sense of the primitive elements of ethics —the greatness and satisfyingness of existence—is not felt to be present and actual.

One of Whitman's disciples has said that if we find anything in him repulsive or offensive, we may be quite sure that there is weakness or defect in ourselves. If that is true, as I firmly believe, the state of society of thirty years ago must, in certain directions, have been a very unhealthy one, for the earlier editions of *Leaves of Grass* were received with an almost universal howl of indignation. The reason thereof lay in a section of the poems called 'Children of Adam,' in which Whitman sings and glorifies the sensuous in man especially with regard to the relation of the sexes. Indecent, in my opinion, these poems are not, but the criticism which universally selects them for discussion and condemnation is extremely indecent. To this discussion, therefore, I will not contribute, but I must call attention to the fact that the 'Children of Adam' are simply the natural realization of Whitman's —genuinely democratic—ideal of human life. In his opinion, this ideal does not consist in the development of certain selected faculties and superiorities, but in the development of man's complete nature. He does not seek to form merely a good man—a man capable of self-command (like Goethe) or a strenuous, helpful man, but an all-round, every way complete man—that is to say, one who, by the exercise of each point of his nature, is capable of finding that which makes him happy and takes him morally forward. In this idea there is doubtless no alarming originality; it is original only in that clearness of vision which perceives all the bearings of the idea, and that unflinching resolution to realize it in practice.

To conclude: There are in Whitman's works three strongly combined qualities which assure to them a lasting worth among mankind. First, we are made aware in him of the working of an intellect whose depth and compass appears more and more astounding the further we penetrate into it. Second, we find in him a wealth of poetic power whose beauty impresses us the more profoundly and lastingly for the very reason that it is not made an end and aim in itself. Third, the fit reader is brought into relationship with something still more unusual and valuable than either intellect or poetry—he finds that an indescribable, magical personal influence streams forth from these leaves; he is not brought into contact with a book but with a man—with a friend, whose spirit, by nothing that we can call a doctrine, but by actual presence, acts upon ours, strengthening, exalting, purifying and liberating. In the above presentment I have merely, or at least principally, touched upon the first, and do not feel at present in a position to enter upon an exposition of the other and more important of these realities. And even from the standpoint of intellect I have dealt with Whitman naturally in the most superficial manner.

50. William James on Whitman

1895

Extract from 'Is Life Worth Living?', *International Journal of Ethics* (October 1895). Reprinted in *The Will to Believe and Other Essays in Popular Philosophy* (1912), pp. 33–5.

William James (1842–1910) was once described by the philosopher Horace M. Kallen as 'leader of the movement known as pragmatism and most renowned and representative of the thinkers of America'. He was the brother of the novelist Henry James, but unlike his brother whose taste for Whitman appears to have been a matter of slow growth, his own was more spontaneous and immediate. He has discussed Whitman's mysticism in *Varieties of Religious Experience*. Here, his main stress is upon Whitman's optimism and lack of a sense of evil in the universe, which is his connecting link with Rousseau. Henry James senior, it is said, 'found something of the consolation and security he was seeking' in the works of Swedenborg. His son found it possible, therefore, to appreciate more vividly than many others the importance to individuals which writers off the beaten intellectual track might acquire.

With many men the question of life's worth is answered by a temperamental optimism which makes them incapable of believing that anything seriously evil can exist. Our dear old Walt Whitman's works are the standing text-book of this kind of optimism. The mere joy of living is so immense in Walt Whitman's veins that it abolishes the possibility of any other kind of feeling:—

To breathe the air, how delicious!
To speak, to walk, to seize something by the hand! . . .
To be this incredible God I am! . . .
O amazement of things, even the least particle!
O spirituality of things!

I too carol the Sun, usher'd or at noon, or as now, setting;
I too throb to the brain and beauty of the earth and of all the growths of the earth. . . .

I sing to the last the equalities, modern or old,
I sing the endless finales of things,
I say Nature continues—glory continues.
I praise with electric voice,
For I do not see one imperfection in the universe,
And I do not see one cause or result lamentable at last.

So Rousseau, writing of the nine years he spent at Annecy, with nothing but his happiness to tell:—

How tell what was neither said nor done nor even thought, but tasted only and felt, with no object of my felicity but the emotion of felicity itself! I rose with the sun, and I was happy; I went to walk, and I was happy; I saw 'Maman,' and I was happy; I left her, and I was happy. I rambled through the woods and over the vine-slopes, I wandered in the valleys, I read, I lounged, I worked in the garden, I gathered the fruits, I helped at the indoor work, and happiness followed me everywhere. It was in no one assignable thing; it was all within myself; it could not leave me for a single instant.

If moods like this could be made permanent, and constitutions like these universal, there would never be any occasion for such discourses as the present one. No philosopher would seek to prove articulately that life is worth living, for the fact that it absolutely is so would vouch for itself, and the problem disappear in the vanishing of the question rather than in the coming of anything like a reply. But we are not magicians to make the optimistic temperament universal; and alongside of the deliverances of temperamental optimism concerning life, those of temperamental pessimism always exist, and oppose to them a standing refutation. In what is called 'circular insanity,' phases of melancholy succeed phases of mania, with no outward cause that we can discover; and often enough to one and the same well person life will present incarnate radiance to-day and incarnate dreariness tomorrow, according to the fluctuations of what the older medical books used to call 'the concoction of the humors.' In the words of the newspaper joke, 'it depends on the liver.' Rousseau's ill-balanced constitution undergoes a change, and behold him in his latter evil days a prey to melancholy and black delusions of suspicion and fear. Some men seem launched upon the world even from their birth with souls as incapable of happiness as Walt Whitman's was of gloom, and they have left us their messages in even more lasting verse than his,—the exquisite Leopardi, for example; or our own contemporary, James Thomson, in that pathetic book, *The City of Dreadful Night*, which I think is less well-known than it should be for its literary beauty, simply because men are afraid to quote its words,—they are so gloomy, and at the same time so sincere.

51. Max Nordau on Whitman

1895

Extract from Max Nordau, *Degeneration*, translated from the German (1895), pp. 231–2.

Max Simon Nordau (1849–1923), Hungarian Jewish author, was born in Budapest and practised medicine in his native city. His novels, stories and essays are generally forgotten, but his attack upon modern art and modern artists entitled *Degeneration* was translated into many languages and became somewhat fashionable in many circles where the new aesthetic phenomena were both puzzling and infuriating. Dr Nordau is also an important figure in the history of Zionism in which he was an early associate of Theodore Herzl whom he joined, at a critical point in that movement, when Herzl wished to accept the British Government's offer of territory in Uganda for settlement by the Jews instead of setting their hearts upon Palestine which was at that time under the rule of the Turks.

I should like here to interpolate a few remarks on Walt Whitman, who is likewise one of the deities to whom the degenerate and hysterical of both hemispheres have for some time been raising altars. Lombroso ranks him expressly among 'mad geniuses.'* Mad Whitman was

* Lombroso, *Genie und Irrsinn*, p. 322: 'Walt Whitman, the poet of the modern Anglo-Americans, and assuredly a mad genius, was a typographer, teacher, soldier, joiner, and for some time also a bureaucrat, which, for a poet, is the queerest of trades.'

This constant changing of his profession Lombroso rightly characterizes as one of the signs of mental derangement. A French admirer of Whitman, Gabriel Sarrazin (*La Renaissance de la Poésie anglaise*, 1798–1889; Paris, 1889, p. 270, footnote), palliates this proof of organic instability and weakness of will in the following manner: 'This American facility of changing from one calling to another goes against our old European prejudices, and our unalterable veneration for thoroughly hierarchical, bureaucratic routine-careers. We have remained in this, as in so many other respects, essentially narrow-minded, and cannot understand that diversity of capacities gives a man a very much greater social value.' This is the true method of the æsthetic windbag, who for every fact which he does not understand finds roundly-turned phrases with which he explains and justifies everything to his own satisfaction.

without doubt. But a genius? That would be difficult to prove. He was a vagabond, a reprobate rake, and his poems contain outbursts of erotomania so artlessly shameless that their parallel in literature could hardly be found with the author's name attached. For his fame he has to thank just those bestially sensual pieces which first drew to him the attention of all the pruriency of America. He is morally insane, and incapable of distinguishing between good and evil, virtue and crime. 'This is the deepest theory of susceptibility,' he says in one place, 'without preference or exclusion; the negro with the woolly head, the bandit of the highroad, the invalid, the ignorant—none are denied.' And in another place he explains he 'loves the murderer and the thief, the pious and good, with equal love.' An American driveller, W. D. O'Connor, has called him on this account 'The good gray Poet.' We know, however, that this 'goodness,' which is in reality moral obtuseness and morbid sentimentality, frequently accompanies degeneration, and appears even in the cruellest assassins, for example, in Ravachol.

He has megalomania, and says of himself:

From this hour I decree that my being be freed from all restraints and limits.
I go where I will, my own absolute and complete master.
I breathe deeply in space. The east and the west are mine.
Mine are the north and south. I am greater and better than I thought myself.
I did not know that so much boundless goodness was in me. . . .
Whoever disowns me causes me no annoyance.
Whoever recognises me shall be blessed, and will bless me.

He is mystically mad, and announces: 'I have the feeling of all. I am all, and believe in all. I believe that materialism is true, and that spiritualism is also true; I reject nothing.' And in another still more characteristic passage:

Santa Spirita [*sic!*], breather, life,
Beyond the light, lighter than light,
Beyond the flames of hell, joyous, leaping easily above hell,
Beyond Paradise, perfumed solely with mine own perfume,
Including all life on earth, touching, including God, including Saviour and
  Satan,
Ethereal, pervading all, for without me what were all? what were God?
Essence of forms, life of the real identities . . .
Life of the great round world, the sun and stars, and of man, I, the general soul.

In his patriotic poems he is a sycophant of the corrupt American vote-buying, official-bribing, power-abusing, dollar-democracy, and a cringer to the most arrogant Yankee conceit. His war-poems—the much renowned *Drum Taps*—are chiefly remarkable for swaggering bombast and stilted patter.

His purely lyrical pieces, with their ecstatic 'Oh!' and 'Ah!', with their soft phrases about flowers, meadows, spring and sunshine, recall the most arid, sugary and effeminate passages of our old Gessner,[1] now happily buried and forgotten.

As a man, Walt Whitman offers a surprising resemblance to Paul Verlaine, with whom he shared all the stigmata of degeneration, the vicissitudes of his career, and, curiously enough, even the rheumatic ankylosis. As a poet, he has thrown off the closed strophe as too difficult, measure and rhyme as too oppressive, and has given vent to his emotional fugitive ideation in hysterical exclamations, to which the definition of 'prose gone mad' is infinitely better suited than it is to the pedantic, honest hexameters of Klopstock.[2] Unconsciously, he seemed to have used the parallelism of the Psalms, and Jeremiah's eruptive style, as models of form. We had in the last century the *Paramythien* of Herder,[3] and the insufferable 'poetical prose' of Gessner already mentioned. Our healthy taste soon led us to recognise the inartistic, retrogressive character of this lack of form, and that error in taste has found no imitator among us for a century. In Whitman, however, his hysterical admirers commend this *réchauffé* of a superannuated literary fashion as something to come; and admire, as an invention of genius, what is only an incapacity for methodical work. Nevertheless, it is interesting to point out that two persons so dissimilar as Richard Wagner and Walt Whitman have, in different spheres, under the pressure of the same motives, arrived at the same goal—the former at 'infinite melody,' which is no longer melody; the latter at verses which are no longer verses, both in consequence of their incapacity to submit their capriciously vacillating thoughts to the yoke of those rules which in 'infinite' melody, as in lyric verse, govern by measure and rhyme.

[1] Salomon Gessner (1730–88) Swiss poet, painter and etcher, whose 'Pastoral Idylls' were composed in a rhythmical prose. Some of his work in English translation was appreciated by Scott, Byron and Wordsworth.

[2] Gottlieb Friedrich Klopstock (1724–1803), German poet, whose epic *Der Messias*, was written in hexameters. It was translated into seventeen languages. He is better known now for his lyric odes.

[3] Johann Gottfried von Herder (1744–1803), German poet and philosopher, broke with classicism and became the pioneer of the '*Sturm und Drang*' movement. He exercised an influence upon Goethe and helped to spread an appreciation of the excellences of Gothic art. In one of his works *Uber den Ursprung der Sprache* (1772), he is credited with having laid the foundations of the science of comparative philology.

52. William Dean Howells on Whitman

1895

Extract from William Dean Howells, 'First Impressions of Literary New York', *Harper's Magazine* (June 1895). Reprinted under the title 'Walt Whitman at Pfaff's' in the *Conservator* (June 1895), pp. 61–2.

Walt Whitman, . . . when the *Saturday Press* took [him] up, had as hopeless a cause with the critics on either side of the ocean as any man could have. It was not till long afterward that his English admirers began to discover him, and to make his countrymen some noisy reproaches for ignoring him; they were wholly in the dark concerning him when the *Saturday Press*, which first stood his friend, and the young men whom the *Press* gathered about it, made him their cult. No doubt he was more valued because he was so offensive in some ways than he would have been if he had been in no way offensive, but it remains a fact that they celebrated him quite as much as was good for them. He was often at Pfaff's with them, and the night of my visit he was the chief fact of my experience. I did not know he was there until I was on my way out, for he did not sit at the table under the pavement, but at the head of one further into the room. There, as I passed, some friendly fellow stopped me and named me to him, and I remember how he leaned back in his chair, and reached out his great hand to me, as if he was going to give it to me for good and all. He had a fine head, with a cloud of Jovian hair upon it, and a branching beard and mustache, and gentle eyes that looked most kindly into mine, and seemed to wish the liking which I instantly gave him, though we hardly passed a word, and our acquaintance was summed up in that glance and the grasp of his mighty fist upon my hand. I doubt if he had any notion who or what I was beyond the fact that I was a poet of some sort, but he may possibly have remembered seeing my name printed after some very Heinesque verses in the *Press*. I did not meet him again for twenty years, and then I had only a moment with him when he was reading the proofs of his poems in Boston. Some years later I saw him for the last time, one day after his lecture on Lincoln, in that city, when he came down from the platform to speak with some hand-shaking friends who had gathered about him. Then and always he gave me the sense of a sweet and true soul, and I felt in him a spiritual dignity which I will not try to reconcile with his printing in the forefront of his book a passage from a private letter of Emerson's though I believe he would not have seen such a thing as most other men would, or thought ill of it in another. The spiritual purity which I felt in him no less than the dignity is something that I will no more try to reconcile with what denies it in his page; but such things we may well leave to the adjustment of finer balances than we have at hand. I will make sure only of the greatest benignity in the presence of the man. The apostle of the rough, the uncouth, was the gentlest person; his barbaric yawp, translated into the terms of social encounter, was an address of singular quiet, delivered in a voice of winning and endearing friendliness.

As to his work itself, I suppose that I do not think it so valuable in effect as in intention. He was a liberating force, a very 'imperial anarch' in literature; but liberty is never anything but a means, and what Whitman achieved was a means and not an end, in what must be called his verse. I like his prose, if there is a difference, much better; there he is of a genial and comforting quality, very rich and cordial, such as I felt him to be when I met him in person. His verse seems to me not poetry, but the materials of poetry, like one's emotions; yet I would not misprize it, and I am glad to own that I have had moments of great pleasure in it. Some French critic quoted in the *Saturday Press* (I cannot think of his name) said the best thing of him when he said that he made you a partner of the enterprise, for that is precisely what he does, and that is what alienates and what endears in him, as you like or dislike the partnership. It is still something neighborly, brotherly, fatherly, and so I felt him to be when the benign old man looked on me and spoke to me.

53. John Burroughs on Whitman

1896

Conclusion of John Burroughs, *Whitman: A Study* (1896), pp. 263–8. John Burroughs (1837–1921), American naturalist, is one of the earliest, most impressive and weighty disciples of Whitman. He was born in New York State and in his early years engaged in a variety of pursuits: teaching, journalism, farming and fruit-raising. He was for nine years a clerk in the Treasury Department in Washington, and in 1867 he wrote an influential little book entitled *Notes on Walt Whitman as poet and person*. In 1871, he began with *Wake-Robin* a series of books on birds and flowers and came to be regarded as to some extent a successor of Thoreau as an essayist on the plants and animals in the human environment. He lived a long life and was a prolific author. His books include, in addition to his essays on out-of-door life, a volume of poems and two books of travel sketches dealing with England and France.

After all I have written about Whitman, I feel at times that the main thing I wanted to say about him I have not said, cannot say; the best about him cannot be told anyway. 'My final merit I refuse you.' His full significance in connection with the great modern movement; how he embodies it all and speaks out of it, and yet maintains his hold upon the primitive, the aboriginal; how he presupposes science and culture, yet draws his strength from that which antedates these things; how he glories in the present, and yet is sustained and justified by the past; how he is the poet of America and the modern, and yet translates these things into universal truths; how he is the poet of wickedness, while yet every fibre of him is sound and good; how his page is burdened with the material, the real, the contemporary, while yet his hold upon the ideal, the spiritual, never relaxes; how he is the poet of the body, while yet he is in even fuller measure the poet of the soul; in fact, how all contradictions are finally reconciled in him,—all these things and more, I say, I feel that I have not set forth with the clearness and emphasis the subject demanded. Other students of him will approach him on other lines, and will disclose meanings that I have missed.

Writing about him, as Symonds said, is enormously difficult. At times I feel as if I was almost as much at sea with regard to him as when I first began to study him; not at sea with regard to his commanding genius and power, but with regard to any adequate statement and summary of him in current critical terms. One cannot define and classify him as he can a more highly specialized poetic genius. What is he like? He is like everything. He is like the soil which holds the germs of a thousand forms of life; he is like the grass, common, universal, perennial, formless; he is like your own heart, mystical yearning, rebellious, contradictory, but ever throbbing with life. He is fluid, generative, electric; he is full of the germs, potencies, and latencies of things; he provokes thought without satisfying it; he is formless without being void; he is both Darwinian and Dantesque. He is the great reconciler, he united and harmonized so many opposites in himself. As a man he united the masculine and feminine elements in a remarkable degree; he united the innocent vanity of the child with the self-reliance of a god. In his moral aspects, he united egoism and altruism, pride and charity, individualism and democracy, fierce patriotism and the cosmopolitan spirit; in his literary aspects he united mysticism and realism, the poet and prophet, the local and the universal; in his religious aspects he united faith and agnosticism, the glorification of the body and all objective things, with an unshakable trust in the reality of the invisible world.

Rich in the elements of poetry, a London critic says, almost beyond any other poet of his time, and yet the conscious, elaborate, crystallic, poetic work which the critic demanded of him, carefully stopping short of, quite content to hold it all in solution, and give his reader an impulse rather than a specimen.

I have accepted Whitman entire and without reservation. I could not do otherwise. It was clear enough to me that he was to be taken as a whole or not at all. We cannot cut and carve a man. The latest poet brings us poetic wares, curiously and beautifully carved and wrought specimens, some of which we accept and some of which we pass by. Whitman brings us no cunning handicraft of the muses: he brings us a gospel, he brings us a man, he brings us a new revelation of life; and either his work appeals to us as a whole, or it does not so appeal. He will not live in separate passages, or in a few brief poems, any more than Shakespeare or Homer or Dante, or the Bible, so lives.

The chief thing about the average literary poet is his poetic gift, apart from any other consideration; we select from what he brings us as we select from a basket of fruit. The chief thing about Whitman is the personality which the poetic gift is engaged in exploiting; the excitement of our literary or artistic sense is always less than the excitement of our sense of life and of real things. We get in him a fixed point of view, a new vantage-ground of personality from which to survey life. It is less what he brings, and more what he is, than with other poets. To take him by fragments, picking out poetic tidbits here and there, rejecting all the rest, were like valuing a walk through the fields and woods only for the flowers culled here and there, or the bits of color in the grass or foliage. Is the air, the sunshine, the free spaces, the rocks, the soil, the trees, and the exhilaration of it all, nothing? There are flowers in Whitman, too, but they are amid the rocks or under the trees, and seem quite unpremeditated and by the way, and never the main concern. If our quest is for these alone, we shall surely be disappointed.

> In order to appreciate Whitman's poetry and his purpose, [says Joel Chandler Harris] it is necessary to possess the intuition that enables the mind to grasp in instant and express admiration the vast group of facts that make man,—that make liberty,—that make America. There is no poetry in the details; it is all in the broad, sweeping, comprehensive assimilation of the mighty forces behind them,—the inevitable, unaccountable, irresistible forward movement of man in the making of this republic.

And again:

> Those who approach Walt Whitman's poetry from the literary side are sure to be disappointed. Whatever else it is, it is not literary. Its art is its own, and the melody of it must be sought in other suggestions than those of metre. . . . Those who are merely literary will find little substance in the great drama of Democracy which is outlined by Walt Whitman in his writings,—it is no distinction to call them poems. But those who know nature at first hand—who know man, who see in this Republic something more than a political government—will find therein the thrill and glow of poetry and the essence of melody. Not the poetry that culture stands in expectation of, nor the melody that capers in verse and metre, but those rarer intimations and suggestions that are born in primeval solitudes, or come whirling from the vast funnel of the storm.

How admirable! how true! No man has ever spoken more to the point upon Walt Whitman.

The appearance of such a man as Whitman involves deep world-forces of race and time. He is rooted in the very basic structure of his age. After what I have already said, my reader will not be surprised when I tell him that I look upon Whitman as the one mountain thus far in our literary landscape. To me he changes the whole aspect, almost the very climate, of our literature. He adds the much-needed ruggedness, breadth, audacity, independence, and the elements of primal strength and health. We owe much to Emerson. But Emerson was much more a *made* man than was Whitman,—much more the result of secondary forces, the college, the church, and of New England social and literary culture. With all his fervid humanity and deeply ingrained modernness, Whitman has the virtues of the primal and the savage. *Leaves of Grass* has not the charm, or the kind of charm, of the more highly wrought artistic works, but it has the incentive of nature and the charm of real things. We shall not go to it to be soothed and lulled. It will always remain among the difficult and heroic undertakings, demanding our best moments, our best strength, our morning push and power. Like voyaging or mountain-climbing, or facing any danger or hardship by land or sea, it fosters manly endeavor and the great virtues of sanity and self-reliance.

54. William Sloane Kennedy on Whitman

1896

Extract from William Sloane Kennedy, *Reminiscences of Walt Whitman* (London, 1896), pp. 162–90.

William Sloane Kennedy (1850–1929) was one of the most polemically effective admirers of Whitman. He is the author of *The Fight of a Book for the World: A companion volume to Leaves of Grass* (1926) which traces the varying fortunes of Whitman's book during the decades. Like Burroughs and other disciples of Whitman, he asks that the poet be accepted as a whole, even while recognizing the existence of imperfections and faults. He even attempts a rationalization of the catalogues and inventories of Whitman which most of those whose appreciation is more lukewarm have been content to abandon.

After this preliminary survey I come at length to Whitman, who is one of the few writers in the world besides Swinburne able to compose symphonic word-music. It can be indubitably proved that his poetic art, *as shown in his most finished productions*, the rhythmic chants,—and especially in his later poems,—is profoundly consonant with the laws of nature and symphonic music; and that conversely and necessarily, therefore, the whole body of English poetry, with the exception of a few lyrical masterpieces, is composed (technically or metrically considered) upon a system as false to nature as it is to the higher harmonies of music.

The great gain in casting nobler and longer works in non-rhyming form is release from the degrading task of sentence-sawing and twisting, and the fixing of the attention on the message to be spoken. Nor is this offering the least encouragement to idleness or inferior work. It is precisely the most difficult thing in the world for a poet or painter to imitate nature's spontaneity. In the first place, his songs must be the pulsations of a profoundly musical nature; and second, while allowing the hand of the Unconscious to wander over the darkling strings of his soul, he must yet know how to so subtly mingle himself in the creative process as, by the higher instinct of his culture, to guide all to a supreme musical expression and shaping which shall surpass the careless work of the pseudo-naturalist in the exact measure of the deeper thought and wider intellectual range they represent. This psychical performance is the pinnacle of the soul's art-life, the farthest point reached by the fountain in its sunward leap. Here the circle of intellectual growth returns to its starting point, and the mind of man comes into electric and vital contact with the Soul of Nature, partaking by hidden inlet of her high powers and virtues.

Let it be premised that to the creations of the seer-poets technique adds very little value. The supreme art of these poets is to forget all art, to have a high moral or emotional aim, and noble passion, and let the style flow spontaneously out of these. Indeed, if the whole mind of *any* poet is directed chiefly to artistic form, he will never attain supreme artistic form. Plato has said, 'Art is the expression of the highest moral energy.' Poetry is not a thing of yard-sticks and tinkling brasses, but is 'the measure of the intensity of the human soul.' Where the air is densest, as on the plains, there the roll of the thunder and the splendor of the lightning are most sublime. The greater number of current poems are to the mind what cork is to water: they have form, but no weight, and refuse to sink into the memory; they are like brooks without water. 'Genius is nothing but love,' said W. M. Hunt: 'whatever the artist paints must be from the heart's blood, if it is only two marks on a shingle.' But poetry to-day has become partly a matter of trick, as it was with Simmias of Rhodes, who wrote verses in the shape of an altar, an egg, a double-edged axe, etc. About the only emotion excited in our breasts by this all-prevalent brand of poetry is that which we feel in looking at the contortions of a circus gymnast. No matter about the thought, but only see how the juggler keeps those nine rhymes going in the air at once! How deftly he managed that difficult line! (and twisted the neck of his thought in doing it). The painful interest we feel in a milliner with her mouth full of pins (as in Maria Edgeworth's 'Mademoiselle Panache'), that is how the average sonneteer affects us. I repeat, the style of the poem will flow spontaneously and in original forms from noble aim and passion. And never doubt that there are as many ways of expressing poetic thought as there are original souls. 'Never was a song good or beautiful which resembled any other,' said Pierre d'Auvergne. We should always expect from a great artist a new style, one that must win its way into favor through abuse, as in the case of Turner, Victor Hugo, Shakspere. 'The melange of existence is but an eternal font of type, and may be set up to any text, however different—with room and welcome, at whatever time, for new compositors.'

It is passing strange how incapable otherwise intelligent persons are of true critical judgments. The A, B, C, of criticism is to put yourself in an author's place, judge him by what he proposed to attain. Now, Walt Whitman, from the very start, gave notice in the preface to his first volume that, in his opinion, the time had come to 'break down the barriers of form between prose and poetry' (*Specimen Days*, pp. 226 and 322); and he proceeded to illustrate his theory in poems—when, lo! a chorus of jeering voices exclaiming, 'These "poems" are half prose: do you call such and such lines poetry?'* No, my bat-eyed ones, we do not: did we not distinctly premise the contrary,—that the work was to be partly in prose? Now, as to the poetical portions of *Leaves of Grass*, let us see if they meet the tests of true art. Beyond question there are certain fundamentals which will never be found lacking in pure poetry. One of these is *Music*, and another is *Form*.

There is music and music,—the simple ballad of the harper and the intricate symphony of the modern composer. Whitman, as has often been said, is the Wagner of poets. As Wagner abandoned the cadences of the old sonatas and symphonies,—occurring at the end of every four, eight, or sixteen bars,—so Whitman has abandoned the measured beat of the old rhymed see-saw poetry, after having himself thoroughly tried it, as the early poems appended to his prose volume attest. In the old operas you were always let down every few seconds by the regularly recurrent cadences: in the dramas of Wagner you never touch ground, but soar, like an eagle or a planet, in great, spiral, Geryon-flights of harmony. So with Whitman poetry has now become an instrument breathing a music in so vast a key that even the stately wheelings and solemn pomp of Milton's verse seem rather formal and mechanical. Whitman's dithyrambic chants, with their long, winding

* I suppose the chief bar to the action of the imagination, and stop to all greatness in this present age of ours, is its mean and shallow love of jest; so that if there be in any good and lofty work a flaw, failing, or undipped vulnerable part, where sarcasm may stick or stay, it is caught at, and pointed at, and buzzed about, and fixed upon, and stung into as a recent wound is by flies; and nothing is ever taken seriously or as it was meant, but always, if it may be, turned the wrong way, and misunderstood; and, while this is so, there is not, nor cannot be, any hope of achievement of high things. Men dare not open their hearts, if we are to broil them on a thorn-fire.—*John Ruskin*.

fiords of sound, require—like summer thunder or organ music—perspective of the ear, if the phrase will be allowed: they must be considered in vocal mass, and not in parts; and, when so considered, it will be found that nearly every page is held in solution by a deep-running undertone of majestic rhythm.* 'Harmony latent,' said Heracleitus, 'is of more value than that which is patent.' In the matter of orchestral word-music, Whitman, in his rhythmic chants, does at any rate more than any other mortal has yet accomplished. Only consider how inferior, for the expression of deep emotion, the cold, solitary, inarticulate words of ink and paper are to music:—

The swift contending fugue,—the wild escape
  Of passions,—long-drawn wail and sudden blast,
The low sad mutterings and entangled dreams
  Of viols and basoons, . . .

The trumpet-cries of anger and despair,
  The mournful marches of the muffled drum;
The bird-like flute-notes leaping into air;—

how will you imprison the vague-sweet and mysterious suggestions of the voices of these children of sound in lifeless, breathless words?

I do not affirm that every part of Whitman's work is musical. There are prosaic intervals in all poetry—in Tennyson's, Shakspere's, and Browning's as much as in any,—only with them the prose is masked in the *form* of poesy, without possessing its lyric soul. But what I do affirm is that the proportion of poetry to prose in *Leaves of Grass* is no less than in any other poet's work, and that the proportion of *symphonic* music—rude at times, if you choose—is immensely greater than in the compositions of any other bard. I cannot quote to illustrate, because I should have to quote whole poems. Read the Sea Chants, Drum Taps, 'Italian Music in Dakota,' 'Proud Music of the Storm,' 'That Music always around Me,' 'Vigil Strange,' 'The Singer in the Prison,' 'Pioneers, O Pioneers,' and the 'Burial Hymn of Lincoln,' and you will catch the interior music I speak of. It will be different from what

* For the benefit of people who have no musical ear I will adduce the testimony of Mrs. Fanny Raymond Ritter, wife of the Professor of Music at Vassar College, who speaks of the strong rhythmical pulsing musical power of *Leaves of Grass* (Bucke, p. 157), and also that of one who belongs to the native home of music—Signor Enrico Nencioni of Italy, who in an article published in the *Nuova Antologia* magazine of Rome, August, 1885, affirms with emphasis the existence of a 'grandiosa e musicale struttura' in Whitman's poetry.

you expected: it will not remind you of a church choir; but it is there, nevertheless.

'In the rhythm of certain poets,' says Emerson, 'there is no manufacture, but a vortex or musical tornado, which falling on words and the experience of a learned mind whirl these materials into the same grand order as planets or moons obey, and seasons and monsoons.' That is the kind of rhythm you will find in the best of Whitman's chants. For twenty years Whitman absorbed the strains of the best singers of the world in the New York operas, and many of his lines were written down while hearing the music, or immediately after (Bucke, p. 157),—a fact that gives us the key to many a bit of wonderful melody that sparkles out of his interspaces of prose. The little poem, 'Weave in, my Hardy Life,' when analysed and divided as the ordinary poets would divide it, turns out to be made up of regular four-foot iambic lines, with two three-foot iambics and one or two lines long or short by a foot—licenses which every poet takes. I add the poem entire, with the lines cut up in the ordinary unnatural way. But first let us have the three opening lines as they stand on the poet's page:—

Weave in, weave in, my hardy life,
Weave yet a soldier strong and full for great campaigns to come,
Weave in red blood, weave sinews in like ropes, the senses, sight weave in.

The ordinary method would be as follows. (At the close of each of Whitman's lines I place a perpendicular bar):—

Weave in, weave in, my hardy life, |
Weave yet a soldier strong and full
   For great campaigns to come, |
Weave in red blood, weave sinews in
Like ropes, the senses, sight weave in, |
Weave lasting sure, weave day and night
The weft, the warp, incessant weave, tire not, |
(We know not what the use O life,
   Nor know the aim, the end,
   Nor really aught we know, |
But know the work, the need goes on
And shall go on, the death-envelop'd march
Of peace as well as war goes on,) |
For great campaigns of peace the same
The wiry threads to weave, | we know not why
Or what, yet weave, forever weave. |

Now, one may venture to say that, if these musical lines had been written in the above orthodox way, not a critic would have peeped. But the awful heresy of originality! The daring to be natural! Nor is this poem a solitary exception. If the reader will turn to pages 366 and 368 of *Leaves of Grass*, and read the poems 'By Broad Potomac's Shore,' 'From Far Dakota's Cañons,' 'What Best I see in Thee,' and 'Spirit that formed this Scene,' he will discover that the iambic movement in these is almost perfect, containing only such variations as nature approves and as the most cultivated musical sense indorses. And these instances might be multiplied many times, especially from the more recent poems,—as 'Of that Blithe Throat of Thine,' published in *Harper's Monthly*, Jan., 1885; 'If I should need to name, O Western World' (Philadelphia *Press*, 1884); and 'Red Jacket from Aloft' (1884). 'To a Man-of-War-Bird' is a poem almost purely iambic in form: so are 'Ethiopia saluting the Colors,' 'World, take Good Notice,' 'Delicate Cluster,' 'Joy, Shipmate, Joy.' There is plenty of music in Whitman's poems, if you only have the ear to detect it, and are not fooled by the visible form, or mould, the poet has chosen.

As to form, poetry may legitimately be divided into two groups or styles,—the sculpturesque and the pictorial. Hitherto the poets have only attempted to create in the sculpturesque, or Greek, style. All Greek art is based on the principle of form, summed up in the saying of Plato, 'Beauty is proportion,' and in the dictum of a modern Greek (the poet Goethe), 'Die Kunst ist nur Gestaltung,' 'Art is form alone.' But Walt Whitman exfoliates the art of poetry into a wider air and range. He would make it less artificial, give it more of the grandeur of nature. 'Poetic style,' he says, 'when address'd to the soul, is less definite form, outline, sculpture, and becomes vista, music, half-tints, and even less than half-tints. True, it may be architecture; but again it may be the forest wild-wood, or the best effect thereof, at twilight, the waving oaks and cedars in the wind, and the impalpable odor.'

If you see nothing to like in Walt Whitman's lines, you will see nothing to please you in the long leaves of coloured lights that rock in sumptuous idleness on the waves, nothing in the purple-floating richness of the flower-de-luce, nothing in the exquisite clare-obscure, soft craterous glooms, and rolling dream-drapery emergent from the locomotive's funnel, nothing in the bobolincoln's pretty little orchestra,—gurgle, whistle, trill, and steady undertone of chime,—nothing in the great bell's resonant roar and long, tapering after-hum; for in all these forms and sounds there is the vague irregularity and asymmetry of all natural phenomena.

But to come closer to the details of our poet's art in this matter of form. As I have said, the fatal defect of the ten-syllable, or heroic, line is that it is too short. To fit your delicate fancy with blank verse, you have got to mangle its joints. But Whitman never breaks a verse on the wheel. So far as I can discover, about the average number of syllables required to express a single poetical thought is from sixteen or twenty to twenty-five.* I at least affirm that about one half of all simple poetical thoughts require that much articulated breath to get them uttered. Every one of Whitman's lucid Greek pages illustrates the statement. His work is nearly always blocked out into lines or periods the length of which corresponds with the natural length of the thoughts. As, for example, in these lines:—

O Western orb sailing the heaven,
Now I know what you must have meant as a month since I walk'd,
As I walk'd in silence the transparent shadowy night,
As I saw you had something to tell as you bent to me night after night,
As you droop'd from the sky low down as if to my side, (while the other stars all look'd on,)
As we wander'd together the solemn night, (for something I know not what kept me from sleep.)
As the night advanced, and I saw on the rim of the west how full you were of woe,
As I stood on the rising ground in the breeze in the cool transparent night,
As I watch'd where you pass'd and was lost in the netherward black of the night,
As my soul in its trouble dissatisfied sank, as where you sad orb,
Concluded, dropt in the night, and was gone.

These flowing epic lines are the counterpart in English of Homer's

* The opening lines of the Sapphic 'Hymn to the Aphrodite' show that the law is as old as Greece:—

Ποικιλόθρον' 'αθάνατ' Αφρόδιτα,
Παὶ Δίος δολοπλόκε, λισσομαί σε
Μή μ' ἄσαισι, μήτ' 'ονίγισι δάμνα,
Πότνια θῦμον.[1]

Compare also the opening sentences of the Iliad and the Odyssey.

[1] Translation of Sappho:

Aphrodite, daughter of Zeus, undying
Goddess, throned in glory, of love's beguilements,
Do not now with frenzy and desperation
Utterly crush me.

hexameters, and are the only possible hexameters for us. They have the required weight and momentum, are strong enough to bear the pressure of the thought, and are the first true, unborrowed heroics ever written in a Germanic tongue. It is doubtless true, as Dr. O. W. Holmes has pointed out, that the ten-syllable line owes much of its impressiveness to the sense of difficulty we have in the reading, since a longer respiration than ordinary is required for each line; but this advantage will not overbalance the other defects. Ours is an age of great and difficult thoughts. Now, a great poet always reflects the ideas and passions of his own day. And just as in a painting showing action all the lines must be agitated or undulating, in sympathy with the leading emotional purpose, and not horizontal, angular, and regular, as in a painting showing repose, so our poet's irregular and fluent twenty-syllable lines are in harmony with the agitated nature of his leading motives,—as well as with the spirit of the age,—and suit the largeness of his themes.

55. Henry James on Whitman

1898

Review of Whitman's posthumous *Calamus*, an extract from Henry James, 'American Letter', *Literature* (16 April 1898), p. 453.

For an earlier statement by James, see No. 27 (and see Introduction, pp. 9–10).

What sense shall I speak of as affected by the series of letters published, under the title of *Calamus*, by Dr. R. M. Bucke, one of the literary executors of Walt Whitman? The democratic would be doubtless a prompt and simple answer, and as an illustration of democratic social conditions their interest is lively. The person to whom, from 1868 to

1880, they were addressed was a young labouring man, employed in rough railway work, whom Whitman met by accident—the account of the meeting, in his correspondent's own words, is the most charming passage in the volume—and constituted for the rest of life a subject of a friendship of the regular 'eternal,' the legendary sort. The little book appeals, I daresay, mainly to the Whitmanite already made, but I should be surprised if it has actually failed of power to make a few more. I mean by the Whitmanite those for whom the author of *Leaves of Grass* is, with all his rags and tatters, an upright figure, a *successful* original. It has in a singular way something of the same relation to poetry that may be made out in the luckiest—few, but fine—of the writer's other pages; I call the way singular because it squeezes through the narrowest, humblest gate of prose.

There is not even by accident a line with a hint of style—it is all flat, familiar, affectionate, illiterate colloquy. If the absolute natural be, when the writer is interesting, the supreme merit of letters, these, accordingly, should stand high on the list. (I am taking for granted, of course, the interest of Whitman.) The beauty of the natural is, here, the beauty of the particular nature, the man's own overflow in the deadly dry setting, the personal passion, the love of life plucked like a flower in a desert of innocent, unconscious ugliness. To call the whole thing vividly American is to challenge, doubtless, plenty of dissent—on the ground, presumably, that the figure in evidence was no less queer a feature of Camden, New Jersey, than it would have been of South Kensington. That may perfectly be; but a thousand images of patient, homely, American life, else undistinguishable, are what its queerness—however startling—happened to express. In this little book is an audible New Jersey voice, charged thick with such impressions, and the reader will miss a chance who does not find in it many odd and pleasant human harmonies. Whitman wrote to his friend of what they both saw and touched, enormities of the common, sordid occupations, dreary amusements, undesirable food; and the record remains, by a mysterious marvel, a thing positively delightful. If we ever find out why, it must be another time. The riddle meanwhile is a neat one for the sphinx of democracy to offer.

56. John Jay Chapman on Whitman

1898

Extracts from John Jay Chapman, *Emerson and Other Essays* (1898), pp. 119, 121, 125. Quoted in Moulton's *Library of Literary Criticism of English and American Authors*.

Walt Whitman has given utterance to the soul of the tramp. . . . . In Whitman's works the elemental parts of a man's mind and the fragments of imperfect education may be seen merging together, floating and sinking in a sea of insensate egotism and rhapsody, repellent, divine, disgusting, extraordinary. . . . The attraction exercised by his writings is due to their flashes of reality. Of course the man was a poseur, a most horrid mountebank and ego-maniac. His tawdry scraps of misused idea, of literary smartness, of dog-eared and greasy reminiscence, repel us. The world of men remained for him as his audience, and he did to civilized society the continuous compliment of an insane self-consciousness in its presence. . . . It is doubtful whether a man ever enjoyed life more intensely than Walt Whitman, or expressed the physical joy of mere living more completely. He is robust, all tingling with health and the sensations of health. All that is best in his poetry is the expression of bodily well-being.

57. Thomas Wentworth Higginson on Whitman

1899

Extract from Thomas Wentworth Higginson, *Contemporaries* (1899), p. 83.

Higginson (1823–1911), the friend and editor of Emily Dickinson, was a prolific writer, a clergyman, editor of the *Atlantic Monthly* and a colonel, commanding the first black regiment during the Civil War. He was an early reader of Whitman and must have mentioned him in his reply to Miss Dickinson's first letter to him (15 April 1862), for on 25 April we find her writing to him: 'You speak of Mr. Whitman—I never read his Book—but was told that he was disgraceful—'

The essential fault of Whitman's poetry was well pointed out by a man of more heroic nature and higher genius, Lanier, who described him as a dandy. Of all our poets, he is really the least simple, the most meretricious, and this is the reason why the honest consciousness of the classes which he most celebrates,—the drover, the teamster, the soldier, —has never been reached by his songs. He talks of labor as one who has never really labored; his 'Drum-Taps' proceed from one who has never personally responded to the tap of the drum. This is the fatal and insurmountable defect; and it is because his own countrymen instinctively recognize this, and foreigners do not, that his following has always been larger abroad than at home. But it is also true that he has, in a fragmentary and disappointing way, some of the very highest ingredients of a poet's nature: a keen eye, a ready sympathy, a strong touch, a vivid but not shaping imagination. In his cyclopaedia of epithets, in his accumulated directory of details, in his sandy wastes of iteration, there are many scattered particles of gold—never sifted out by him, not always abundant enough to pay for the sifting, yet unmistakable gold. He has something of the turgid wealth, the self-conscious and mouthing amplitude of Victor Hugo, and much of his broad, vague, indolent desire for the welfare of the whole human race; but he has none of Hugo's structural power, his dramatic or melodramatic instinct, and his occasionally terse and brilliant condensation. It is not likely that he will ever have that place in the future which is claimed for him by his English admirers or even by the more cautious endorsement of Mr. Stedman: for, setting aside all other grounds of criticism, he has phrase, but not form—and without form there is no immortality.

58. Santayana on Whitman

1900

Extract from George Santayana, 'The Poetry of Barbarism', *Interpretations of Poetry and Religion* (1900), pp. 174–87.

The poetry of barbarism is not without its charm. It can play with sense and passion the more readily and freely in that it does not aspire to subordinate them to a clear thought or a tenable attitude of the will. It can impart the transitive emotions which it expresses; it can find many partial harmonies of mood and fancy; it can, by virtue of its red-hot irrationality, utter wilder cries, surrender itself and us to more absolute passion, and heap up a more indiscriminate wealth of images than belong to poets of seasoned experience or of heavenly inspiration. Irrational stimulation may tire us in the end, but it excites us in the beginning; and how many conventional poets, tender and prolix, have there not been, who tire us now without ever having excited anybody? The power to stimulate is the beginning of greatness, and when the barbarous poet has genius, as he well may have, he stimulates all the more powerfully on account of the crudity of his methods and the recklessness of his emotions. The defects of such art—lack of distinction, absence of beauty, confusion of ideas, incapacity permanently to please—will hardly be felt by the contemporary public, if once its attention is arrested; for no poet is so undisciplined that he will not find many readers, if he finds readers at all, less disciplined than himself.

These considerations may perhaps be best enforced by applying them to two writers of great influence over the present generation who seem to illustrate them on different planes—Robert Browning and Walt Whitman. They are both analytic poets—poets who seek to reveal and express the elemental as opposed to the conventional; but the dissolution has progressed much farther in Whitman than in Browning, doubtless because Whitman began at a much lower stage of moral and ntellectual organization; for the good will to be radical was present in both. The elements to which Browning reduces experience are still passions, characters, persons; Whitman carries the disintegration further and knows nothing but moods and particular images. The world of Browning is a world of history with civilization for its setting and with the conventional passions for its motive forces. The world of Whitman is innocent of these things and contains only far simpler and more chaotic elements. In him the barbarism is much more pronounced; it is, indeed, avowed, and the 'barbaric yawp' is sent 'over the roofs of the world' in full consciousness of its inarticulate character; but in Browning the barbarism is no less real though disguised by a literary and scientific language, since the passions of civilized life with which he deals are treated, as so many 'barbaric yawps,' complex indeed in their conditions, puffings of an intricate engine, but aimless in their vehemence and mere ebullitions of lustiness in adventurous and profoundly ungoverned souls.

Irrationality on this level is viewed by Browning with the same satisfaction with which, on a lower level, it is viewed by Whitman; and the admirers of each hail it as the secret of a new poetry which pierces to the quick and awakens the imagination to a new and genuine vitality. It is in the rebellion against discipline, in the abandonment of the ideals of classic and Christian tradition, that this rejuvenation is found. Both poets represent, therefore, and are admired for representing, what may be called the poetry of barbarism in the most accurate and descriptive sense of this word. For the barbarian is the man who regards his passions as their own excuse for being; who does not domesticate them either by understanding their cause or by conceiving their ideal goal. He is the man who does not know his derivations nor perceive his tendencies, but who merely feels and acts, valuing in his life its force and its filling, but being careless of its purpose and its form. His delight is in abundance and vehemence; his art, like his life, shows an exclusive respect for quantity and splendour of materials. His scorn for what is poorer and weaker than himself is only surpassed by his ignorance of what is higher.

II

WALT WHITMAN

The works of Walt Whitman offer an extreme illustration of this phase of genius, both by their form and by their substance. It was the singularity of his literary form—the challenge it threw to the conventions of verse and of language—that first gave Whitman notoriety: but this notoriety has become fame, because those incapacities and solecisms which glare at us from his pages are only the obverse of a profound inspiration and of a genuine courage. Even the idiosyncrasies of his style have a side which is not mere perversity or affectation; the order of his words, the procession of his images, reproduce the method of a rich, spontaneous, absolutely lazy fancy. In most poets such a natural order is modified by various governing motives—the thought, the metrical form, the echo of other poems in the memory. By Walt Whitman these conventional influences are resolutely banished. We find the swarms of men and objects rendered as they might strike the retina in a sort of waking dream. It is the most sincere possible confession of the lowest—I mean the most primitive—type of perception. All ancient poets are sophisticated in comparison and give proof of longer intellectual and moral training. Walt Whitman has gone back to the innocent style of Adam, when the animals filed before him one by one and he called each of them by its name.

In fact, the influences to which Walt Whitman was subject were as favourable as possible to the imaginary experiment of beginning the world over again. Liberalism and transcendentalism both harboured some illusions on that score; and they were in the air which our poet breathed. Moreover he breathed this air in America, where the newness of the material environment made it easier to ignore the fatal antiquity of human nature. When he afterward became aware that there was or had been a world with a history, he studied that world with curiosity and spoke of it not without a certain shrewdness. But he still regarded it as a foreign world and imagined, as not a few

Americans have done, that his own world was a fresh creation, not amenable to the same laws as the old. The difference in the conditions blinded him, in his merely sensuous apprehension, to the identity of the principles.

His parents were farmers in central Long Island and his early years were spent in that district. The family seems to have been not too prosperous and somewhat nomadic; Whitman himself drifted through boyhood without much guidance. We find him now at school, now helping the labourers at the farms, now wandering along the beaches of Long Island, finally at Brooklyn working in an apparently desultory way as a printer and sometimes as a writer for a local newspaper. He must have read or heard something, at this early period, of the English classics; his style often betrays the deep effect made upon him by the grandiloquence of the Bible, of Shakespeare, and of Milton. But his chief interest, if we may trust his account, was already in his own sensations. The aspects of Nature, the forms and habits of animals, the sights of cities, the movement and talk of common people, were his constant delight. His mind was flooded with these images, keenly felt and afterward to be vividly rendered with bold strokes of realism and imagination.

Many poets have had this faculty to seize the elementary aspects of things, but none has had it so exclusively; with Whitman the surface is absolutely all and the underlying structure is without interest and almost without existence. He had had no education and his natural delight in imbibing sensations had not been trained to the uses of practical or theoretical intelligence. He basked in the sunshine of perception and wallowed in the stream of his own sensibility, as later at Camden in the shallows of his favourite brook. Even during the civil war, when he heard the drum-taps so clearly, he could only gaze at the picturesque and terrible aspects of the struggle, and linger among the wounded day after day with a canine devotion; he could not be aroused either to clear thought or to positive action. So also in his poems; a multiplicity of images pass before him and he yields himself to each in turn with absolute passivity. The world has no inside; it is a phantasmagoria of continuous visions, vivid, impressive, but monotonous and hard to distinguish in memory, like the waves of the sea or the decorations of some barbarous temple, sublime only by the infinite aggregation of parts.

This abundance of detail without organization, this wealth of perception without intelligence and of imagination without taste, makes the singularity of Whitman's genius. Full of sympathy and receptivity, with a wonderful gift of graphic characterization and an occasional rare grandeur of diction, he fills us with a sense of the individuality and the universality of what he describes—it is a drop in itself yet a drop in the ocean. The absence of any principle of selection or of a sustained style enables him to render aspects of things and of emotion which would have eluded a trained writer. He is, therefore, interesting even where he is grotesque or perverse. He had accomplished, by the sacrifice of almost every other good quality, something never so well done before. He has approached common life without bringing in his mind any higher standard by which to criticise it; he has seen it, not in contrast with an ideal, but as the expression of forces more indeterminate and elementary than itself; and the vulgar, in this cosmic setting, has appeared to him sublime.

There is clearly some analogy between a mass of images without structure and the notion of an absolute democracy. Whitman, inclined by his genius and habits to see life without relief or organization, believed that his inclination in this respect corresponded with the spirit of his age and country, and that Nature and society, at least in the United States, were constituted after the fashion of his own mind. Being the poet of the average man, he wished all men to be specimens of that average, and being the poet of a fluid Nature, he believed that Nature was or should be a formless flux. This personal bias of Whitman's was further encouraged by the actual absence of distinction in his immediate environment. Surrounded by ugly things and common people, he felt himself happy, ecstatic, overflowing with a kind of patriarchal love. He accordingly came to think that there was a spirit of the New World which he embodied, and which was in complete opposition to that of the Old, and that a literature upon novel principles was needed to express and strengthen this American spirit.

Democracy was not to be merely a constitutional device for the better government of given nations, not merely a movement for the material improvement of the lot of the poorer classes. It was to be a social and a moral democracy and to involve an actual equality among all men. Whatever kept them apart and made it impossible for them to be messmates together was to be discarded. The literature of democracy was to ignore all extraordinary gifts of genius or virtue, all distinction drawn even from great passions or romantic adventures. In Whitman's works, in which this new literature is foreshadowed, there is accordingly not a single character nor a single story. His only hero is Myself, the 'single separate person,' endowed with the primary impulses, with health, and with sensitiveness to the elementary aspects of Nature. The perfect man of the future, the prolific begetter of other perfect men, is to work with his hands, chanting the poems of some future Walt, some ideally democratic bard. Women are to have as nearly as possible the same character as men: the emphasis is to pass from family life and local ties to the friendship of comrades and the general brotherhood of man. Men are to be vigorous, comfortable, sentimental, and irresponsible.

This dream is, of course, unrealized and unrealizable, in America as elsewhere. Undeniably there are in America many suggestions of such a society and such a national character. But the growing complexity and fixity of institutions necessarily tends to obscure these traits of a primitive and crude democracy. What Whitman seized upon as the promise of the future was in reality the survival of the past. He sings the song of pioneers, but it is in the nature of the pioneer that the greater his success the quicker must be his transformation into something different. When Whitman made the initial and amorphous phase of society his ideal, he became the prophet of a lost cause. That cause was lost, not merely when wealth and intelligence began to take shape in the American Commonwealth, but it was lost at the very foundation of the world, when those laws of evolution were established which Whitman, like Rousseau, failed to understand. If we may trust Mr. Herbert Spencer, these laws involve a passage from the homogeneous to the heterogeneous, and a constant progress at once in differentiation and in organization—all, in a word, that Whitman systematically deprecated or ignored. He is surely not the spokesman of the tendencies of his country, although he describes some aspects of its past and present condition: nor does he appeal to those whom he describes, but rather to the *dilettanti* he despises. He is regarded as representative chiefly by foreigners, who look for some grotesque expression of the genius of so young and prodigious a people.

Whitman, it is true, loved and comprehended men; but this love and comprehension had the same limits as his love and comprehension of Nature. He observed truly and responded to his observation with genuine and pervasive emotion. A great gregariousness, an innocent tolerance of moral weakness, a genuine admiration for bodily health and strength, made him bubble over with affection for the generic human creature. Incapable of an ideal passion, he was full of the milk of human kindness. Yet, for all his acquaintance with the ways and thoughts of the common man of his choice, he did not truly understand him. For to understand people is to go much deeper than they go themselves; to penetrate to their characters and disentangle their inmost ideals. Whitman's insight into man did not go beyond a sensuous sympathy; it consisted in a vicarious satisfaction in their pleasures, and an instinctive love of their persons. It never approached a scientific or imaginative knowledge of their hearts.

Therefore Whitman failed radically in his dearest ambition: he can never be a poet of the people. For the people, like the early races whose poetry was ideal, are natural believers in perfection. They have no doubts about the absolute desirability of wealth and learning and power, none about the worth of pure goodness and pure love. Their chosen poets, if they have any, will be always those who have known how to paint these ideals in lively even if in gaudy colours. Nothing is farther from the common people than the corrupt desire to be primitive. They instinctively look toward a more exalted life, which they imagine to be full of distinction and pleasure, and the idea of that brighter existence fills them with hope or with envy or with humble admiration.

If the people are ever won over to hostility to such ideals, it is only because they are cheated by demagogues who tell them that if all the flowers of civilization were destroyed its fruits would become more abundant. A greater share of happiness, people think, would fall to their lot could they destroy everything beyond their own possible possessions. But they are made thus envious and ignoble only by a deception: what they really desire is an ideal good for themselves which they are told they may secure by depriving others of their preëminence. Their hope is always to enjoy perfect satisfaction themselves; and therefore a poet who loves the picturesque aspects of labour and vagrancy will hardly be the poet of the poor. He may have described their figure and occupation, in neither of which they are much interested; he will not have read their souls. They will prefer to him any sentimental story-teller, any sensational dramatist, any moralizing poet; for they are hero-worshippers by temperament, and are too wise or too unfortunate to be much enamoured of themselves or of the conditions of their existence.

Fortunately, the political theory that makes Whitman's principle of literary prophecy and criticism does not always inspire his chants, nor is it presented, even in his prose works, quite bare and unadorned. In *Democratic Vistas* we find it clothed with something of the same poetic passion and lighted up with the same flashes of intuition which we admire in the poems. Even there the temperament is finer than the ideas and the poet wiser than the thinker. His ultimate appeal is really to something more primitive and general than any social aspirations, to something more elementary than an ideal of any kind. He speaks to those minds and to those moods in which sensuality is touched with mysticism. When the intellect is in abeyance, when we would 'turn and live with the animals, they are so placid and self contained,' when we are weary of conscience and of ambition, and would yield ourselves for a while to the dream of sense, Walt Whitman is a welcome companion. The images he arouses in us, fresh, full of light and health and of a kind of frankness and beauty, are prized all the more at such a time because they are not choice, but drawn perhaps from a hideous and sordid environment. For this circumstance makes them a better means of escape from convention and from that fatigue and despair which lurk not far beneath the surface of conventional life. In casting off with self-assurance and a sense of fresh vitality the distinctions of tradition and reason a man may feel, as he sinks back comfortably to a lower level of sense and instinct, that he is returning to Nature or escaping into the infinite. Mysticism makes us proud and happy to renounce the work of intelligence, both in thought and in life, and persuades us that we become divine by remaining imperfectly human. Walt Whitman gives a new expression to this ancient and multiform tendency. He feels his own cosmic justification and he would lend the sanction of his inspiration to all loafers and holiday-makers. He would be the congenial patron of farmers and factory hands in their crude pleasures and pieties, as Pan was the patron of the shepherds of Arcadia: for he is sure that in spite of his hairiness and animality, the gods will acknowledge him as one of themselves and smile upon him from the serenity of Olympus.

59. Basil de Selincourt on Whitman

1914

Extracts from Basil de Selincourt, 'The Problem of the Form', *Walt Whitman: A Critical Study* (1914), pp. 55–72, 74–5, 78–83, 87–9, 91–3.

Among Basil de Selincourt's books are: *Giotto* (London, 1905), *William Blake* (London, 1909), *The English Secret, and other essays* (London, 1923), *Pomona, or the future of English* (London, 1926) and *Anne D. Sedgewick, a portrait in letters* (London, 1936), Basil de Selincourt.

See Introduction, pp. 13–14.

His rhythm and uniformity he will conceal in the roots of his verses, not to be seen of themselves, but to break forth loosely as lilacs on a bush, and take shapes compact as the shapes of melons or chestnuts or pears.[1]

Salient among the problems with which Whitman and his work confront us is that of the form in which his poetic impulse clothed itself. To what extent are his Leaves a natural and coherent growth? To what extent are their shapes vital shapes? And how are we to discern what is vital in them from what is trivial or redundant? To answer these questions involves analysing, however cursorily, the relation of the form to the matter in poetry as a whole. It is arguable that the highest kind of poetry rejects a rhythmical plan or predetermined scheme of any kind: that its form can be determined by nothing else than the creative impulse which takes as it arises the form proper to it. The attainment of poetry will in this view be the attainment of complete freedom. Can any one believe that the true poem is dependent for its unity upon preserving an equal number of stresses in a line or lines in a stanza? Its unity lies surely in the fact that it proceeds from a continuously developing emotion; and this, as it grows to the light,

[1] Whitman's Preface to the initial edition of *Leaves of Grass* in 1855.

will open here a leaf and there a tendril and here again a bud or a flower, all unpredictably and each in shape and size responsive to the various degrees of light that fall upon it, adaptable to no pattern. So Walt Whitman must have argued; and some of the greatest monuments of emotional literature exist to assure us that he was not wrong in believing that the essence of poetry overflows all its moulds. His *Leaves of Grass* was a deliberate challenge to the conventional ideas of what is beautiful and appropriate in verse.

> What to such as you anyhow such a poet as I? therefore leave my works,
> And go lull yourself with what you can understand, and with piano-tunes,
> For I lull nobody, and you will never understand me!

It is a bracing if not a reassuring note. Whitman in fact challenged so much that we shall do well to search for the residue left unchallenged by him. What is the ground common to him and other poets?

The poet uses language and summons before our minds, as language must do, an array of thoughts and images, his object being to communicate the feeling which these thoughts and images arouse in him. The feeling sometimes includes and transcends the thought and imagery, sometimes merely insinuates itself among the thoughts, touching their surfaces; however that may be, it is more for the sake of the feeling than for their own sake that the thoughts and images are presented; the feeling is the determining principle, the creative centre of the work. Shelley's

> Hail to thee, blithe spirit,
> Bird thou never wert—

is not a piece of perverse ornithology. It denies a fact in order to establish an emotion. And to guard it against a literal interpretation, the denial is couched in a peculiar form; it is made rhythmically.

If a friend is with me and I use the expression 'How delightful!' he can gauge at once from his knowledge of my character and from the tone of my voice what kind of delight I am experiencing and how much of it; but the words, printed upon the page of a book, suggest no more than that some unknown person has experienced an unknown quantity of a feeling of which we know no more than that he thought or professed to think it pleasant. Now the problem in poetry is to find some substitute for the tone of the voice. The printed symbols are to be redeemed from dumbness and so ordered that we shall recover in them the quality of the poet's mood, the breath and emphasis of his expression. They are to be the embodiment, not the mere record, of his experience. We are to find in them the unique spiritual impulse out of which they came.

To convey this organic effect poetry falls back upon something more primitive than words. Birds and animals communicate their feelings to one another by variations of tone which the whole fraternity recognises and which we ourselves can recognise to have a direct significance. Besides varying the tone they express themselves also by varying the rhythm of their cries. That highly-strung creature, the blackbird, conveys excitement in screams which are not only shrill but also punctuated and distributed in an expressive pattern. The coo of the turtle-dove in its unflagging persistency and that of the wood-pigeon in its soft retarded pressures would express, even without help from the quality of the notes, that brooding domesticity which is characteristic of both these birds. Not only the tone of the voice, then, but, as we see by these primitive examples, its rhythm also, assumes a natural impress from the feeling of the utterer. It follows that in so far as words can be made rhythmical, their rhythm, as dictated by the poet's feeling, will convey to us immediately as we hear it, the feeling which it is his purpose to convey.

So far we have Whitman with us wholeheartedly. His native instinct for rhythmical expression is indeed abnormally powerful.

> I behold from the beach your crooked inviting fingers,

he writes of the sea in his first great poem, and the rhythm of the line beckons of itself unmistakably. A little later we have

> Cushion me soft, rock me in billowy drowse,

and the rhythm lulls now and assuages. Effects like these are common in *Leaves of Grass*, and a great part of the pleasure it gives us depends upon them. Differences arise when we go further and consider the conditions under which language and rhythm are best associated. In poetry we have as a rule not only rhythm but metre—a measurable something which is common to one line after another, one stanza after another, a uniform pattern which underlies their subtly varying forms. Why is this? If rhythm is an immediate expression of feeling, we might have expected rhythm and feeling to change obviously together, as, in *Leaves of Grass*, they actually do. Putting aside our experience of poetry and habit of mind in regard to it, we see that its regularity is a curiously artificial product and calls for explanation.

The explanation is to be looked for in the nature of the rhythm in words and the limitations and difficulties imposed by it upon the poet's art. One of the commonest fallacies of the prosodist is that of supposing that our normal pronunciations are susceptible of precise metrical analysis; that certain syllables are long, definitively, and certain other syllables definitively short. On the contrary, the problem of prosody is to strike averages; not to discover the length of syllables, but why and how it is convenient for certain purposes to regulate or conventionalise their length. When we speak with feeling, we here dwell on a syllable or on a word, there run rapidly forward, crowding a number of unimportant words or syllables together. We do this easily and naturally; and we can do it because words have no strongly inherent rhythm of their own. Their meaning as words does not depend upon the length of time it takes us to pronounce them. And so far as their relation to feeling goes, they are indeterminate matter. They do not dictate a rhythm to us; the more intense our feeling, the more natural we find it to dictate to them, and to no matter what combination of them, any rhythm we will. Feelings, in live speech, are in fact irrepressible, and can safely be left to declare themselves after their own fashion.

This being so, the tendency of language has been to consider clearness and practical convenience in the formation and articulation of words, so that we may be provided with a medium for the accurate exchange of information and ideas. Here then is the poet's difficulty. The purposes of language are opposed to his purposes. For the expression of his feeling he must find in words and make to appear from within through his use of them the rhythms which feeling ordinarily forces upon them from without. Like the pigeon or the blackbird, he feels a certain measure or pulsation appropriate to the emotion he has to convey; but in order to convey it he must find words to suggest it, and how is this to be done? The emotion which we convey in speech takes its own rhythm and pulls the words this way and that to make them fit it. In poetry the rhythm of the emotion must somehow find its embodiment in the words so that as we read the words we recognise the rhythm and feel the emotion. And since the same words are susceptible of different rhythms according to the emotion we put into them, how is it possible for us to arrive at the poet's rhythm and emotion through his words?

In brief, when we see a line of poetry before us, to what is due our confidence that we feel its rhythm as the poet intended it to be felt?

A child said *What is the grass?* fetching it to me with full hands;
How could I answer the child? I do not know what it is any more than he.

If we ask half a dozen of our friends to read this aloud to us, we shall probably find that to each of them the four clauses have a slightly different shape and cadence. In particular the value of the words *said*, *is*, *to*, *me*, in the first line will be variously interpreted, while, in the second, rhythmical ambiguity will extend to as many perhaps as eleven syllables. For example, we may read:—

How could I answer the child?

or:—

How could I answer the child?

or:—

How could I answer the child?

and again:—

I do not know what it is any more than he

or:—

I do not know what it is any more than he

or:—

I do not know what it is any more than he.

and so on almost indefinitely. Our disposition at first will be to assure ourselves that this perplexity is fictitious; that to discuss the rhythm of the lines is academical; that the version which seems most natural to ourselves is the correct one. Let me place my own version before the reader as a test:—

A child said *What is the grass?* fetching it to me with full hands;
How could I answer the child? I do not know what it is any more than he.

I must not flatter myself he will accept it. And though I have marked where, to my ear, the stresses fall, I may still have failed to convey to him what seems to me to be the cadence of the lines. Now uncertainty of this kind is, in varying degrees, unavoidable where the rhythm is free; that is, where each line is its own law and pattern. And yet, unless the rhythm is communicated with exactitude,—wherever, that is, the poet fails to make clear to his reader what cadence he intends,—the words are liable to lose their poetic quality and to become lifeless. It is here that metre can assist us; as a rhythmical scheme separable from the words and exemplified in them it provides a basis for mutual understanding.

Now the more mutual understanding is set up between the poet and his reader, the wider, the more resourceful becomes, clearly, the poet's vehicle of expression. Reflecting again upon the lines of Whitman just quoted, we observe that our uncertainty as to their exact rhythmical intention is hardly distinguishable from our uncertainty as to the exact shade of meaning he intends them to convey. What does this imply? It implies surely a great sacrifice of expressive power. For if the subtleties of a poet's rhythm are only appreciable as the result of an appreciation of the subtleties of his meaning, it is clear that they cannot contribute anything to that meaning on their own account. But when the rhythm follows a plan, we take its broad outlines for granted; it is something known; and this means that we have attention to spare for the turns, the syncopations, the irregularities, which contribute so much to its expressiveness.

Again, the effect of a regular rhythm, perhaps as a result of its directness and immediacy, is very soon played out; and to sustain it, to keep the attention, variations must be introduced. The language of rhythm, in its more developed phases, involves (as every musician knows) a constant play of anticipation and surprise. Effects are produced, meanings are conveyed, by preparing the mind to expect one thing and giving it another. Hardly is a rule laid down before, now in one, now in another direction, it is disregarded. And it is in these variations, this embroidery, that the value of rhythm as a medium of progressive communication really consists. But, obviously, if you are to depart from a rule, you must have a rule to depart from. Variations imply a theme. The significance of the irregularities is their deliberate and measurable deviation from a recognised basis of regularity. It is to metre, then, that the poet turns for a basis of regularity against which his irregularities may play. Without it, he is limited to the broadest outlines for his rhythmical expression, to shapes that will impose themselves on the unguided attention; and even these broad outlines will often be ambiguous. For subtler play of rhythm he will be obliged to fall back upon the relation of sound to sense, and, instead of adding rhythmical to linguistic effects, derive the one from the other.

Thus the first question which criticism has to answer in regard to the form of Whitman's poems is this: how far in discarding metre did he reckon with the value of what he discarded? how much intelligence and craftsmanship, how much technical experience lay behind his choice of spontaneous methods? This decided, we shall be able to ask to what extent his apparent irregularities conceal an order equivalent to that attained in the conventional regularities of other poets.

A curious feature of *Leaves of Grass* is the frequency with which lines of a conventional pattern are introduced in stanzas which, as stanzas, are completely free. The hexameter is quite a favourite; elegiac couplets several times occur; the ordinary blank verse line is, of course, the commonest of all. More than this, even rhymes are resorted to occasionally. The natural tendency of criticism is to take these manifestations as a tacit admission by the poet, only the more significant if it was unconscious, of the virtue of the forms against which he was in rebellion. Mr. Paul Elmer More even goes so far as to say that the 'prevalent effect' of *Leaves of Grass* is 'that of a hexametric cadence such as probably preceded the schematisation of the Homeric poems,' and his opinion clearly is that the perception and acknowledgment of this by Whitman himself would logically have involved him in a similar schematisation of his own work. But Mr. More exaggerates the relative frequency of hexameters, even if we include under that heading a generous measure of hexametristic lines. And his view of Whitman generally is hardly sympathetic enough to reveal to him the positive grounds on which Whitman's rejection of common forms was based. Sometimes, no doubt, a sort of instinct for formal composition takes Whitman, as it might seem, at unawares; he has written one or two splendid poems in which the quality of his inspiration appears to demand from him a consistent flow of rhythm, and only habit, it might be argued, leads him to refuse this: Some of the most majestic lines in 'Prayer of Columbus' and 'Song of the Universal' take a familiar pattern:—

Shadowy vast shapes smile through the air and sky.

or:—

Love like the light silently wrapping all,

and these poems, with a few others, might, perhaps, be called metrical in their entirety, examples of a frustrated and magnified blank verse.

But I know of no poem which can fairly be said to imply the hexameter as a base. And, in the compositions just alluded to, it must be noted that the magnificence of the verse is bound up with its frustration. If the 'Song of the Universal' is great, its theme makes it so; the versification is fumbling, and descends more than once into a merely metristic prettiness. Indeed the poem, in spite of its beauty and triumph at the close, is a laboured piece of work. The opening paragraphs, in particular, betray a weak search for adventitious decoration, a feature which is of all others the most uncharacteristic of *Leaves of Grass* as a whole. Lines like

> As from tall peaks the modern overlooking,
> Successive fiats absolute issuing,

would have been enough to destroy a lesser poem, and their weakness lies precisely in their relation to a norm; they have so far demeaned themselves as to become Iambics! Thus even those poems which come nearest to metre owe their strength to their disdain of it.

As a general rule the appearance in his work of the waifs and strays of rhyme and rhythm has a disquieting effect. They are momentary, miscalculated ebullitions. Children of fashion that have lost their way they are jostled by the Bohemian crowd, which bestows upon them and receives from them unkindly glances.

> Thou Mother with thy equal brood,
> Thou varied chain of different States, yet one identity only,
> A special song before I go I'd sing o'er all the rest,
> For thee, the future.

Could any passage be more accurately calculated than this to give displeasure? The trivial skipping motion on a hackneyed idea in the second line, the meandering complacency of the third line,—first wilful violation of a rhythm we have been led to expect, then foolish insistence on a rhythm which is not worth having when we have got it,—all these things are bad enough to prepare us for the worse that follows. The pity of it too is that the disorder, the clash of poetry, pedantry, and piano-tunes, is enjoyed, deliberately aimed at. The opening lines of the 'Song of the Broad Axe' are another flagrant example:—

> Weapon shapely, naked, wan,
> Head from the mother's bowels drawn,
> Wooded flesh and metal bone, limb only one and lip only one,
> Gray-blue leaf by red-heat grown, helve produced from a little seed sown,
> Resting the grass amid and upon,
> To be lean'd and to lean on.

Half concealed by wayward printing, we have here in effect an eight-line stanza, in which the lines are all equivalent and all rhyme together. The one or two touches in it of descriptive genius, the beautiful use of the word 'wan', are not enough to redeem the whole from absurdity; and again we must note that the absurdity has been sought out, enjoyed. Another poem, which begins in high declamatory style:—

And now gentlemen,

lets us down after a little into the lamest jog trot:—

Having studied the new and antique, the Greek and Germanic systems,
Kant having studied and stated, Fichte and Schelling and Hegel,

hexameters as worthless, as meaningless as, once more, they are intentional. Turn even to that noble threnody, 'When Lilacs Last in the Dooryard Bloom'd,' and on the very threshold a sheer barbarism confronts you:—

Ever-returning spring, trinity sure to me you bring.

What does this betray if not a childish, under the circumstances a fatuous and even wanton, pleasure in a silly jingle of words?* There

* After long turning over in my mind, tasting and retasting, the tercet of which this is the first line, I have come to suspect in it a concealed rhythmical intention which would make such harsh terms unjustifiable. The line at first sight scans:—

/ / / / / / /
Ever-returning spring, trinity sure to me you bring,

and in this form is, to me, anathema. Yet Whitman, who could write a line like:—

Will you not little shells to the tympans of temples held . . .

cannot complain if readers attribute to him other barbarisms. The true scansion of the tercet seems, however, to be this:—

/ / / / / /
Ever-returning spring, | trinity sure to me you bring, |
/ / / / / /
Lilac blooming perennial | and drooping star in the west |
/ / /
And thought of him I love. |

There is, that is to say, a sequence of five members, each of them bearing three accents; and these trinities of accents are, I suppose, a conscious symbolic reinforcement of the idea of the trinity of recollections. The whole conformation of the stanza would, according to this reading, be the result of scrupulous and delicate adjustments; and the purpose of the opening rhyme might be to prepare the reader's attention for an unusual effect. As a further instance of what looks like conscious moulding to a norm, it may be observed that the rather curious accentuation 'su re to me you bri ng' is echoed at the transition between the next two members very beautifully ('-e nnial and dro op-'). But the uncertainty attaching to all this is instructive. Whitman seems to be trying here to obtain effects to which a scheme is indispensable. And it is a good instance of the risks of metrical antinomianism that it should permit so much care to be directed to communicating what after all remains obscure.

is no need to multiply examples. Clearly Whitman's refusal of metre was the refusal of innocence, not of experience. One must doubt whether his ear was capable of receiving the disciplined music of such verse as Milton's, whether, in fact, the verse of all the greatest poets did not seem sing-song to him. Certainly, whatever determined his choice of irregularity, his perception of the meaning of conventional forms, his instinct and practice in the use of them, were at a primitive level. He is far from being unsusceptible to the charms of metre. But they are Circe charms to him. Crying out for an ideal of nonchalance and ease he escapes a temptress.

The poem, as Whitman conceives it, is to remain fundamentally a conversation. It is to be the expression by me to you of the feelings which are as much yours as mine, and would undoubtedly have been expressed by you to me but for the accident of my being the more garrulous fellow of the two. It is to act in the field of spiritual needs much as the more modern kind of advertisement does in the field of material needs, button-holing its client, assuring him that he is a brother, and confiding to him its knowledge of the common perplexities of the life of man. How easily this atmosphere of confidence and familiarity raises a smile! It subsists largely upon illusions; but the illusions are harmless, for they deceive nobody; and they are really worth entertaining, even if they are a little wearisome and overpersistent at times; for with them come large reinforcements of that genuine raciness and diffused good feeling which are part of America's contribution to the civilisation of the world. There was more of strength and perception and courage than there was of weakness in Whitman's determination to turn this unpromising stuff to poetic uses. The impromptu confab, in which equal takes equal aside for a few words (or not so few!), this he felt to be typical not only of his country but also of his country's ideals.

The form of Whitman's conversational poem depends on the course the conversation takes and the temper which has initiated it; and whether the form is perfect or not in a particular case we can decide only by familiarising ourselves with the unique requirements of the case in point. Thus, in the example that follows, the tone of conversation has passed into that of soliloquy; the mood is too intimate, too remote, to admit of the idea of any but an impersonal utterance; we picture the soul of the poet addressing as it were some shadow of itself:—

Tears! tears! tears!
In the night, in solitude, tears,
On the white shore dripping, dripping, suck'd in by the sand,
Tears, not a star shining, all dark and desolate,
Moist tears from the eyes of a muffled head;
O who is that ghost? that form in the dark, with tears?
What shapeless lump is that, bent, crouch'd there on the sand?
Streaming tears, sobbing tears, throes, choked with wild cries;
O storm, embodied, rising, careering with swift steps along the beach!
O wild and dismal night storm, with wind—O belching and desperate!
O shade so sedate and decorous by day, with calm countenance and regulated pace,
But away at night as you fly, none looking—O then the unloosen'd ocean,
Of tears! tears! tears!

The form here is of such exquisite sensitiveness that it is with an effort we remember the offences its author could commit. The lines 'O who is that ghost' and 'What shapeless lump is that' serve just to maintain the air of realistic familiarity that Whitman loves. He takes advantage of the ballast they provide to soar up into heights of suggestion and impressionism where he is equally at home. The storm, the human creature out in it, exchange forces, appearance, personality almost, from line to line. The tears are the rain, but who is it that is weeping? The night, the tempest, the seashore are part of the solitude and the despair they cover, part of the outpouring of passion and sorrow which they liberate, echo and absorb. And how does language take the impress of hints so vague and so conflicting and of an integration so profound? All through the piece alliteration, though never obtruding itself, and indeed never appearing till it is sought out, adds significance to the choice of the words by coaxing the reader to dwell upon them and so helping him to pass naturally over gaps, whether of grammar or idea which might otherwise check him; he may observe next how every line, sensitive to the cadence of the first, divides itself sympathetically into a succession of lesser impulses, of which there are usually, but not always, three; and finally, as the sign of a still more vital sensitiveness, he will note the repetition of the keynote of the piece, the word 'tears.' The word is not only repeated, but variously placed in successive lines, so that by maintenance of the emphasis upon it its structural significance may be fully brought out. Then, at what is structurally the centre of the piece, there is a cessation; four lines of release and tumult follow which are silent of it; and so we are prepared for the beauty and inevitability of the final cadence in which it returns.

In Tears! Tears! Tears! we have a piece of poetic architecture which is at once completely original and completely satisfying. To measure the achievement it represents, let us oppose to it an example of merely conventional melodiousness. Here, from Spenser's *Teares of the Muses* (a poem which extends to 600 lines), is the first verse of the mourning of Melpomene:—

> O who shall powre into my swollen eyes
> A sea of teares that neuer may be dryde,
> A brasen voice that may with shrilling cryes
> Pierce the dull heauens and fill the ayer wide,
> And yron sides that sighing may endure,
> To waile the wretchednes of world impure?

A passage like this brings vividly before us a vicious tendency to which verse-writing is subject even in the hands of true poets—when the form evokes rather than expresses the feelings of which it is the mould. To call the tendency vicious is not to deny that it sometimes produces exquisite poetry, if never poetry of a kind which Whitman would have recognised. And though he would have been wrong to see nothing but artifice and insincerity in it, these are, nevertheless, besetting dangers. Let any reader, who will deal strictly with himself, turn the pages of his most cherished master;—how many works will he find of which he can say that their form, however appropriate to the feeling, completely fills it, that nowhere a line, a phrase, a word has been inserted for form's sake? The sincerer our devotion to poetry, the more readily we recognise that even in works called great, the form is apt to be a convenient mantle which, though it serves indeed to reveal the living gestures of the poet, serves also to give an average effect of dignity to transitional moments, when he is recovering from one gesture and preparing for the next. Form, as Whitman made use of it, avoids this pitfall. Not pre-existing as a mould to be filled, it cannot attract the feeling that is to fill it. It waits upon the feeling, and the feeling when it comes is the more likely to be genuine and sincere.

Whitman's failures, numerous as they are, do not affect his stature as a poet. His successes, and the fact that his successes include some of the longest and most audacious of his works, suffice to establish his power in conception and creation and the quality of his touch as an executant. Among his greatest gifts is his command of the music of words, the freedom with which he can throw off phrases equally remarkable for their significance and for their beauty. And it is worth noting here that the free structure of his work enabled it in a peculiar degree to accommodate the concentrations of poetic motive to which this gift gave rise. We know how the vague films of the oyster shell are knitted into a pearl under the influence of a creature vaguer, filmier than ourselves. Similarly in Whitman, poetry is, on the one hand, diffused, a nourishing, penetrating fluid, a living milk; on the other hand, it is always ready to crystallise itself at need; and the two conditions, instead of destroying, seem naturally to explain and support one another. His form, not demanding a poetical manner from him, is not cast down by the appearance of the jewel of poetry when occasion brings it forth, but is ready, exists in fact, to provide a natural setting for it.

O baffled, balk'd, bent to the very earth,

he cries out, in one of his most solemn moments, using accents and entering with them into an atmosphere that recalls the religious illumination and self-effacement of an Ezekiel or an Isaiah. In all but the next line he is

Aware now that amid all that blab whose echoes recoil upon me I have not once had the least idea who or what I am.

And how can we but wonder that in these two utterances, apparently so different in tone, a community of substance and feeling should announce itself! The fact is indubitable. Both take their place in a paragraph permeated, irradiated, by the splendour of its opening line.

This is but another way of saying that Whitman in the bulk of his work had found by intuition the form which his genius required. His conception of poetry, his poetic habit, demanded, on the one side, spontaneity; they demanded, on the other, universal simplicity and receptiveness. The forms of poetry are artificial. Language submits to discipline in order to assume them, and disciplined language cannot express spontaneous feelings. The appearance of spontaneousness can only be obtained by an allowance for the requirements of the form, by an imaginative effort so perfect that we are unaware it has been made. This involves a certain conventionalisation of the feeling to be expressed. Most of the shades, the hesitations, the convergences, the conflicts of impulse have to be obliterated. The tentative processes of growth escape, as it were, through the meshes of the measured line and stanza; what these give to us is the clear movement and outline which, when the growth is achieved, represent and announce its characteristic features. There is a sense, obviously, in which such handling was beyond Whitman's scope; there is a sense also in which it was not good enough to attract him. His nature was too crude for poetry; but it was also too sensitive; poetry was, in a sense, too crude for him. One of the most perfect of his compositions takes for its theme a metaphysical, an elusive, yet for all that a very familiar emotion—'The Terrible Doubt of Appearances'—and the poet reaches his climax of perplexity in the amazing line:—

> Maybe seeming to me what they are (as doubtless they indeed but seem) as from my present point of view, and might prove (as of course they would) nought of what they appear, or nought anyhow, from entirely changed points of view;

This heap of stumbling contraries, this litter of words, this rubble of ideas, is in its place pure poetry. Whitman's point is to express the disorder, the commotion of feeling which accompanies a certain confusion and distress of the mind, to express the state of reasonable, of seemingly final, uncertainty, before which philosophy itself becomes powerless, and to express this in such a way that having felt it we may also feel its resolution:—

> To me these and the like of these are curiously answer'd by my lovers, my dear friends,
> When he whom I love travels with me or sits a long while holding me by the hand,
> When the subtle air, the impalpable, the sense that words and reason hold not, surround us and pervade us,
> Then I am charged with untold and untellable wisdom, I am silent, I require nothing further . . .

Everything in the piece, every word and detail, every repetition and parenthesis, every concession and modification, is part of a single effect; and the effect, when we have it, is an effect of beauty, a revelation of life in its conditions and inner principle, a picture of spiritual growth and conquest. All depends upon Whitman's fearless use of a form which aimed primarily at the expression of gradations, and which rejected set patterns as too clumsy to admit of faithfulness to the imperceptible ebb and flow and interplay of vital emotion.

Bibliography

ALLEN, EVIE ALLISON, 'A checklist of Whitman publications 1945–1960' in Gay Wilson Allen, *Walt Whitman as Man, Poet and Legend*, Southern Illinois University Press, 1961, pp. 179–244, deserves Mrs Allen's description of it as 'comprehensive'.

ALLEN, G. W., *Walt Whitman Abroad*, Syracuse University Press (1955): extensive listing from virtually all continental European countries and many of those of Asia and South America.

ANONYMOUS, *Leaves of Grass Imprints, American and European Criticisms on 'Leaves of Grass,'* Boston, Thayer & Eldridge, 1860: quotes extensively from many of the earliest articles in America and in England and supplements the similarly motivated selection of criticism which is in the Appendix to the second (1856) edition of the *Leaves*; this supplementary gathering helped publicize the third edition.

BLODGETT, HAROLD, *Walt Whitman in England*, Cornell University Press: valuable account of Whitman's English reception.

BUCKE, R. M., *Walt Whitman*, Glasgow, 1884: an edition of the biography initially published in 1883 and containing supplementary selections of English criticism of Whitman compiled by Edward Dowden.

——, HARNED, T. and TRAUBEL, H. (literary executors of Whitman), *In Re Walt Whitman*, Philadelphia, 1893: contains a number of continental European criticisms of Whitman as well as the first authoritative admission of the authorship of his self-reviews.

HOLLOWAY, E. and SAUNDERS, H. S., 'Bibliography of Walt Whitman', *Cambridge History of American Literature*, New York, Putnam's, 1918, vol. II, pp. 551–81; extensive listing of reactions to the poet in English, but rather skimpy on foreign criticism.

KENNEDY, WILLIAM S., *The Fight of a Book for the World: A companion volume to Leaves of Grass*, West Yarmouth, Mass., 1926: competent account of the vicissitudes in the early reputation of Whitman.

TANNER, J. T. F., 'Walt Whitman bibliographies: A chronological listing, 1902–1964', *Bulletin of Bibliography*, vol. 25, no. 5, Jan.–Apr. 1968: listing sixty-eight separate bibliographies.

TANNER, J. T. F., *Walt Whitman: A supplementary bibliography, 1961–1967*, Kent State University Press, 1968: takes up at the point where E. A. Allen's *Checklist* ended.

THORP, W., 'Whitman' in *Eight American Authors*, New York, 1956, pp. 271–318, with a bibliographical supplement by J. Chesley Matthews in the edition published by W. W. Norton in 1963.

TRIGGS, OSCAR L., a bibliography of Walt Whitman, *Complete Writings of Walt Whitman*, New York and London, Putnam's, 1902, vol. X, pp. 139–233: has, despite many gaps and inaccuracies, a historical interest as the first attempt to grapple with the problem of Whitman's reception in an exhaustive way.

WHITE, W., quarterly listings of new items in Whitman bibliography in the *Walt Whitman Review* by one of its editors, from 1955 to the present time.

Index

INDEX OF WHITMAN'S WORKS SPECIFICALLY MENTIONED

INDEX OF NAMES

References in italic are to texts by indexed persons

INDEX OF JOURNALS

...CAL HERITAGE SERIES

... B. C. SOUTHAM

...coming

...	...tham
BROWNING	Boyd Litzinger and Donald Smalley
BYRON	Andrew Rutherford
THOMAS CARLYLE	Jules Paul Seigel
CLOUGH	Michael Thorpe
COLERIDGE	J. R. de J. Jackson
DICKENS	Philip Collins
DRYDEN	James and Helen Kinsley
GEORGE ELIOT	David Carroll
HENRY FIELDING	Ronald Paulson and Thomas Lockwood
FORD MADOX FORD	Frank MacShane
THOMAS HARDY	R. G. Cox
HAWTHORNE	J. Donald Crowley
HENRY JAMES	Roger Gard
JOHNSON	James T. Boulton
JAMES JOYCE (in 2 vols)	Robert H. Deming
KEATS	G. M. Matthews
KIPLING	Roger Lancelyn Green
D. H. LAWRENCE	R. P. Draper
MEREDITH	Ioan Williams
MILTON	John T. Shawcross
EZRA POUND	Eric Homberger
ROCHESTER	David Farley-Hills
SCOTT	John O. Hayden
SPENSER	R. M. Cummings
SWIFT	Kathleen Williams
SWINBURNE	Clyde K. Hyder
TENNYSON	John D. Jump
THACKERAY	Geoffrey Tillotson and Donald Hawes
ANTHONY TROLLOPE	Donald Smalley
MARK TWAIN	Frederick Anderson
WALT WHITMAN	Milton Hindus
OSCAR WILDE	Karl Beckson